Microsoft®
Windows 7 Your Way
Speed Up and Customize Windows

Michael Miller

800 East 96th Street,
Indianapolis, Indiana 46240 USA

Microsoft® Windows 7 Your Way: Speed Up and Customize Windows

Copyright © 2010 by Pearson Education, Inc.

ISBN-13: 978-0-7897-4286-5
ISBN-10: 0-7897-4286-1

Library of Congress Cataloging-in-Publication Data:

Miller, Michael, 1958-

  Microsoft Windows 7 your way : speed up and customize windows / Michael Miller.

        p. cm.

  ISBN 978-0-7897-4286-5

  1. Microsoft Windows (Computer file) 2. Operating systems (Computers) I. Title.

  QA76.76.O63M5621665 2010

  005.4'46—dc22

                                                    2009042722

Printed in the United States of America

First Printing: December 2009

Trademarks

Warning and Disclaimer

Bulk Sales

Que Publishing offers excellent discounts on this book when ordered in quantity for bulk purchases or special sales. For more information, please contact

   U.S. Corporate and Government Sales

   1-800-382-3419

   corpsales@pearsontechgroup.com

For sales outside of the U.S., please contact

   International Sales

   international@pearson.com

Associate Publisher
Greg Wiegand

Acquisitions Editor
Rick Kughen

Development Editor
Rick Kughen

Managing Editor
Patrick Kanouse

Project Editor
Mandie Frank

Indexer
Cheryl Lenser

Proofreader
Geneil Breeze

Technical Editor
Todd Meister

Publishing Coordinator
Cindy Teeters

Designer
Anne Jones

Compositor
Bronkella Publishing LLC

Contents at a Glance

Table of Contents

About the Author

Michael Miller has written more than 90 non-fiction how-to books over the past two decades; his books have collectively sold more than one million copies worldwide. He has written many books about the Windows operating system, dating from *Using Windows 95* (written in 1995). His more recent books include Que's *Absolute Beginner's Guide to Computer Basics, Easy Computer Basics, Your First Notebook PC, Speed It Up! A Non-Technical Guide for Speeding Up Slow Computers, Wireless Networking with Microsoft Windows Vista,* and *How Microsoft Windows Vista Works.*

Mr. Miller has established a reputation for clearly explaining technical topics to non-technical readers and for offering useful real-world advice about complicated topics. More information can be found at the author's website, located at www.molehillgroup.com.

Dedication

To Collin and Hayley—who always want it their *way.*

Acknowledgments

Thanks to the usual suspects at Que, including but not limited to Greg Wiegand, Rick Kughen, Mandie Frank, and technical editor Todd Meister.

We Want to Hear from You!

As the reader of this book, *you* are our most important critic and commentator. We value your opinion and want to know what we're doing right, what we could do better, what areas you'd like to see us publish in, and any other words of wisdom you're willing to pass our way.

As an associate publisher for Que Publishing, I welcome your comments. You can email or write me directly to let me know what you did or didn't like about this book—as well as what we can do to make our books better.

Please note that I cannot help you with technical problems related to the topic of this book. We do have a User Services group, however, where I will forward specific technical questions related to the book.

When you write, please be sure to include this book's title and author as well as your name, email address, and phone number. I will carefully review your comments and share them with the author and editors who worked on the book.

Email: feedback@quepublishing.com

Mail: Greg Wiegand
         Associate Publisher
         Que Publishing
         800 East 96th Street
         Indianapolis, IN 46240 USA

Reader Services

Visit our website and register this book at informit.com/register for convenient access to any updates, downloads, or errata that might be available for this book.

Introduction

You want your burger with just the right fixings. You want your new car in your favorite color and configuration. You want your web browser's home page to deliver the news and information you specify. You want your iPod to play your personalized playlists. So why shouldn't you want to have Windows your way, too?

I've been writing about Windows for fifteen or so years now, and I know the first thing that most users do when they get a new computer is personalize the desktop with their own background images. People want to make Windows their own—to create their own custom copy of the operating system. They want their copy of Windows to look and feel like it was designed just for them.

Changing the desktop background is just one small step in what can be a long and involved personalization process. The reality is that there's a lot about Windows you can customize, if you put your mind to it. In fact, there's much more you can configure than most users realize.

That's where this book comes in. *Windows 7 Your Way* is your guide to configuring the way Microsoft's new operating system looks and acts. I'll show you not only how to change the desktop background, but also how to create a desktop slideshow, change window colors and transparencies, and personalize the items on the taskbar and Start menu. And all that's in just the first five chapters!

You see, Windows 7 is the most customizable version of Windows yet. Not only can you change Windows' look and feel, you can also change the operating system's default programs, which applications are associated with which file types, and what different users are allowed to do when logged on. Then there's everything you can do with digital pictures and music, all sorts of network configuration settings, little tweaks for using a notebook PC on the road...well, as I said, there's a lot you can change.

And the changes aren't limited to superficial settings. There are also lots of things you can do to make Windows run faster—which is always desirable. Speeding up your system's performance is the ultimate example of running Windows *your way*.

What's in This Book

Windows 7 Your Way is all about customizing and optimizing Windows 7 on your computer system. Obviously, it covers all the new features of Windows 7; there's something here for everyone!

To present all the various ways you can configure Windows 7 your way, this book contains 28 chapters, divided into 6 major parts. Each part walks you through a different way to have Windows your way, from basic interface personalization to hard-core system tweaks:

- **Part I: Personalizing Windows—Your Way** presents all the things you can do to reconfigure Windows 7's basic settings. That includes personalizing the desktop, of course, but also working with the taskbar and Start menu, as well as setting Windows' default programs. This is easy stuff that makes a big difference in terms of how Windows looks and feels.

- **Part II: Managing Windows Data and Media—Your Way** is all about working with various types of files. You'll learn how to personalize Windows Explorer, as well as advanced methods of managing files and folders. There's also a lot here about working with digital media files (photos, music, and videos), including using Windows Media Center to play your media files in your living room—and throughout your house.

- **Part III: Managing Windows Users and the Network—Your Way** is where you learn all about configuring Windows' user accounts—and Windows' User Account Control feature. There's also a lot here about network configuration, including how to share files and devices over the network.

- **Part IV: Optimizing Windows Online—Your Way** connects you to the Internet—and helps you speed up your Internet connection. You'll learn how to customize the Internet Explorer web browser, how to change default web browsers, and how to use IE's new InPrivate Browsing mode to anonymously surf the Web. You'll also learn how to surf *safely*—and avoid all the pesky nuisances that plague the Internet.

- **Part V: Using Windows on the Road—Your Way** is the section to read if you have a notebook PC. Windows 7 offers a lot of configuration options for mobile users, as well as ways to extend your notebook's battery life.

- **Part VI: Optimizing Windows Performance—Your Way** presents many ways to speed up your Windows-based PC. You'll learn how to prepare for optimization (think: protecting your data), manage your system security, remove unwanted programs and files, work with hard drives and system memory, and even tweak the Windows Registry for some high-level performance improvements. There's also a section on running problem programs, including using the new Windows XP Mode with older applications. And we wrap things up with a section on troubleshooting Windows problems—those annoying crashes and freezes that keep you from using Windows any which way.

That's a lot of stuff—but then again, there's a lot you can configure in Windows 7. When you're done, your version of Windows will be unique; you'll truly have Windows 7 *your way.*

Who Can Use This Book

You don't have to be a technical expert to use this book; many of the procedures discussed here require nothing more than a few clicks of the mouse. It helps if you know your way around the Windows desktop, of course, and there are a few more advanced options that require either tweaking the Windows Registry or performing simple hardware upgrades. But in general, just about anybody can perform most of the customization and optimization presented here.

One thing, though: This book is written specifically for computers running Microsoft Windows 7. If you have an older version of Windows, not all the instructions here will apply. (Although some will; Win7 isn't *that* much different from Windows Vista and Windows XP.)

How to Use This Book

I hope that this book is easy enough to read that you don't need instructions. That said, a few elements bear explaining.

First, this book contains several special elements, presented in what we in the publishing business call "margin notes." There are different types of margin notes for different types of information, as you see here.

note

This is a note that presents information of interest, even if it isn't wholly relevant to the discussion in the main text.

tip

This is a tip that might prove useful for whatever it is you're in the process of doing.

caution

This is a caution that something you accidentally do might have undesirable results.

Because some of the solutions presented in this book involve third-party software utilities or new hardware devices, you'll find web page addresses in the text accompanying the mentions of these products. When you see one of these addresses (also known as a URL), you can go to that web page by entering the URL into the address box in your web browser. I've made every effort to ensure the accuracy of the web addresses presented here, but given the ever-changing nature of the Web, don't be surprised if you run across an address or two that's changed. For that matter, some of the products and prices presented here are likely to change by the time you read this text. I apologize in advance, but that's the way the world works.

There's More Online...

When you need a break from reading, feel free to go online and check out my personal website, located at www.molehillgroup.com. Here you'll find more information about this book and other books I've written. And if you have any questions or comments, feel free to email me directly at win7yourway@molehillgroup.com. I can't guarantee I'll respond to every email, but I do guarantee I'll read them all.

Do It *Your Way*

With all these preliminaries out of the way, it's now time to get started. Put on your reading glasses, fire up your mouse, and get ready to configure Windows 7 *your way!*

1

Configuring Basic Settings

To configure Windows your way, you need to start with the basics.
That means learning what tools to use—and how to use them.
That's right, we're talking configuration essentials, starting with the
Windows Control Panel

Using the Control Panel

Most of Windows' configuration settings are set via a utility called
the Control Panel. In reality, the Control Panel is just a folder or
library that contains lots of individual configuration utilities (also
called *applets*); it's through these utilities that the actual configuration takes place.

How the Control Panel Works

You open the Control Panel by clicking the Start menu and selecting
Control Panel; that's easy enough. What you see next is the default
Control Panel, shown in Figure 1.1. This view of the Control Panel is
designed for the casual user, with shortcuts to take you directly to
various configuration options.

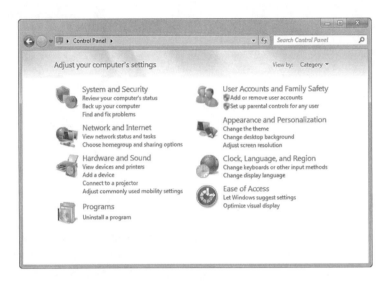

FIGURE 1.1

The Windows 7 Control Panel, in default Category view.

The default Control Panel is organized into eight sections, each corresponding to a type of task:

- System and Security, with separate links to Review Your Computer's Status, Back Up Your Computer, and Find and Fix Problems.

- Network and Internet, with separate links to View Network Status and Tasks and Choose Homegroup and Sharing Options.

- Hardware and Sound, with separate links to View Devices and Printers, Add a Device, Connect to a Projector, and Adjust Commonly Used Mobility Settings.

- Programs, with a separate link to Uninstall a Program.

- User Accounts and Family Safety, with separate links to Add or Remove User Accounts and Set Up Parental Controls for Any User.

- Appearance and Personalization, with separate links to Change the Theme, Change Desktop Background, and Adjust Screen Resolution.

- Clock, Language, and Region, with separate links to Change Keyboards or Other Input Methods and Change Display Language (Ultimate Edition only).

- Ease of Access, with separate links to Let Windows Suggest Settings and Optimize Visual Display.

Click any of the major section links and you see a new set of links. For example, when you click Appearance and Personalization, you see the screen shown in Figure 1.2, with major sections for Personalization, Display, Desktop Gadgets, Taskbar and Start Menu, Ease of Access Center, Folder Options, and Fonts. Under each section are additional links that lead directly to specific configuration utilities.

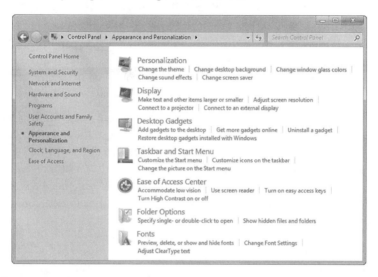

FIGURE 1.2

The Control Panel's Appearance and Personalization screen.

Keep clicking through the links and you're eventually led to the utility used to configure a particular setting. For example, when you click the Personalization link, Windows displays the Personalization window; when you click the Folder Options link, Windows displays the Folder Options dialog box. It may take a few clicks, but eventually you get to where you want to go.

So this is what I meant when I said that the Control Panel is actually a folder that holds various configuration utilities or applets. It's the individual utilities that enable configuration, but you get to those utilities via the Control Panel.

note

Not to be confusing, but the individual configuration utilities in the Control Panel are sometimes themselves called control panels. I prefer the term configuration utility, just to keep things clear.

Configuring the Control Panel

The only problem with the Windows 7 Control Panel is that, in an attempt to make it easier for casual users to figure out how to do what they want to do, Microsoft effectively buried most of the configuration utilities several layers beneath the surface. In short, you have to make too many clicks to get to each configuration utility.

There's a way around this problem, however—which happens to be our first customization tip in the book. In Windows 7, you can accept the default Control Panel display (all those easy-to-understand links) or you can reconfigure the appearance of the Control Panel to display the configuration utilities themselves.

The default display is called the Category view, but there are two other views you can enable. Pull down the View By list at the top right corner of the Control Panel and you see options for Large Icons and Small Icons. Both of these views list all the individual configuration utilities in the Control Panel window. The two views are identical save for the size of the icons; the Large Icons view (shown in Figure 1.3) uses larger icons than does the Small Icons view.

FIGURE 1.3

Displaying the Control Panel in Large Icons view.

note

In previous versions of Windows, the Control Panel Large Icons view was known as the Classic view.

With either of the Icons views, you can go directly to the configuration utility you want. Just click an icon and you open the appropriate window or dialog box, no additional click-throughs required. It's a whole lot quicker than using the default Category view—assuming you know what utility is used for which type of configuration.

Understanding the Configuration Utilities

Since you'll be using most (if not all) of these configuration utilities throughout this book to configure Windows your way, it helps to know a little bit about the individual configuration utilities. To that end, Table 1.1 details all the Windows 7 configuration utilities and what they do.

Table 1.1   Control Panel Configuration Utilities

Utility	Description
Action Center	Displays the Action Center, used to manage most of Windows' security and maintenance operations.
Administrative Tools	Displays a list of administrative tools used for advanced Windows management.
AutoPlay	Lets you choose what happens when you insert specific devices or types of media.
Backup and Restore	Opens the Windows Backup utility for backing up and restoring system data.
BitLocker Drive Encryption	Enables encryption of complete drives for enhanced security. (Available only with Enterprise and Ultimate editions.)
Color Management	Enables configuration of color management profiles for enhanced display.
Credential Manager	Stores and manages user names and passwords for various websites and programs.
Date and Time	Opens Date and Time dialog box to configure system date, time, and time zone.
Default Programs	Lets you choose the default programs Windows uses to open specific file types.
Desktop Gadgets	Lets you select gadgets to display on the Windows desktop.
Device Manager	Opens the Device Manager to manage and configure all device drivers installed on your system.
Devices and Printers	Displays and manages external devices connected to your computer—printers, scanners, and so on.
Display	Manages all display settings—text size, resolution, brightness, color, and the like.
Ease of Access Center	Manages accessibility tools.

Table 1.1   Continued

Utility	Description
Folder Options	Opens the Folder Options dialog box to configure folder appearance and operation.
Fonts	Displays the Fonts window for installing and deleting system fonts.
Getting Started	Displays the Getting Started window, useful for new users and those new to Windows 7.
HomeGroup	Helps you set up and configure a network HomeGroup.
Indexing Options	Displays the Indexing Options dialog box for configuring what locations on your system are indexed for Windows' search tool.
Internet Options	Displays the Internet Properties dialog box for configuring Internet Explorer options.
Keyboard	Displays the Keyboard Properties dialog box for configuring keyboard operations.
Location and Other Sensors	Configures sensors that detect your computer's location (if installed).
Mouse	Displays the Mouse Properties dialog box for configuring mouse and pointer operations and appearance.
Network and Sharing Center	Opens the Network and Sharing Center for configuring network connections.
Notification Area Icons	Selects which icons appear in the notification area of the Windows taskbar.
Parental Controls	Configures the Parental Controls feature for monitoring children's computer use.
Performance Information and Tools	Rates your computer's performance and enables access to performance-enhancing tools (adjust visual effects, adjust indexing options, adjust power settings, and so forth).
Personalization	Displays the Personalization utility for changing desktop themes, backgrounds, colors, sounds, and screen savers.
Phone and Modem	Opens the Phone and Modem dialog box for systems utilizing modems for dial-up connections.
Power Options	Lets you adjust your system's power options for both AC and battery use. (For notebook computers only.)
Programs and Features	Lets you uninstall programs from your system, as well as turn specific Windows features on or off.
Recovery	Opens the System Restore utility for restoring your system to a previous operational point.
Region and Language	Displays the Region and Language dialog box for configuring your system's location and language. (Ultimate Edition only.)
RemoteApp and Desktop Connections	Enables remote connection to desktops and programs at a workplace.
Sound	Opens the Sound dialog box for configuring system sounds and audio.
Speech Recognition	Configures Windows' speech recognition tools.

Table 1.1   Continued

Utility	Description
Sync Center	Enables data synchronization between devices.
System	Displays information about your computer system and enables access to the Device Manager, System Properties dialog box, and other system tools.
Taskbar and Start Menu	Displays the Taskbar and Start Menu Properties dialog box for configuring appearance and operation of the Windows taskbar and Start menu.
Troubleshooting	Displays a list of troubleshooters to help diagnose system problems.
User Accounts	Lets you make changes to user accounts on your system.
Windows CardSpace	Launches the Windows Cardspace utility for securely managing information exchanged with participating websites.
Windows Defender	Launches the Windows Defender anti-spyware utility.
Windows Firewall	Enables or disables the Windows Firewall for preventing computer attacks.
Windows Mobility Center	Displays the Windows Mobility Center for configuring essential notebook computer settings. (For notebook computers only.)
Windows Update	Manages updates to the Windows operating system.

note

Windows 7 Ultimate Edition has one setting you won't find in any other edition—the ability to change the display language. This lets you convert your English-language version of Windows to a French or Finnish or Filipino version. (Normally you'd have to purchase a new version of Windows in that language.) Select Region and Language in the Control Panel to access this feature.

In addition to these standard configuration utilities, some programs and hardware you install on your system place their own configuration utilities in the Control Panel. For example, my Toshiba notebook installed a CD/DVD Drive Acoustic Silencer item in the Control Panel that lets me set my computers' CD/DVD drive to either normal or quiet mode; Sun's Java application installs a Java control panel to manage its software. Other software and hardware install similar utilities—most of which are only visible when you display the Control Panel in one of the Icons modes. So it's likely that your computer will have a few more Control Panel items than the ones listed in Table 1.1

note

Some Control Panel items can also be accessed elsewhere in Windows. For example, you can display the Personalization utility either from the Control Panel or by right-clicking anywhere on the desktop and selecting Personalize from the pop-up menu; the same Personalization window appears either way.

If you're like me and frequently access these individual configuration utilities, you'll find that the Icons views are the preferred way to display the Control Panel. If, however, you only infrequently configure these utilities, the default Category view is probably a little more user friendly.

> **note**
>
> For ease of explanation, this book assumes that you configure the Control Panel for one of the Icons views. That is, I'll say something like "Open the Control Panel and select User Accounts," rather than going through the multiple click-throughs in the Category display.

Configuring the Control Panel Start Menu Display

For power users and speed freaks, there's an even faster way to access individual Control Panel utilities—directly from the Start menu. Let me show you how.

By default, when you open the Start menu and click Control Panel, the Control Panel opens in its own window. You can, however, configure the Start menu so that the individual configuration utilities appear as a submenu when you select the main Control Panel menu item, as shown in Figure 1.4. Just follow these steps:

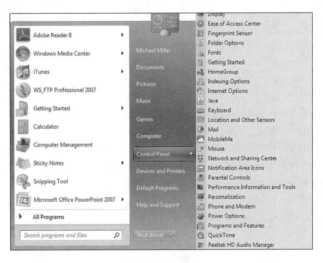

FIGURE 1.4

The Control Panel displayed as a menu on the Start menu.

1. From the Control Panel, select Taskbar and Start Menu.

2. When the Taskbar and Start Menu Properties dialog box appears, click the Start Menu tab.

3. Click the Customize button.

4. When the Customize Start Menu dialog box appears, as shown in Figure 1.5, go to the Control Menu item and check Display as a Menu.

5. Click OK; then click OK again to close both the dialog boxes.

Click Display as a Menu to have your
Control Panel open in fly-out menu style.

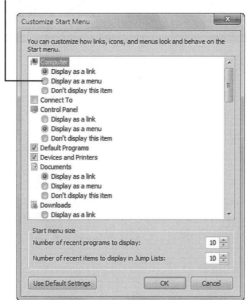

FIGURE 1.5

Configuring the Control Panel item on the Start menu.

Voila! When you click Start, Control Panel, you now see a large submenu of all the available configuration utilities. Click any submenu item to launch that utility.

Other Ways to Configure Windows

The Control Panel isn't the only way to configure Windows. Let's examine two more common approaches that you may encounter.

Right-Click Menus

As you're probably aware, Windows is highly right-clickable. That is, most items on the screen do something when you right-click them. (That's distinguished from the normal left-click operation, which typically opens or launches an item.)

In most instances, right-clicking an item displays a pop-up menu, like the one shown in Figure 1.6. This menu is item-specific, meaning that the options on the menu are specific to the item being clicked. For example, right-clicking an open area of the desktop brings up a different menu than does right-clicking the Start menu button/orb. The menus are fine-tuned for individual items.

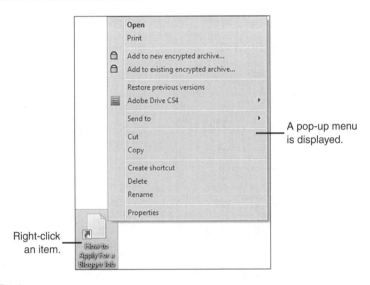

FIGURE 1.6

The pop-up menu you see when you right-click the Windows taskbar.

note

When you right-click an item on the new Windows 7 taskbar, you display not a pop-up menu but a *jump list*—typically a list of common commands for that program, as well as that program's most recently opened documents.

One common option on most right-click menus is the Properties option. In most instances, clicking this option displays a Properties dialog box for that item. It's this dialog box that enables you to configure various settings for the selected item.

So if in doubt, right-click the item you wish to configure. Chances are it will lead you to that item's Properties dialog box—and the configuration option you seek.

Windows Registry

Another place you find configuration options is in the Windows Registry. Without going into all the nitty gritty details, the Registry is a giant database of configuration settings for Windows and Windows applications; it's what the operating system itself uses for configuration. Indeed, when you make a configuration change via the Control Panel, that change is stored in the Registry.

That being the case, one way to make configuration changes is to edit those settings in the Registry. This isn't that hard to do, but it does require a bit of technical surety, as it's possible to really mess up your system if you make the wrong Registry change. For that matter, editing the Registry is not recommended for everyone; in fact, some experts don't recommend it for anyone—other than hard-core techies, of course. I'm not that opposed to recommending Registry edits, but do understand if any given reader isn't comfortable doing so.

The Registry is edited via a utility called the Registry Editor (or just Regedit). There's no direct way to open this utility, however. (That's Microsoft's way of keeping non-techies away.) What you have to do is open the Start menu and enter **regedit** into the search box. The Regedit program appears in the search results list; click this item to launch the Editor.

Once the Registry Editor is open, as shown in Figure 1.7, you navigate to specific settings (called *keys*) to make your changes. The Registry is densely packed with obscure entries, so it definitely pays to know what you're doing before you get in over your head.

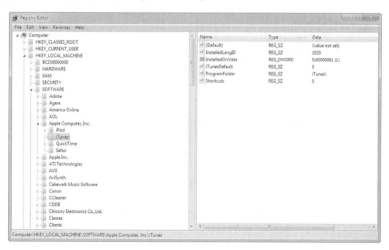

FIGURE 1.7

Configuring the Windows Registry via the Registry Editor.

---

note

The Registry is so important to configuring Windows your way that I devote an entire chapter to its use. Learn more in Chapter 27, "Tweaking the Windows Registry." Don't fiddle with Registry settings until you've read that chapter and taken appropriate steps to protect yourself in case you make a mistake.

Changing Your PC's Time and Date

Let's try out some of what we learned in this chapter by configuring some basic Windows system settings. There's a lot more where this comes from, which we'll cover in subsequent chapters; for now, this should help you get your hands dirty with configuration basics.

The first system setting we'll configure is your computer's time and date setting. In Windows 7, the time and date are displayed at the far right of the taskbar. You can even display a larger analog clock and the current month's calendar, as shown in Figure 1.8, by clicking the normal time and date display.

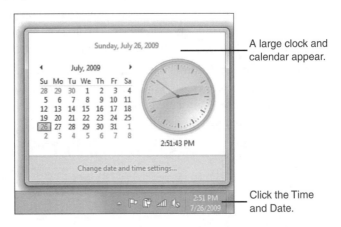

FIGURE 1.8

Click the time and date display in the taskbar to display an analog clock and current-month calendar.

Displaying the Date and Time Dialog Box

You make all date and time-related changes via the Date and Time dialog box, shown in Figure 1.9. There are a number of ways to get to this dialog box; you can:

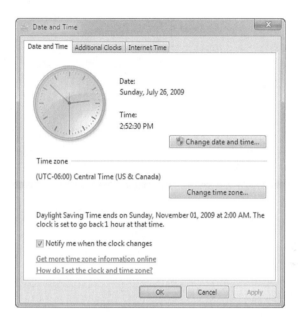

FIGURE 1.9

Configuring your system's time and date from the Date and Time dialog box.

- Click the time and date area on the taskbar to display the calendar and clock; then click Change Date and Time Settings.

- Right-click the time and date area on the taskbar and select Adjust Date/Time from the pop-up menu.

- Open the Control Panel and select Date and Time.

Changing Date and Time

To change the date and time, follow these steps:

1. From the Date and Time dialog box, select the Date and Time tab.

2. Click the Change Date and Time button.

3. When the Date and Time Settings dialog box appears, as shown in Figure 1.10, click the desired date on the calendar; use the right and left arrows to cycle back and forward through the months.

4. Adjust the control under the clock to select a new time.

5. Click OK to close the dialog box.

FIGURE 1.10

Changing Windows' date and time.

Changing Time Zone

The time you select in Windows is tied to a specific time zone. To change your time zone, follow these steps:

1. From the Date and Time dialog box, select the Date and Time tab.

2. Click the Change Time Zone button.

3. When the Time Zone Settings dialog box appears, as shown in Figure 1.11, pull down the Time Zone list and select the appropriate time zone.

4. If you want Windows to automatically change the time when Daylight Saving Time changes (and you probably do), check the Automatically Adjust Clock for Daylight Saving Time option.

5. Click OK to close the dialog box.

Displaying Additional Clocks

Windows can display multiple clocks for multiple time zones, which is quite useful when you're traveling. To display another clock, follow these steps:

1. From the Date and Time dialog box, select the Additional Clocks tab, shown in Figure 1.12.

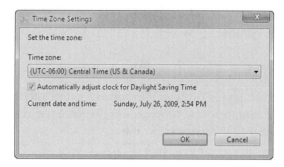

FIGURE 1.11

Changing Windows' time zone settings.

2. Check the first Show This Clock option.

3. Pull down the Select Time Zone list and select the time zone for the clock you want to display.

4. Enter a name for this clock in the Enter Display Name box.

5. Click OK to close the dialog box.

FIGURE 1.12

Displaying additional clocks for different time zones.

To add another clock, check the second Show This Clock option and repeat steps 3 and 4.

Synchronizing Time Over the Internet

Windows is configured by default to connect to the Internet and get the current time from the time.windows.com server. If you'd rather synchronize to another time server, follow these steps:

1. From the Date and Time dialog box, select the Internet Time tab.

2. Click the Change Settings button.

3. When the Internet Time Settings dialog box appears, as shown in Figure 1.13, pull down the Server list and make another selection.

4. Click the Update Now button to synchronize your computer with the new time server.

5. Click OK to close the dialog box.

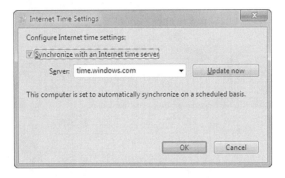

FIGURE 1.13

Synchronizing your computer with a different Internet time server.

Changing Your Computer's Name

Here's another fairly important system change that's relatively easy to make. Your computer came from the factory with some sort of default name, or maybe you opted to change the name when you were first setting up Windows. In any case, you're not stuck with that initial name; it's easy enough to change the name of your computer in Windows.

note

The name you assign your computer is important because that's what other users see when they access your computer over a network.

Here's how to do it:

1. Open the Control Panel and select System.

2. This opens the window shown in Figure 1.14, which displays all manner of information about your system—the kind of processor you have, how much memory is installed, and so forth. The current name of your computer is listed here (as Computer Name); click the Change Settings link.

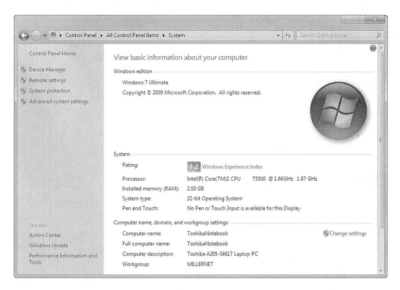

FIGURE 1.14

Viewing information about your computer system.

3. When the System Properties dialog box appears, as shown in Figure 1.15, make sure the Computer Name tab is selected.

4. If you want to change the *description* (not the name—not yet) assigned to your computer, enter a new description into the Computer Description box.

5. To rename your computer, click the Change button.

6. When the Computer Name/Domain Changes dialog box appears, as shown in Figure 1.16, enter a new name into the Computer Name box.

7. Click OK to save your changes.

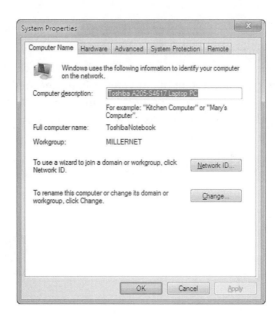

FIGURE 1.15
Opening the System Properties dialog box.

FIGURE 1.16
Changing your computer's name.

The change you make doesn't take effect until you restart your computer. When prompted to do so, click the Restart Now button. On restart, your computer will be known by its new name.

note

You can also use the Computer Name/Domain Changes dialog box to change the name of your computer's network workgroup. Learn more in Chapter 12, "Managing Network Connections."

The Bottom Line

Configuring Windows 7 your way is easy when you know what to do. One of the key tools for configuring Windows is the Control Panel—which itself can be configured for easier use. From there you can configure all sorts of system settings, including resetting the date and time and changing your computer's name. In most cases, it's as easy as making a few mouse clicks!

2

Setting Default Programs

One of the nice changes in Windows 7 is that you're no longer tied down to Microsoft's default programs, such as Windows Media Player and Internet Explorer. If you want to use another program for specific operations, it's easy to change what launches automatically. In fact, Microsoft doesn't even include a lot of the applications it used to include with Windows XP and Vista—although you can still download them, for free, if you like.

Windows 7 also makes it easy to change what programs are associated with specific types of files, as well as what happens when you insert specific types of media and devices. It's all a matter of configuring Windows 7 your way—with your choice of programs.

Changing Default Programs

Let's start with the programs that Windows uses to perform specific types of tasks. For example, when you want to browse the Web, Windows by default launches its own Internet Explorer web browser; when you want to send an email message, it launches Windows Mail or Outlook Express.

That's the way it worked in previous versions of Windows, anyway. In Windows 7, things are different; now you can easily choose which programs Windows uses by default.

Behind the Change

Why did Microsoft make this change? Microsoft says it's all about giving its users the freedom of choice, but that's not it at all. You see, Microsoft has been subject to a number of antitrust lawsuits over the years, accusing the company of monopolizing the market for various types of applications. Microsoft's unbundling of core applications (discussed later in this chapter) and enabling easier change of default programs is simply a reaction to those lawsuits. Change isn't always given, but it is sometimes taken—in this case, by concerned users (and competing software companies) around the world.

note

These changes go even further in Europe, where action by the European Union forced Microsoft to fully remove Internet Explorer from Windows 7.

Whatever the impetus, being able to change Windows' default programs truly results in your being able to configure and use Windows your way. You're no longer locked into Microsoft's default applications; you can pick and choose what programs you want to use for all sorts of basic tasks.

Let's say, for example, that you're an iPod user and would prefer to use iTunes as your media player. Right now, when you insert an audio CD, it launches Windows Media Player by default; you'd rather not see WMP at all, and want to have iTunes launched instead. Well, that's what these changes are all about—changing the default programs for common operations. Changing from Windows Media Player to iTunes is now easy to do.

What You Can Change

What programs are we talking about changing? Essentially, these are applications that Windows uses for core operations, as detailed in Table 2.1.

Table 2.1   Windows Default Applications

Operation	Default Application	Optional Programs[1]
Email program	None	Microsoft Outlook, Mozilla Firebird, Windows Live Mail
Instant messaging	None	AOL Instant Messenger, Google Talk, ICQ, Windows Live Messenger, Yahoo! Messenger
Java virtual machine	None	Sun JVM
Media player	Windows Media Player	iTunes, QuickTime, RealPlayer, Windows Media Center
Web browser	Internet Explorer	Google Chrome, Mozilla Firefox, Opera, Safari

1 The applications listed here are commonly chosen alternates; other applications are available.

All of these applications are somewhat self-explanatory, with the exception of the Java virtual machine, or JVM. This is a plug-in for your web browser that enables the running of Java-based web applications. Back in the Windows XP days, Microsoft supplied its own JVM, but it discontinued it several years back. Today the only real option is Sun's JVM (Sun being the developer of Java), but since many older systems might still have the Microsoft JVM installed, the option to change the default is there if you upgraded to Windows 7 from an older version of the operating system.

Changing the Defaults

In Windows 7, Microsoft makes it easy to select any program you have installed on your PC as the default program for these core operations. Here's how to do it:

1. Open the Windows Start menu and select Default Programs. (Alternately, you can also open the Control Panel and select Default Programs from there.)

2. When the Default Programs window appears, as shown in Figure 2.1, click Set Program Access and Computer Defaults.

3. When the Set Program Access and Computer Defaults window opens, as shown in Figure 2.2, click the down arrow to expand the Custom section.

4. For each operation listed, check the program you want to use as the default application.

5. Click the OK button when done.

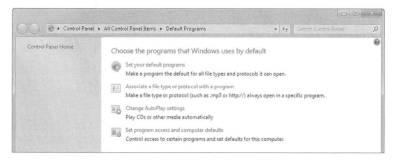

FIGURE 2.1

The Default Programs window.

Toggle the arrow and up and down
to show and hide custom options.

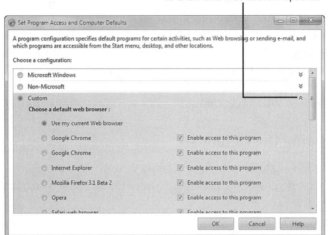

FIGURE 2.2

Changing program defaults.

note

When you change a default program, you don't physically remove the previous program from your computer's hard drive. To uninstall a program, see Chapter 23, "Removing Unnecessary Files and Programs."

Remember, you can only set a program as your default if you have it installed on your computer. So, for example, if you want to switch from Internet Explorer to Mozilla Firefox, you first have to download and install Firefox on your PC. To that end, Table 2.2 lists the URLs where you can download many of the third-party programs you might want to switch to using this procedure. All of these programs are free.

tip

If you don't want to make changes for a given operation—that is, if you want to continue using the current default application—check the Use My Current option.

Table 2.2   Third-Party Programs Download Information

Application	Download URL
AOL Instant Messenger	www.aim.com
Google Chrome	www.google.com/chrome

Application	Download URL
Google Talk	www.google.com/talk
ICQ	www.icq.com
iTunes	www.apple.com/itunes
Mozilla Firefox	www.mozilla.com/firefox
Mozilla Thunderbird	www.mozillamessaging.com
Opera	www.opera.com
QuickTime	www.apple.com/quicktime
RealPlayer	www.real.com
Safari	www.apple.com/safari
Sun JVM	www.java.com/getjava
Windows Live Mail	download.live.com
Windows Live Messenger	download.live.com
Yahoo! Messenger	messenger.yahoo.com

Changing File Type Defaults

When you think of default programs, you may also think about the programs that launch when you open a file of a given type. This has to do with which programs are associated with which file types.

You can think of file type association as a big table. In one column you have all the available file extensions that define the various file types. In the other column you have the programs that are linked to each file extension. It's a simple thing, really.

So, for example, you might have the JPG file extension (for JPEG type image files) associated with Adobe Photoshop Elements. When you double-click a JPG file in Windows Explorer, it launches Photoshop Elements and displays the clicked file.

Problems come when you don't like your current associations. Maybe you'd rather use Paint Shop Pro to edit your JPG files; that means you need to change the JPG association from Photoshop Elements to Paint Shop Pro.

tip

By default, Windows hides the extensions when it displays filenames. To display extensions in Windows 7, open the Control Panel and select Folder Options. When the Folder Options dialog box appears, select the View tab; then, in the Advanced Settings list, *uncheck* the Hide Extensions for Known File Types option. Click OK when finished.

Fortunately, this another type of default setting you can have your way in Windows 7. There are two approaches you can take: Assign a variety of file types to a given program, or assign a program to a given file type. I'll show you both.

Assigning File Types to an Application

If you want a given application to open a variety of file types (for example, if you want an image editing program to open all image file types), follow these steps:

1. Open the Windows Start menu and select Default Programs. (Alternately, you can also open the Control Panel and select Default Programs from there.)

2. When the Default Programs window appears, click Set Your Default Programs.

3. When the Set Your Default Programs window appears, as shown in Figure 2.3, select a program in the Programs list.

4. To have this program open all the file types that it can, click Set This Program as Default.

5. If you'd rather pick and choose which file types this program opens, click Choose Defaults for This Program. When the next screen appears, check the file types you want to associate with this program, then click Save.

6. Click OK to save your changes.

Assigning an Application to a File Type

Conversely, you can work in the opposite direction—assign a specific application to each available file type. Here's how that works:

1. Open the Windows Start menu and select Default Programs. (Alternately, you can also open the Control Panel and select Default Programs from there.)

2. When the Default Programs window appears, click Associate a File Type or Protocol with a Program.

3. When the next screen appears, as shown in Figure 2.4, select a file type from the list.

4. Click the Change Program button.

5. When the Open With dialog box appears, as shown in Figure 2.5, select one of the recommended programs, or click the Browse button to browse for the program you want. Click OK when done.

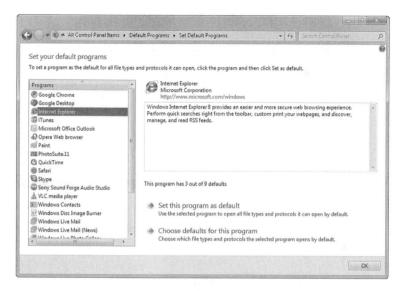

FIGURE 2.3

Assigning file types to a given application.

6. Repeat steps 3 to 5 to change additional file type associations.

7. Click Close when done.

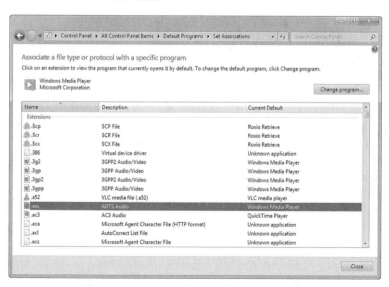

FIGURE 2.4

Selecting a file type to associate.

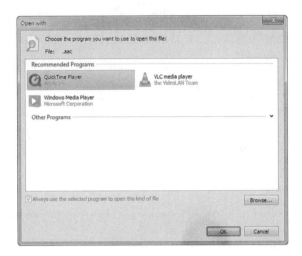

FIGURE 2.5

Selecting an application to associate with a file type.

tip

It's probably easier to use the first method to make wholesale association changes than to use the second method to fine-tune the association list.

Downloading New Applications from Windows Live Essentials

Let's talk a bit about the applications that come bundled with Windows. In the early days of computer operating systems (I'm talking DOS here, for you old-timers), the only thing you got when you installed an operating system was the operating system itself; in the DOS days, you didn't even get a graphical user interface. Over the years, however, Microsoft began to bundle more and more auxiliary utilities and applications with the OS, from a basic text editor (Notepad) to a calculator to a web browser to a photo editing program.

It's difficult to argue that a photo editing program is a core component of the operating system. It's not. It is convenient to users who now don't have to purchase and install a separate photo editing program. That's fine and dandy, but a bit damaging to those competing companies that are attempting to make money from selling photo editing software. It's downright non-competitive, in many eyes.

Some of those eyes are legal eyes, and as noted previously, Microsoft has taken a lot of flak for trying to dominate new markets by including non-core applications in the Windows operating system. Microsoft responds to those complaints in Windows 7 by unbundling some of these applications.

This unbundling is good for competing software companies, but not necessarily good for users, who now have to go out and purchase programs that they used to get for free in previous versions of Windows. Except that you can still get them for free—you just have to download them manually.

What's Not There Anymore

So what applications did Microsoft unbundle from Windows 7? Here's the list; these are all programs that used to be installed automatically in previous versions of Windows, but are no longer included as part of the installation routine:

- Windows Mail (email)
- Windows Messenger (instant messaging)
- Windows Movie Maker (video editing)
- Windows Photo Gallery (photo editing and organization)

If you're used to using these programs, you won't find them in Windows 7—at least, not by default.

note

As noted previously, Internet Explorer is also unbundled in European versions of Windows but still included as part of the U.S. package.

tip

While Microsoft removed these applications from Windows 7, some PC manufacturers may still install the new versions of these programs themselves—so don't be surprised if these programs are still on the Start menu of some new computers.

Downloading Windows Live Essentials

So Microsoft removed these programs from Windows 7—but didn't get rid of the programs altogether. Instead, Microsoft now offers these applications for free download as part of the new Windows Live Essentials program. As part of this program, the names of the programs have been changed (to include "Windows Live" in the title), and a few new programs have been made available.

Here's what you can download—for free:

- Windows Live Family Safety, for monitoring and controlling your children's Internet access
- Windows Live Mail, for sending and receiving email
- Windows Live Messenger, for instant messaging
- Windows Live Movie Maker, for editing digital movies
- Windows Live Photo Gallery, for viewing, organizing, and editing digital photos
- Windows Live Toolbar, for searching the Web (using Windows Live Search) directly from your web browser
- Windows Live Writer, for creating blog posts on Blogger, Wordpress, TypePad, and other blogging services

note

Windows Live Essentials is just one part of Microsoft's larger Windows Live family of websites, which include Hotmail email, Office Live tools, and the Bing search engine.

This is probably a good solution for all involved. Competing software publishers don't face unfair competition by having similar apps included as part of the default Windows installation. Users can still get the free programs by downloading them. And users aren't forced to install *all* these programs; you can save hard disk space by only downloading the programs you need. Like I said, kind of a win-win situation.

To download and install any or all of these applications, follow these steps:

1. Point your web browser to download.live.com, shown in Figure 2.6.
2. Click the Download button.
3. When you see the File Download dialog box, click Run.
4. If you see a User Account Control prompt, click Yes.
5. You now see the Windows Live window, shown in Figure 2.7. Check those applications you want to install.
6. Click Install to begin the download and installation.

FIGURE 2.6

The Windows Live Essentials website.

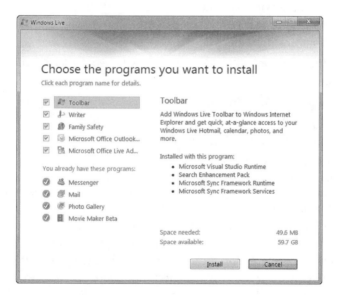

FIGURE 2.7

Selecting which applications to install.

Configuring AutoPlay Settings

There's one last program default type of operation that you can configure to run your way. I'm talking about Windows' AutoPlay settings—what Windows does when you insert a particular type of media, or attach a given device.

For example, what do you want to have happen when you insert an audio CD in your computer's CD drive? Do you want to play the CD, and if so, using what media player program? Or do you want to automatically rip the CD to your hard drive? Or do you want to do nothing—and be prompted every time you perform this operation?

That's what AutoPlay is all about. You can configure Windows to automatically perform the operation you select, using the program you select, every time you insert media or connect a device. It's a real time-saver, once you do the initial configuration.

Here's what you need to do:

1. Open the Windows Start menu and select Default Programs. (Alternately, you can also open the Control Panel and select Default Programs from there.)

2. When the Default Programs window appears, click Change AutoPlay Settings.

3. When the AutoPlay window appears, as shown in Figure 2.8, pull down the first item list and select an action.

4. Repeat step 3 for all listed media and devices.

5. Click Save when done.

For example, when you pull down the list next to Audio CD, you see a number of different possible actions—Play Audio CD Using Windows Media Player, Play Audio CD Using iTunes (if you have iTunes installed), Import Songs Using iTunes, Open Folder to View Files Using Windows Explorer, Take No Action, Ask Me Every Time, and so forth. If you always want to play a CD using WMP, select that option. If you always want to rip a CD to your iTunes library, select the Import Songs Using iTunes option. If you don't want to do the same thing every time you insert a CD, select the Ask Me Every Time option. You get the idea.

You'll need to make this choice for each type of media and device listed, from audio CDs and DVD movies to all the devices you've installed on your system—digital cameras, iPods, and so forth. Once you get it set up, however, you won't have to be bothered every time you insert a disc or connect a camera; Windows will know what to do.

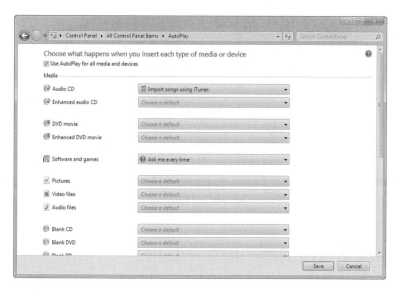

FIGURE 2.8

Configuring Windows' AutoPlay options.

tip

To use AutoPlay whenever you insert or connect media or a device, check the Use AutoPlay for All Media and Devices option.

The Bottom Line

Windows works with a lot of different programs in a lot of different ways. Your life gets easier if you configure Windows to always use the programs you want to do the things you want to do. That's why it's worth your time to configure Windows' default programs, file associations, and AutoPlay actions—it speeds up your day-to-day operations when Windows does them your way.

3

Customizing the Desktop

Pretty much the first thing I do when I get a new computer (after I work through all the startup and installation stuff, that is) is go to work on the desktop. I like to personalize the way my desktop looks; I want my own background image, collection of shortcut icons, gadgets, and the like. I'm like most folks in this matter; I want to customize the Windows desktop to fit both the way I work and my personality.

All of which leads us to this chapter, which I know will be the most read chapter in the book. It's also one of the longest, as there are a lot of things you can customize in Windows 7. After all, personalizing the desktop is the most visually apparent way to have Windows your way!

Changing Desktop Themes

Let's start with the big picture—not just the desktop background, but also the window color, system sounds, and screen saver. In Windows 7, all these elements are organized together into what Microsoft calls *themes*. Windows 7 includes a number of these pre-configured themes—and you can create your own, as well.

tip

Some styles include desktop *slideshows*, where multiple desktop backgrounds are displayed in order.

Choosing an Existing Theme

The easiest way to deal with themes is to choose one that Microsoft includes with Windows 7. These themes include the generic Windows 7 theme, as well as Architecture, Characters, Landscapes, Nature, Scenes, and United States themes.

To apply one of these pre-existing themes, follow these steps:

1. Open the Control Panel and select Personalization. (Alternately, right-click anywhere on the desktop and click Personalize from the pop-up menu.)

2. When the Personalization window appears, as shown in Figure 3.1, click the new theme you want to apply.

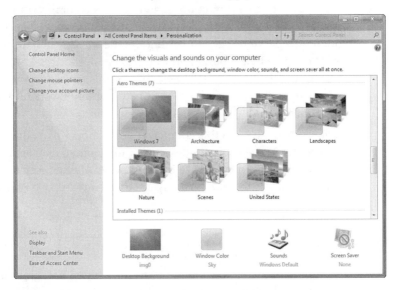

FIGURE 3.1

Use the Personalization window to change Windows' theme, desktop background, window colors, sounds, and screen saver.

The new theme is applied as soon as you click it in the Personalization window, no Save or OK button to click. This means you can see how the theme looks while you're still in the Personalization window—and change to another theme if you don't like the one you first selected.

Finding New Themes Online

The themes that ship with Windows 7 aren't the only themes available. Microsoft makes available a variety of additional themes online; here's how you find them:

1. From the Personalization window, scroll down to and click the Get More Themes Online link.

2. This opens Microsoft's Personalize Your PC web page in your web browser, as shown in Figure 3.2. Make sure the Themes tab is selected.

3. Find the theme you want, and then click the Download button.

4. When the Save As dialog box appears, navigate to the location where you want to save your themes (the My Themes folder in the Documents library is a good choice), and then click Save.

5. Open Windows Explorer, navigate to where you saved the new theme, and then double-click it.

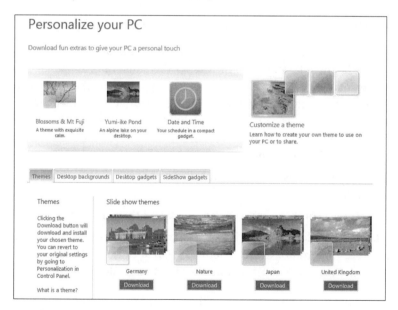

FIGURE 3.2

Browsing new themes online at Microsoft's Personalize Your PC page.

This opens and applies the new theme, as well as installs it in the Personalization window for future use. The next time you open the Personalization window, the new theme will appear in the My Themes section.

tip

Microsoft's Personalize Your PC page (windows.microsoft.com/en-US/windows7/downloads/personalize) also includes desktop backgrounds and gadgets you can download, all for free.

Of course, this isn't the only place you can find new Windows 7 themes. There are a number of sites on the Web that offer themes for downloading, most of them for free. Here is a sampling of such sites you might want to check out:

- Windows 7 Center (windows7center.com/windows-7-themes/)
- Windows 7 Themes (www.windows7themes.net)

caution

Some shady sites offering themes for downloading are rife with computer viruses. Use vigilance when finding Windows themes, desktop backgrounds, and the like to download—and do your downloading only from reputable sites.

Finding Windows 7's Hidden Themes

Then there are the *hidden* themes that come with Windows 7 but aren't visible by default. These are themes for the different countries or regions where Windows 7 is available. By default, you see the theme for your country; for example, if you're in the U.S., you see the United States theme. But there are also themes included for Australia, Canada, Great Britain, and South Africa, if you know where to look for them—which you now do, by following these instructions:

1. Open Windows Explorer and navigate to the c:\Windows\winsxs\ folder.

2. Enter ***.theme** into the search field, and then click Enter.

3. You should now see a list of files; included in this list are files named AU (Australia), CA (Canada), GB (Great Britain), US (United States), and ZA (Australia). Double-click the theme file you want to install.

As before, the theme you click will be immediately applied and thereafter appear in the Personalization window.

Creating a New Theme

You can also create your own themes, from your own combination of background images, colors, sounds, and screen saver. Get everything just the way you like it, then save it as a theme; when you want to return to this particular setup, just switch to this theme and you're all set.

Here's how to create and save a new theme in Windows 7:

1. Apply the desktop background, colors, sounds, and screen saver you want for the theme.

2. Your choices now appear in the Personalization window as an Unsaved Theme. Click this theme to select it.

3. With the unsaved theme selected, right-click this theme in the window and select Save Theme.

4. When prompted, give the theme a name and click the Save button.

This new theme now appears in the Personalization window for you to select in the future.

Changing the Desktop Background

You don't have to change the entire theme to personalize Windows. Windows 7 lets you change each element of the theme individually, starting with the desktop background.

Choosing a Static Background

Windows 7 offers a wide selection of pictures you can use for your desktop background; you can also opt to have a plain-colored background, or choose any other picture on your PC. All you have to do is follow these steps:

1. From the Control Panel, select Personalize. (Alternately, right-click anywhere on the desktop and click Personalize from the pop-up menu.)

2. When the Personalization window appears, click Desktop Background.

3. This opens the Desktop Background window, shown in Figure 3.3. Click the Picture Location list and select what kind of background you want—Windows Desktop Backgrounds, Pictures Library, Top Rated Photos, or Solid Colors.

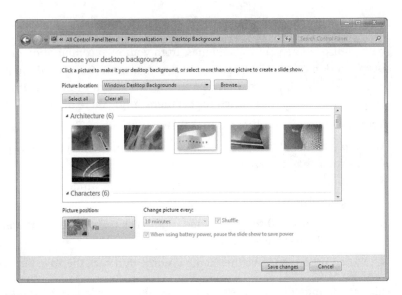

FIGURE 3.3
Choosing a new background for your Windows desktop.

---

tip

You can apply any digital picture stored on your computer as a desktop background. Just click the Browse button in the Desktop Background window and browse for the folder that contains the picture you want; the pictures within that folder will then be displayed in the Desktop Background window.

---

4. Scroll through the list of options until you find the background you want. Select by the background by clicking it; this automatically applies the background to your desktop.

5. To determine how the picture fills your desktop, click the Picture Position list and select Fill, Fit, Stretch, Tile, or Center.

6. Click Save Changes.

A word on those picture position options, which are used when you have a picture that doesn't fill the entire desktop:

- Fill enlarges the photo so that the smallest side fits on the computer screen, as shown in Figure 3.4. This will place the larger side of the photo off the screen.

- Fit enlarges the photo so that the largest side of the photo fits on the computer screen, as shown in Figure 3.5. This will leave colored bars on the smallest sides of the photo.

- Stretch stretches the photo to fill the entire screen, as shown in Figure 3.6. This typically results in either tall, thin people (stretching the photo taller) or short, fat people (stretching the photo wider).

- Tile repeats a smaller photo in a tile pattern across the screen, as shown in Figure 3.7.
- Center places a smaller photo dead center on the screen, with colored space all around it, as shown in Figure 3.8.

FIGURE 3.4

A smaller desktop background with the Fill option.

This image has been fit to the screen with empty space to either side.

FIGURE 3.5

A smaller desktop background with the Fit option.

This image has been stretched to fit the desktop.

FIGURE 3.6

A smaller desktop background with the Stretch option.

FIGURE 3.7

A smaller desktop background with the Tile option.

Choose whichever option looks best for the picture you select. In most cases Fill does the best job, but there are obvious exceptions—which is why the other options exist.

This image has been centered with empty space all around it.

FIGURE 3.8

A smaller desktop background with the Center option.

tip

To get a precise fit without stretching, crop or resize your photo to match the resolution (in pixels) of your computer display.

Creating a Background Slideshow

Prior to Windows 7, you could only select one picture for the desktop background. Windows 7, however, lets you have multiple desktop backgrounds displayed one after another in desktop slideshow. It's a great way to view all your favorite photos—without having to manually switch backgrounds.

To create a desktop slideshow, follow these steps:

1. From the Control Panel, select Personalize. (Alternately, right-click anywhere on the desktop and click Personalize from the pop-up menu.)

2. When the Personalization window appears, click Desktop Background.

3. From the Desktop Background window, click the Picture Location list and select what kind of background you want—or the location of the desired background image.

4. Check the multiple background images you want to include in the slideshow.

5. To determine how long each background displays, select a value from the Change Picture Every list.

6. To display background images in a random order, click the Shuffle option.

7. Click Save Changes.

The result is an ever-changing desktop background—great for displaying all your favorite images.

Changing the Color Scheme

Windows 7 features the Aero interface, which offers a nice combination of translucent (see-through) colors. You can change the color scheme, however, as well as the level of translucency used in window frames, the taskbar, the Start menu, and other onscreen elements.

caution

If your PC doesn't have enough graphics horsepower, it can't display the translucent Aero interface. In this instance, you'll see the Windows 7 Basic interface instead—which looks similar but doesn't have the translucency and many of the three-dimensional effects. (The Basic interface is also what you'll see if you're running the Windows 7 Starter edition, which doesn't include the Aero interface.)

To change the color and translucency in Windows 7, follow these steps:

1. From the Control Panel, select Personalize. (Alternately, right-click anywhere on the desktop and click Personalize from the pop-up menu.)

2. When the Personalization window appears, click Window Color.

3. When the Window Color and Appearance window appears, as shown in Figure 3.9, click the color scheme you want.

4. To make the onscreen windows more transparent, move the Color Intensity slider to the left. To make the windows more solid, move the slider to the right.

5. Click Save Changes.

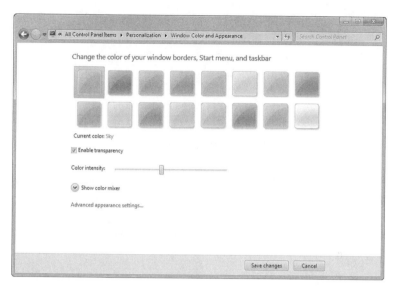

FIGURE 3.9

Choosing a new color scheme and transparency for your Windows desktop.

tip

If you want to choose a custom color, click the Show Color Mixer button in the Windows Color and Appearance window; then fine-tune the selected hue, saturation, and brightness.

Changing Display Resolution

The look and feel of your desktop is also influenced by the resolution of the screen. A larger (higher resolution) desktop lets you view more things onscreen at the same time—even though each item is smaller than before. A smaller (lower resolution) desktop displays fewer items, but they're larger. (This is great if your eyesight is less than perfect.)

You change the size of the desktop by changing Windows' *screen resolution*. Follow these steps:

1. Right-click anywhere on the desktop and select Screen Resolution from the pop-up menu.

2. When the Screen Resolution window appears, as shown in Figure 3.10, click the Resolution button and use the slider to select a new resolution. Move the slider up to set a higher resolution (and display more items on the desktop); move it down to set a lower resolution.

3. Click OK to apply your changes.

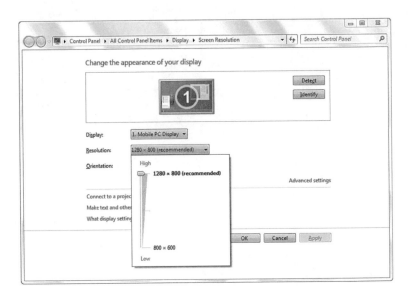

FIGURE 3.10

Use the Resolution slider to change the display size.

tip

To best use all the features of Windows 7, go for a 1024 x 768 or higher resolution. If this setting makes things look too small (a problem if you have a smaller monitor), try the 800 x 600 resolution.

Changing Font and Window Size

If you like the resolution of your display but find the text a little too small to read, you can configure Windows to enlarge the fonts, menus, windows, and other items on the screen to your liking. Here's how to do it:

1. From the Control Panel, select Display.

2. When the Display window appears, as shown in Figure 3.11, select either Smaller (the default size), Medium, or Larger.

3. Click the Apply button.

tip

To enlarge just part of the screen (to more easily read some fine print, for example), use Windows' Magnifier tool. Launch this tool by opening the Start menu and selecting All Programs, Accessories, Ease of Access, Magnifier.

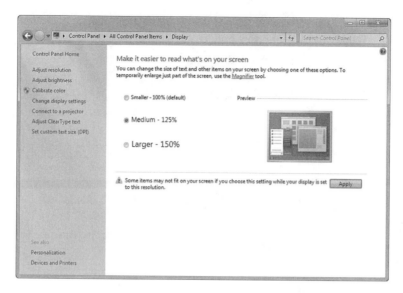

FIGURE 3.11

Choose Medium or Larger to enlarge Windows' fonts, menus, and windows.

Changing Cursor Schemes

The cursor—or *pointer*, as Microsoft likes to call it—is that thing that moves around the computer screen when you move mouse or touchpad. You're used to seeing a few different cursors; the traditional arrow, of course, but also the little "I" you see when inserting the cursor in a document and the hourglass that displays when you're waiting for Windows to do something.

The cursors you see are part of a cursor scheme—and, not surprisingly, Windows lets you change cursor schemes, if you want. Some of the available schemes are a lot easier on the eye (and more usable) than the default scheme.

To change the look of Windows' cursors, follow these steps:

1. From the Control Panel, select Mouse.

2. When the Mouse Properties dialog box appears, select the Pointers tab, shown in Figure 3.12.

3. Pull down the Scheme list and make a new selection.

4. To assign a new cursor within a scheme, select that cursor type in the Customize list, click the Browse button, and then select the cursor you want.

5. If you want to put a drop shadow under the cursors, check the Enable Pointer Shadow option.

6. Click OK to close the dialog box.

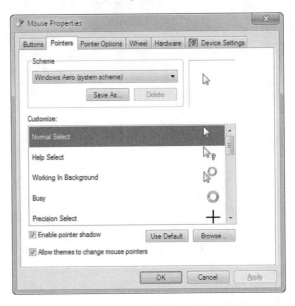

FIGURE 3.12

Changing your system's cursor scheme.

note

Cursor schemes are also saved as part of an overall Windows theme.

The default Windows Aero scheme is nice, but the Black and Inverted schemes might be easier to see if you do a lot of typing on white backgrounds. And if you find the default cursors a bit too small to always see well, choose one of the large or extra large schemes, instead.

tip

On some displays, you may want to display pointer trails (little ghost cursors) to help you keep track of moving cursors. To do this, select the Pointer Options tab and check the Display Pointer Trails option.

For that matter, you can download new cursor schemes from a number of different websites. Try searching for "cursors" at Tucows (www.tucows.com) or Download.com (www.download.com); you should see a big list of cursor schemes you can download for free to your computer. Follow the instructions to install the schemes to the c:\windows\cursors\ folder; some cursors will automatically appear as new schemes in the Scheme list, while others may need to be manually assigned from the Customize list.

Organizing the Desktop

Windows lets you display a variety of shortcut icons on the desktop. These icons function as shortcuts for starting applications and opening documents. Placing a shortcut on your desktop is an alternative to launching items from the Start menu; just double-click the shortcut icon to launch the associated program or document.

Creating New Shortcuts

You can create shortcuts for both applications and individual documents. Here's how to put a new shortcut on the desktop:

1. Use Windows Explorer to navigate to the application or document for which you want to create a shortcut.

2. Right-click the program or file icon and then select Send To, Desktop (Create Shortcut).

But that's just one way to do it. You can also create a shortcut by right-dragging a file icon directly to the desktop, or by right-clicking on the desktop and selecting New, Shortcut from the pop-up menu. However you do it, you end up with a new desktop icon, like the one in Figure 3.13.

FIGURE 3.13

A shortcut icon on the Windows desktop.

> **tip**
>
> To remove a shortcut icon from the desktop, just drag it into the Recycle Bin. (This deletes only the shortcut, of course, not the associated document or application.)

Changing the Name of a Shortcut

When you create a new shortcut icon, the word "Shortcut" is automatically added to the icon's name. You can get rid of this, if you want—or totally change the name of the shortcut to something more easily recognizable. Here's how you do it:

1. Right-click the shortcut on your desktop.

2. When the pop-up menu appears, select Rename.

3. The shortcut's name is now highlighted on your desktop. Use the Delete or Backspace keys to erase parts of the existing name, and then type a new name. Press Enter when you've finished entering the new name.

Changing the Icon Image

By default, a desktop shortcut uses the icon for the document's application. So if you create an icon for an Excel worksheet, you get the Excel worksheet icon for the shortcut.

You don't have to settle for these default icons, however. Windows lets you change the image for any icon, with just a few clicks of the mouse. Here's how to do it.

1. Right-click the shortcut on your desktop.

2. When the pop-up menu appears, select Properties.

3. When the Properties dialog box appears, select the Shortcut tab.

4. Click the Change Icon button.

5. When the Change Icon dialog box appears, as shown in Figure 3.14, select one of the icons displayed, or click the Browse button to browse to a different file and select an icon there.

6. Click OK.

You can find icons in a few different files. I like to browse the included icons in the c:\windows\system32\shell32.dll, c:\windows\system32\imageres.dll, and c:\windows\system32\moricons.dll files.

And here's another place to find icons—in application files. That's right, you can navigate to any program file (.exe) and find an icon for that application stored within; you can apply that icon to any shortcut.

FIGURE 3.14

Selecting a new icon for a desktop shortcut.

tip

Many websites offer individual icons and icon collections for download. Search Google for **Windows icons** and you'll find a bunch.

Arranging Icons on the Desktop

All those desktop icons let you quickly open your most-used programs, but they can really clutter up the look of your Windows desktop. To better arrange your icons, right-click a blank area of the desktop, select Sort By, and choose from one of the following options:

- **Name.** Sorts items alphabetically by filename
- **Size.** Sorts items by file size, from smallest to largest
- **Type.** Sorts items by file type so that files with the same extension are grouped together
- **Date Modified.** Sorts items by date, from oldest to most recent

In addition, you can force all the icons on your desktop to snap to an invisible grid. Just right-click the desktop, click View, and then select Auto Arrange Icons.

Using Gadgets

Here's something that's both neat and useful. Windows 7 lets you add a variety of *gadgets* to the desktop. These gadgets, like the ones shown in Figure 3.15, are actually small utility applications that perform a single simple function. For example, the Clock gadget displays the current time, the Weather gadget reports the current weather conditions and forecast for your area, and so on.

FIGURE 3.15

Gadgets on the Windows desktop.

The intent of these gadgets is to put more content, information, and functions at your fingertips. It's handier to have content modules floating on the desktop than it is to dig through layers of menus to open up each application individually. For that reason, I'm a big fan of gadgets; I think you will be, too.

note

Microsoft first introduced gadgets in Windows Vista, as part of Vista's Sidebar. Microsoft removed the Sidebar from Windows 7, instead enabling you to place gadgets directly on the desktop.

Adding New Gadgets

To add a new gadget to your desktop, follow these steps:

1. Open the Control Panel and select Desktop Gadgets. (Alternately, right-click anywhere on the desktop and then select Gadgets from the pop-up menu.)

2. When the Gadgets window appears, as shown in Figure 3.16, double-click the gadget you wish to add.

Once you've added a gadget to the desktop, you can position it anywhere you want by clicking and dragging the gadget with your mouse. To remove a gadget from your desktop, hover over the gadget and then click the X.

FIGURE 3.16

Adding new gadgets.

caution

Since gadgets are little programs, they draw some system resources all the time. In addition, those gadgets that connect to the Internet for information (such as the Weather and Stocks gadgets) constantly use a small portion of your Internet bandwidth. If you're concerned about conserving system resources, you probably want to minimize the number of gadgets on your desktop.

Finding More Gadgets Online

Only a limited number of gadgets appear in the Gadgets window. Don't fear, however; many more gadgets can be found online. All you have to do is click Get More Gadgets Online from the Gadgets window; this opens your web browser and displays the good old Personalize Your PC page. Click the Desktop Gadgets tab and then click the Get More Desktop Gadgets link.

As you can see in Figure 3.17, this opens the Personalize PC page, with available gadgets sorted by category. At last count there were more than 3,000 gadgets available, so you'll probably be able to find at least one you want to try. Click the Download button for any gadget you want to install.

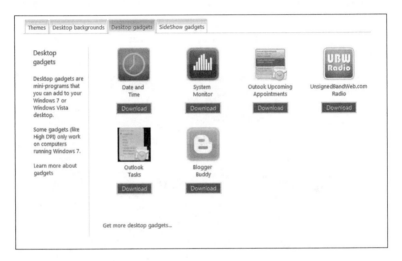

FIGURE 3.17

Browsing for more gadgets online.

Configuring Gadgets

Some gadgets have options for how they're displayed. For example, you can enter your own location into the Weather gadget to display your local weather conditions and forecast. To configure the options for a gadget, right-click the gadget and select Options. Alternately, hover your cursor over the gadget until the Options bar appears, as shown in Figure 3.18, and then click the tool icon. Naturally, the available options differ from gadget to gadget.

FIGURE 3.18

Displaying a gadget's Options bar.

Some gadgets have both a large and a small version; the large version typically displays more information than the smaller one. To switch from one version to another, hover your cursor over the gadget to display the Options bar, and then click the Smaller Size or Larger Size icon.

You can also change how much the desktop shows through a gadget's background. Just right-click the gadget, select Opacity, and then select a percent. The larger the percentage, the less opaque (more solid) the gadget will be.

Using Non-Microsoft Gadgets

Windows 7 gadgets aren't the only gadgets you can put on your desktop. The whole concept of small content modules started with a company called Konfabulator, which created what it called *widgets* for the desktop. Konfabulator was subsequently purchased by Yahoo!, resulting in the now-renamed Yahoo! Widgets.

You can find a whole variety of Yahoo! Widgets to download at widgets.yahoo.com. These widgets operate pretty much like Windows gadgets; they install directly to your desktop and can be moved around wherever you want.

Another source of desktop gadgets is the Google Desktop. This is a piece of software that has two functions. Google Desktop is a search engine for files on your computer, as well as a host for a variety of gadgets that dock onto the Desktop's sidebar. You can learn more at desktop.google.com.

note

On the Apple side of things, the Dashboard enables users to add a variety of widgets to the Mac desktop.

Applying a Screen Saver

Let's move slightly beyond the desktop to your system's screen saver. As you're probably aware, a screen saver displays moving designs on your computer screen when you haven't typed or moved the mouse for a while.

Originally, screen savers were intended to prevent static images from burning onto monitor screens. While burn-in was an issue with old CRT monitors, today's LCD monitors don't have that problem. Still, screen savers remain popular, for their entertainment value if nothing else.

To activate one of the screen savers included with Windows 7, follow these steps:

1. From the Control Panel, select Personalize. (Alternately, right-click anywhere on the desktop and click Personalize from the pop-up menu.)

2. When the Personalization window appears, click Screen Saver.

3. When the Screen Saver Settings dialog box appears, as shown in Figure 3.19, select a screen saver from the Screen Saver drop-down list.

4. Click the Settings button to configure that screen saver's specific settings (if available).

5. Click OK when you're done.

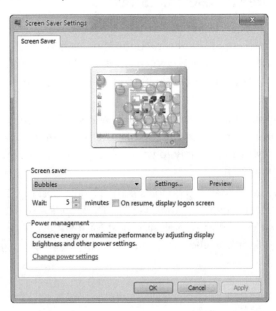

FIGURE 3.19

Selecting a Windows screen saver.

Calibrating Your Monitor

Have you ever edited a digital photo on your computer, made sure it looked great on your monitor, and then printed it—only to discover that the colors didn't look quite the same as they did onscreen? The problem is a common one, and it's due to a miscalibrated monitor.

This leads us to the next bit of configuration, which isn't for Windows itself but rather for your computer monitor—or, in the case of a notebook PC, the built-in display. In most instances, you can adjust the color and brightness controls of your display just as you would the similar controls on a television set to produce the best-looking picture possible.

Here's how it works:

1. Open the Control Panel and select Display.

2. When the Display window appears, select Calibrate Color from the side panel.

3. Click the Next button; then continue clicking Next until you get to the Adjust Gamma screen, shown in Figure 3.20.

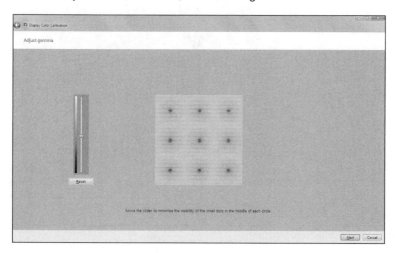

FIGURE 3.20

Adjusting your display's gamma setting.

note

Gamma is the relationship between the brightness of an image pixel and the numerical value of that pixel. Too large a gamma setting results in oversaturated colors; too small a gamma setting results in washed out colors.

4. Move the slider until the small dots in the middle of each circle are minimized; then click Next.

5. Click the Next button until you get to the Adjust Brightness screen.

6. Adjust the brightness control on your monitor until you can just distinguish the dark shirt from the black background, and then click Next.

note

Few notebook PCs have brightness and contrast controls. You typically find these controls on separate computer monitors.

7. Click the Next button until you get to the Adjust Contrast screen.

8. Move the contrast control on your monitor as high as you can without losing the wrinkles and button's on the subject's shirt, and then click Next.

9. Click the Next button until you get to the Adjust Color Balance screen, shown in Figure 3.21.

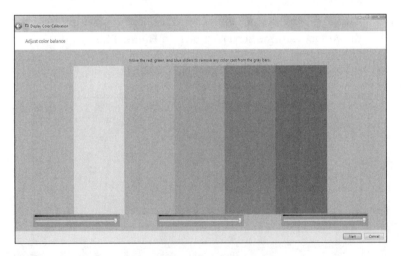

FIGURE 3.21
Adjusting your display's color balance.

10. Adjust the red, green, and blue sliders until you achieve pure gray bars; then click Next.

11. On the next screen, click the Finish button.

12. When the ClearType Text Tuner window appears, check the Turn on ClearType option and click Next.

note

ClearType is a font-smoothing technology that Windows uses to improve the display of text on computer monitors; it works to reduce the jagged edges that might otherwise appear.

13. On the next screen, click the Next button.

14. When the next window appears, as shown in Figure 3.22, click the text sample that looks best to you, and then click Next.

FIGURE 3.22

Fine-tuning the ClearType text.

15. Repeat step 14 for the next three screens.

16. Click the Finish button.

Your display should now look a little better than it did before.

tip

For more precise calibration, purchase a professional color calibration system, such as the Pantone Huey (www.pantone.com) or Spyder3Pro (spyder.datacolor.com). These systems, which include a piece of hardware called a colorimeter that you hang in front of your monitor, typically run a few hundred dollars, and are popular with professional photographers and video editors.

Changing System Sounds

Our last bit of configuration is also a bit outside the confines of the desktop, but it's all part and parcel of the piece. I'm talking about system sounds—you know, the various beeps and boops that Windows makes when you perform specific operations.

Choosing a Sound Scheme

Windows 7 offers a number of built-in sound schemes—combinations of sounds for all appropriate Windows events. You can easily change from one scheme to another, or spend a bit more time to customize the sounds within a scheme. Here's what to do:

> **note**
>
> Sound schemes are also saved as part of your overall Windows theme.

1. Open the Control Panel and select Sound.

2. When the Sound dialog box appears, select the Sounds tab, shown in Figure 3.23.

3. To select a new sound scheme, pull down the Sound Scheme list and make a selection.

4. To change an individual sound event within a scheme, select it in the Program Events list; then pull down the Sounds list and make a new selection. This lets you reassign sounds within a scheme; to choose a sound from outside the scheme, click the Browse button and browse to the sound file you want to use.

5. Click the OK button to close the dialog box.

> **tip**
>
> To preview how a sound sounds, select it and then click the Test button.

Using Your Own Sounds

Here's the real way to have Windows sound your way: Don't limit yourself to the built-in schemes and sounds. Instead, use the Browse button to select other WAV-format sound files stored on your hard drive. With a little advanced planning (such as converting your favorite MP3 files to WAV format, for example), you can have Windows play "We Are the Champions" every time it starts up. Cool!

FIGURE 3.23

Changing Windows' sounds.

---

tip

To convert MP3 song files to WAV format, use an audio editing/conversion program such as Audacity (audacity.sourceforge.net) or TuneCab (www.tunecab.com).

The Bottom Line

Most users like to customize the look and feel of Windows, to make their systems seem a bit more personal. There's a lot to customize in Windows 7, from the coordinated desktop themes to the background images and window colors, to the new desktop gadgets. I particularly like the new desktop slideshows, which make it easy to display a variety of images on the desktop. In any case, take the time to learn everything you can personalize—and then have fun doing so!

4

Customizing the Taskbar

Windows 7 offers many new features not found in previous versions of the operating system. One of the most useful of these features is the new taskbar, which is totally different from anything you've used in previous versions of Windows. It's also highly customizable, which makes it worth our examination.

What's New About the Windows 7 Taskbar

If you've been using Windows for awhile, you're already familiar with the taskbar, that little strip of real estate at the bottom of the desktop. You will find the Windows 7 taskbar, however, to be a bit different from what you're used to.

In previous versions of Windows, the taskbar existed to show you which programs or documents were currently open in Windows. Every open application or document had its own button on the taskbar; you could easily switch from one open window to another by clicking the appropriate taskbar button.

That changed a little with Windows XP, when Microsoft added a Quick Launch toolbar that you could dock to the taskbar. The Quick Launch toolbar could be configured with buttons for your favorite apps, which could then be quickly launched from the toolbar—which, when docked, appeared to be part of the taskbar. In Windows XP, the Quick Launch toolbar was activated by default; it was still around in Windows Vista, but not automatically displayed.

Well, in Windows 7, the taskbar takes on the attributes of the traditional taskbar plus the old Quick Launch toolbar—and a little more.

That is, the Win7 taskbar includes buttons (actually, just icons—no text) that are not just for running applications and documents but also for your favorite applications.

Click an icon to launch an app or click an icon to switch to an open window; taskbar icons exist for both. In this aspect, the new taskbar more than a little resembles the Dock from the Mac OS.

Using the Windows 7 Taskbar

First things first. The Windows 7 taskbar looks different from the taskbar in Windows Vista and previous versions. It's more glass-like than the old taskbar, a little taller as well, and it displays icons, not buttons. There are no labels on the icons, just the icon graphic.

The advantage of this new design is both visual (cleaner look) and practical (the new icons—while larger than the icons on the old text buttons—take up less space on the taskbar). It's easier to see what's what, while at the same time more items are displayed in the same amount of screen real estate.

Understanding Taskbar Icons

That said, you might have some problems figuring out what's what in terms of taskbar buttons. That's because a Win7 taskbar icon can represent a currently open window, a group of open windows (multiple documents for the same applications), or a shortcut to a program that isn't currently running. Unless you look closely, it's difficult to see the difference between different types of icons.

Difficult, yes, but not impossible. Here's the key.

As you can see in Figure 4.1, an icon for a not-yet-open application or document—essentially a shortcut to that app or doc—appears on the taskbar with no border. An icon for an open window has a slight border, while still appearing translucent. An icon for the currently selected open window also has a border, but is less transparent. And if there is more than one document open for a given application (or more than one tab open in a web browser), that app's icon button appears "stacked" to represent multiple instances.

Click a shortcut icon to open the associated application or document. Click an open window icon to display that window front and center.

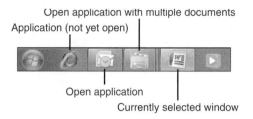

FIGURE 4.1

The different types of icons on the Windows 7 taskbar.

Viewing Taskbar Thumbnails

If you click a multiple-window icon, however, something interesting happens: Windows displays thumbnails for each of that application's open windows, as shown in Figure 4.2. (The same thing happens if you hover the cursor over any open-window icon, actually.)

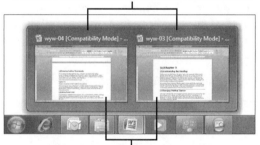

FIGURE 4.2

Viewing document thumbnails from the taskbar.

Move the cursor over a thumbnail, and that window temporarily displays on top of the stack on your desktop, no matter what its actual position. Click a thumbnail to switch to that window, or click the red X on the thumbnail to close the window.

Using Jump Lists

The Windows 7 taskbar becomes even more useful with the addition of Jump Lists—kind of context-sensitive pop-up menus for each icon on the taskbar. To display an icon's Jump List, like the one in Figure 4.3, right-click the icon.

FIGURE 4.3

A Windows 7 taskbar Jump List.

What you see in a Jump List depends to some degree on the application associated with the icon. For example, Windows 7–specific apps will display more specific (and useful) Jump Lists than applications developed prior to Windows 7; an app has to be written specifically to take full advantage of this new feature.

Most Jump Lists contain the following items:

- The most recent documents opened in this application
- A link to open a new instance of this application
- An option to unpin this item from the taskbar (for shortcut icons)
- An option to close the current window (for open-window icons)

Win7-specific apps offer more application-appropriate items on their Jump Lists. For example, Windows Media Player 12 (the new version in Windows 7) has a section for Frequent playlists and albums, as well as a Tasks section with the most-recent program operations.

In short, Windows 7 taskbar Jump Lists are a lot like traditional right-click pop-up menus, but with more useful options. They make the new taskbar icons more useful than they would have been otherwise.

Personalizing the Taskbar

Now that you know what the Windows 7 taskbar does, let's look a little at how to manage the new taskbar—and configure it to look and work your way.

Moving the Taskbar

Ninety nine point nine percent of Windows users display the taskbar at the bottom of the computer screen. That's the default position, after all, and it works pretty well.

That said, you can move the taskbar to any side of the computer screen. You can display it at the top of the screen, or on the right or left sides of the screen. I happen to like the left-side display, shown in Figure 4.4, especially if you have a widescreen monitor; it's a good use of real estate.

FIGURE 4.4

The taskbar moved to the left side of the display.

How do you move the taskbar? It's easy; just follow these steps:

1. Right-click on an open area of the taskbar and select Properties. (Alternately, open the Control Panel and select Taskbar and Start Menu.)

2. When the Taskbar and Start Menu Properties dialog box appears, select the Taskbar tab, shown in Figure 4.5.

3. Pull down the Taskbar Location on Screen list and select the desired location: Bottom, Left, Right, or Top.

4. Click OK.

If you position the taskbar at the top of the screen, the Start menu pulls down instead of popping up. If you position the taskbar at the left side of the screen, the Start menu opens to the right. If you position the taskbar at the right side of the screen, the Start menu opens to the left.

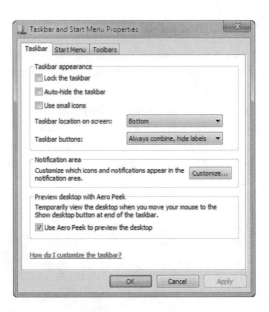

FIGURE 4.5

Use the Taskbar and Start Menu Properties dialog box to configure the taskbar.

Hiding the Taskbar

By default, the taskbar is constantly displayed. But maybe you don't want it taking up all that screen real estate all the time. In which case, you can "auto-hide" the taskbar, so that it doesn't appear onscreen until you move your cursor to the bottom of the screen—which then causes the taskbar to slide back up into view.

To auto-hide the taskbar, follow these steps:

1. Right-click anywhere on the taskbar and select Properties. (Alternately, open the Control Panel and select Taskbar and Start Menu.)

2. When the Taskbar and Start Menu Properties dialog box appears, select the Taskbar tab.

3. Check the Auto-Hide the Taskbar option.

4. Click OK.

Changing the Way Icons Are Displayed

You can also configure the way the taskbar buttons behave. By default, Windows combines multiple documents from a single application into a single button; it also hides the labels for each button. There are other options, however, including never combining multiple documents into a single button, and combining documents only when the taskbar is full. To make your choice, follow these steps:

1. Right-click anywhere on the taskbar and select Properties. (Alternately, open the Control Panel and select Taskbar and Start Menu.)

2. When the Taskbar and Start Menu Properties dialog box appears, select the Taskbar tab.

3. Pull down the Taskbar Buttons list and make a new choice.

4. Click OK.

You can also change the size of the buttons on the taskbar—and thus the taskbar itself. By default, Windows uses what it calls "large icons"; you can easily shrink the size of the toolbar by switching to "small icons." Go to the Taskbar tab in the Taskbar and Start Menu Properties dialog box and check the Use Small Icons option. Uncheck this option to return to the default "large icons" view.

tip

You can also change the color of the taskbar, by changing the overall Windows color scheme. Learn more in Chapter 3, "Customizing the Desktop."

Adding Icons to the Taskbar

If you configure your taskbar smartly, you may seldom use the Windows Start menu. To that end, I create taskbar buttons for my most-used applications and for a handful of my favorite documents. That way everything I need is right on the taskbar, a single click away from opening.

How do you add new buttons to the taskbar? Remember, you can create taskbar buttons for applications or for documents. Here's how to do it:

1. Open the Start menu or Windows Explorer and locate the application or document you want to add to the taskbar.

2. Right-click the item and select Pin to Taskbar from the pop-up menu.

That's pretty easy. It's also easy to remove an item from the taskbar. Just right-click the button to display the Jump List, then select Unpin This Program from the Taskbar.

tip

Even easier, you can open Windows Explorer and drag the icon for the item from any folder onto the taskbar. That pins it!

Rearranging Taskbar Icons

In previous versions of the taskbar, you had no control over the order of taskbar buttons; the order was dictated by the order in which the applications were opened. With Windows 7, you have total control over taskbar icon order. Just use your mouse to drag and drop a taskbar icon into the position you want, and there it stays. That makes for a more consistent—and easier-to-use—taskbar.

Changing the Number of Items in Jump Lists

By default, Windows displays the ten most-recent items in all taskbar Jump Lists. If you'd prefer a shorter list, follow these steps:

1. Right-click anywhere on the taskbar and select Properties. (Alternately, open the Control Panel and select Taskbar and Start Menu.)

2. When the Taskbar and Start Menu Properties dialog box appears, select the Start Menu tab.

3. Click the Customize button to display the Customize Start Menu dialog box.

4. Select a new number from the Number of Recent Items to Display in Jump Lists list.

5. Click OK when finished.

> **tip**
>
> Even better, you can choose not to display any recently opened files in your Jump Lists. Go to the Start Menu tab of the Taskbar and Start Menu Properties dialog box and uncheck the Store and Display Recently Opened Items in the Start Menu and the Taskbar option, then click OK.

Resizing the Taskbar

If you add a lot of icons to the taskbar, you may fill it up. Fortunately, you can resize the taskbar to display two, three, or more rows of buttons, as shown in Figure 4.6. Here's how to do it:

FIGURE 4.6

A taskbar resized to hold two rows of buttons.

1. Right-click on the taskbar and uncheck the Lock the Taskbar option.

2. Use your mouse to grab the top edge of the taskbar, and then drag it upward.

3. When you're done resizing the taskbar, right-click on the taskbar again and re-check the Lock the Taskbar option.

As is obvious, you can't resize the taskbar while the taskbar is locked. So you first have to unlock it and then resize it.

Revisiting the Notification Area

There's another important part of the taskbar, that area on the right side of the taskbar called the notification area. In Windows Vista, this was a very cluttered area, holding icons that represented each and every little application or utility that ran in the background.

note

Microsoft used to call the notification area the system tray, as it served as a tray to hold all sorts of system utilities.

Well, the notification area in Windows 7 is a lot less cluttered than what it used to be. Microsoft wisely took the initiative to de-clutter the notification area to display only a handful of the most useful system icons.

As you can see in Figure 4.7, the Windows 7 notification area contains icons for the following utilities:

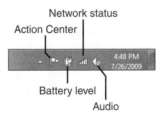

FIGURE 4.7

The streamlined Windows 7 taskbar notification area.

- Action Center (kind of a notification/troubleshooting gateway)
- Battery level (on notebook PCs)
- Network status (also displays wireless status when connected to a WiFi network)
- Audio

In addition, the time and date are displayed on the far right side of the notification area.

Viewing Hidden Icons

What happened to all the other icons you used to find in the notification area? In Windows 7, they're relegated to a Jump List-like pop-up menu that displays when you click the up-arrow to the left of the notification area, as shown in Figure 4.8. This makes for a much cleaner (and smaller) notification area. It's a huge improvement.

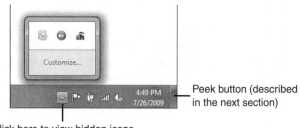

Peek button (described in the next section)

Click here to view hidden icons or to customize the notification area.

FIGURE 4.8

The icons you don't see in the notification area.

Displaying Different Icons

What if you want to display a different notification area icon? Say, for example, you have a status icon for a particular application you've installed that you find useful. How do you get it to show in the new streamlined notification area?

Here's how to do it:

1. Click the up arrow to the left of the notification area, and then click Customize. (Alternately, open the Control Panel and select Notification Area Icons.)

2. When the Notification Area Icons window appears, as shown in Figure 4.9, pull down the list next to a specific utility and select Show Icon and Notifications.

3. To not display an icon, pull down the list next to that utility and select Hide Icon and Notifications.

4. If you want to see notifications from a utility but not display the icon full-time, pull down the list next to that utility and select Only Show Notifications.

5. Click OK.

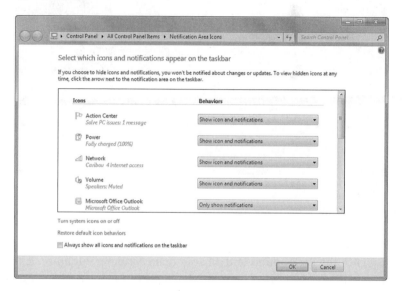

FIGURE 4.9

Configuring icon display for the notification area.

---

tip

To always show all available icons in the notification area, check the Always Show All Icons and Notifications on the Taskbar option.

Peeking at the Desktop

There's one more part of the taskbar that bears discussion, even if there's no configuration involved. That's the (unlabeled) Peek button—actually a thin translucent slice at the far right-hand side of the taskbar, just past the date and time display.

The Peek button activates a new feature of Windows 7 dubbed Aero Peek. Hover your cursor over this button and all the open windows on your desktop go transparent, as shown in Figure 4.10. This lets you see the contents of the desktop below—your desktop background, shortcut icons, and gadgets.

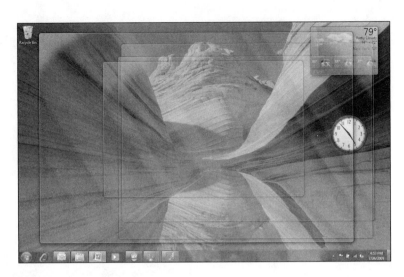

FIGURE 4.10
Peeking at the desktop with Aero Peek.

You can also use the Peek button to gain instant access to your desktop. Just click the Peek button and all your open windows minimize. It's a nifty way to quickly view or access the gadgets and icons on your desktop—and a great new feature of Windows 7.

> **note**
>
> As with past versions, Windows 7 also lets you add individual toolbars (such as the old Quick Launch toolbar) to the taskbar; you do this from the Toolbars tab of the Taskbar and Start Menu Properties dialog box. However, given the new functionality of the Windows 7 taskbar, these toolbars are pretty much unnecessary—and functionally obsolete.

The Bottom Line

The Windows 7 taskbar is different from what you're used to in Windows Vista or Windows XP. In fact, it's so different as to be confusing to some users. Fortunately, you can personalize how the taskbar looks and works—you can move it around the screen, make it slide up from the bottom of the screen, and select just what buttons you want to appear. Same thing with the notification area, which is a lot less crowded this time around. It's all in service of configuring Windows your way!

5

Customizing the Start Menu

So far we've looked at the desktop and taskbar, but there's one more part of the Windows 7 interface that you can have your way. I'm talking about the Start menu, which you can easily customize to look and work the way you want.

Understanding the Start Menu

The Start menu, shown in Figure 5.1, is the menu you see when you click the Start button or "orb" on the Windows taskbar. It's your gateway to all the programs installed on your system, including Windows' system utilities.

The Start menu is divided into two panes. The left pane displays your most recently used programs, as well as any programs you've "pinned" to the menu. The left pane is also where you access the All Programs menu (by clicking the All Programs link), which stores all the programs you've installed on your system.

note

When you "pin" an application to the Start menu, it always appears there, at the top of the left pane.

The right pane of the Start menu contains links to various Windows folders, libraries, and utilities. It's also home to the Power button, which you use to shut down your system.

tip

While the Start menu appears by default at the bottom left side of the screen, you can reposition the Start button to the top or either side of the desktop, by moving the entire taskbar. Learn more in Chapter 4, "Customizing the Taskbar."

FIGURE 5.1

The default Windows 7 Start menu, consisting of left and right panes.

Customizing the Right Pane of the Start Menu

While the Start menu pretty much is the Start menu, there are a few ways you can personalize the way it looks and works for you. For starters, you can change what items appear in the right pane of the Start menu—and how each item behaves.

There are a number of items that appear in the right pane by default— links to your Documents, Pictures, and Music libraries, a submenu of recently opened documents, links to the Control Panel and Help system, and the like. You can remove any or all of these items from the Start menu, or add other items that may be of more use to you.

In addition, some of these items can be displayed in different ways. For example, by default the Documents item opens a Documents window when clicked. However, you can opt to display the Documents item as a menu—that is, when you click it, it displays a submenu of items in the Documents library, as shown in Figure 5.2. This option to display as a link (opens a new window) or a menu (displays a submenu) is available for many right-pane items.

FIGURE 5.2

The Documents item displayed as a menu, not a link.

So how do you customize the right pane of the Start menu? Just follow these steps:

1. Right-click the Start button and select Properties from the pop-up menu. (Alternately, open the Control Panel and select Taskbar and Start Menu.)

2. When the Taskbar and Start Menu Properties dialog box appears, select the Start Menu tab.

3. Click the Customize button.

4. When the Customize Start Menu dialog box appears, as shown in Figure 5.3, scroll to an item you want to appear on the Start menu.

5. If there is only a single check box for that item, check the check box. This will display the item as a link; when clicked, it will open a new window for that item.

6. Some items have three options. To display the item as a link (when clicked, it opens a new window), check the Display as a Link option. To display the item as a menu (when clicked, a submenu opens), select Display as a Menu.

7. If you don't want an item to display on the Start menu, either uncheck the single check box or check the Don't Display This Item option.

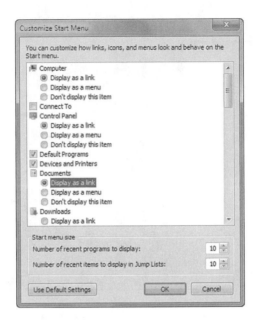

FIGURE 5.3

Customizing the items in the Start menu's right pane.

8. Click OK when done.

So what items can you show in the right pane? Here's a list:

- Computer (AKA My Computer)
- Connect To (displays network and WiFi connections)
- Control Panel
- Default Programs (list of Windows default programs)
- Devices and Printers
- Documents (AKA My Documents)
- Downloads (recent items you've downloaded to your PC)
- Favorites Menu (the Favorites website list from Internet Explorer)
- Games
- Help
- Homegroup (all computers and devices in your network homegroup)
- Music
- Network (all computers and devices on your network)
- Personal Folder
- Pictures

- Recent Items
- Recorded TV
- Run Command
- System Administrative Tools
- Videos

Further Customizing the Start Menu

While you're in the Customize Start Menu dialog box, there are a few display options buried in the items list that you might want to tinker with. Here's what you'll find:

- **Enable Context Menus and Dragging and Dropping.** This option, enabled by default, enables you to reposition items in the left pane of the Start menu (and on the All Programs menu) by dragging and dropping. It also displays pop-up context-sensitive menus when you right-click any Start menu item. Unchecking this option disable drag-and-drop repositioning and pop-up right-click menus.

- **Highlight Newly Installed Programs.** When enabled (which it is by default), this option highlights recently installed programs on the All Programs menu. Unchecking this option results in no items being highlighted.

- **Open Submenus When I Pause on Them with the Mouse Pointer.** Enabled by default, this item displays any available submenus when you hover over a Start menu item. Uncheck this item if you prefer to click to open submenus.

- **Sort All Programs Menu by Name.** When checked (which it is, by default), this items displays all items on the All Programs menu in alphabetical order. When unchecked, items on the All Programs menu are listed in order of installation.

- **Use Large Icons.** The default configuration displays large icons in the Start menu. Uncheck to display smaller icons—and thus reduce the size of the Start menu.

I really like customizing what does and doesn't display on the right side of the Start menu. I'm a particular fan of displaying key items, such as the Control Panel, as menus rather than as links; this makes it easier for me to get to those items I use most often.

tip

To remove any personalization of the Start menu's right pane, click the Use Default Settings button in the Customize Start Menu dialog box.

Pinning and Unpinning Items To and From the Start Menu's Left Pane

In Chapter 4 you learned how to pin items to the taskbar—that is, to place an icon for a document or application on the taskbar, permanently. Well, you can also pin items to the Start menu—in particular, to the top of the left pane, as shown in Figure 5.4. All you have to do is follow these steps:

FIGURE 5.4

Items pinned to the top left pane of the Start menu.

1. Click the Start button to display the Start menu.
2. Click All Programs to open the Programs menu.
3. Navigate to a specific program.
4. Right-click that program to display the pop-up menu.
5. Select Pin to Start Menu.

The program you selected now appears every time you open the Start menu; it doesn't scroll off the menu as you open newer programs, as with the other programs in the left pane. If you ever want to remove a pinned item from the Start menu, just right-click its icon and select Unpin from Start Menu.

tip

Don't like the order of pinned items? Use your mouse to drag an item up or down the pinned list to a new position.

Displaying Fewer Programs on the Start Menu

By default, the left pane of the Start menu displays the ten most-recent applications you've run. If this is too much for you, you can reconfigure the Start menu to display fewer applications at a time.

To display fewer programs, follow these steps:

1. Right-click the Start button and select Properties from the pop-up menu. (Alternately, open the Control Panel and select Taskbar and Start Menu.)

2. When the Taskbar and Start Menu Properties dialog box appears, select the Start Menu tab.

3. Click the Customize button to display the Customize Start Menu dialog box.

4. Select a new number from the Number of Recent Programs to Display list.

5. Click OK when finished.

tip

If you'd rather not display any recent programs in the left pane of the Start menu, go to the Start Menu tab of the Taskbar and Start Menu Properties dialog box and uncheck the Store and Display Recently Opened Programs in the Start Menu option.

Clear Recently Opened Files

See all those right arrows next to items in the Start menu and All Programs menu? Click a right arrow and you see a list of recently opened files for that program. If you'd rather not display your most recent files in this fashion, follow these steps:

1. Right-click the Start button and select Properties from the pop-up menu. (Alternately, open the Control Panel and select Taskbar and Start Menu.)

2. When the Taskbar and Start Menu Properties dialog box appears, select the Start Menu tab, shown in Figure 5.5.

3. Uncheck the Store and Display Recently Opened Items in the Start Menu and the Taskbar option.

4. Click OK.

FIGURE 5.5
Clearing recently opened items from the Start menu.

Changing What the Power Button Does

The Power button is that big button at the bottom right of the Start menu that you typically use to shut down your computer. You can, however, choose to have that big button perform any of the following tasks:

- Shut Down (turns off your PC)
- Hibernate (your open data is saved to your hard disk and your PC is fully powered down)

- Sleep (like Hibernate, except your PC goes into a low-power mode rather than fully powering down)
- Restart (shuts down and then reboots your computer)
- Lock (returns to the Windows logon screen and requires a logon to resume)
- Log Off (logs off the current user from Windows)
- Switch User (enables another user to log on to Windows)

Now, all these options are available when you click the right arrow next to the Power button. But you can assign any of these options to the Power button itself, by following these steps:

1. Right-click the Start button and select Properties from the pop-up menu. (Alternately, open the Control Panel and select Taskbar and Start Menu.)

2. When the Taskbar and Start Menu Properties dialog box appears, select the Start Menu tab.

3. Pull down the Power Button Action list and select a new option.

4. Click the OK button.

Advanced Customizing with the Group Policy Editor

Believe it or not, there are even more things you can tweak about the Start menu, using Windows' Group Policy Editor. The Group Policy Editor is a system-level utility that isn't directly accessible from the Control Panel or any other menu; you have to launch the program manually.

What does the Group Policy Editor enable you to change? Lots of things! The settings in the Group Policy Editor—technically called *policies*—affect not only the Start menu, but also other Windows functions. There's a lot here to work with!

How do you launch and use the Group Policy Editor? Follow these steps:

1. Click the Start button, enter **gpedit.msc** into the search box, and then press Enter.

2. When the Group Policy Editor window appears, as shown in Figure 5.6, select in the navigation pane User Configuration, Administrative Templates, Start Menu and Taskbar.

3. In the contents pane, double-click the setting you want to change.

4. A new window for that setting now appears, like the one shown in Figure 5.7. Check the Enabled option.

5. Click OK to close the setting window.

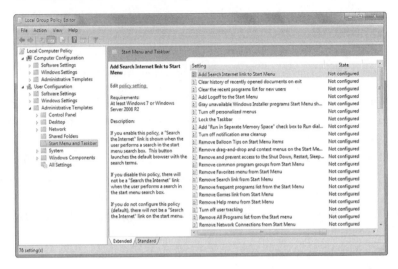

FIGURE 5.6

Using the Group Policy Editor to customize the Start menu.

FIGURE 5.7

Enabling a setting.

So what settings can you change with the Group Policy Editor? Well, some of these settings are the same as what we've discussed previously; others can only be changed via the Group Policy Editor. In particular, the Group Policy Editor enables you to remove items from the Start menu that you just don't use—and can't be removed by any other method.

So there are a lot of "remove" options in the Group Policy Editor. Here's what you can change in the Start Menu and Taskbar section alone:

- Add Search Internet link to Start menu
- Clear history of recently opened documents on exit
- Clear the recent programs list for new users
- Add Logoff to the Start menu
- Gray unavailable Windows Installer programs Start menu shortcuts
- Turn off personalized menus
- Lock the taskbar
- Add "Run in Separate Memory Space" check box to Run dialog box
- Turn off notification area cleanup
- Remove Balloon Tips on Start menu items
- Remove drag-and-drop and context menus on the Start menu
- Remove and prevent access to the Shut Down, Restart, Sleep, and Hibernate commands
- Remove common program groups from Start menu
- Remove Favorites menu from Start menu
- Remove Search link from Start menu
- Remove frequent programs list from Start menu
- Remove Games link from Start menu
- Remove Help menu from Start menu
- Turn off user tracking
- Remove All Programs list from Start menu

caution

That's right—you can actually remove the All Programs menu from the Start menu! Not that you should, of course; without the All Programs menu, you won't be able to access a list of installed programs.

- Remove Network Connections from Start menu
- Remove pinned programs list from Start menu

- Do not keep history of recently opened documents
- Remove Recent Items menu from Start menu
- Do not use the search-based method when resolving shell shortcuts
- Do not use the tracking-based method when resolving shell shortcuts
- Remove Run menu from Start menu
- Remove Default Programs link from Start menu
- Remove Documents icon from Start menu
- Remove Music icon from Start menu
- Remove Network icon from Start menu
- Remove Pictures icon from Start menu
- Do not search communications
- Remove Search Computer link
- Remove See More Results/Search Everywhere link
- Do not search for files
- Do not search Internet
- Do not search programs and Control Panel items
- Remove programs on Settings menu
- Prevent changes to Taskbar and Start menu Settings
- Remove Downloads link from Start menu
- Remove Homegroup link from Start menu
- Remove Recorded TV link from Start menu
- Remove user's folders from Start menu
- Remove Videos link from Start menu
- Force classic Start menu
- Remove Clock from the system notification area
- Prevent grouping of taskbar items
- Do not display any custom toolbars in the taskbar
- Remove access to the context menus for the taskbar
- Hide the notification area
- Remove user folder link from Start menu
- Remove user name from Start menu
- Remove links and access to Windows Update
- Change Start menu power button

- Show QuickLaunch on taskbar
- Remove the "Undock PC" button from Start menu
- Add the Run command to the Start menu
- Remove logoff on the Start menu
- Remove the Action Center icon
- Remove the networking icon
- Remove the battery meter
- Remove the volume control icon
- Turn off feature advertisement balloon notifications
- Do not allow pinning items in Jump Lists
- Do not allow pinning programs to the taskbar
- Do not display or track items in Jump Lists from remote locations
- Turn off automatic promotion of notification icons to the taskbar
- Lock all taskbar settings
- Prevent users from rearranging toolbars
- Turn off all balloon notifications
- Remove pinned programs from the taskbar
- Prevent users from moving taskbar to another screen dock location
- Prevent users from resizing the taskbar
- Turn off taskbar thumbnails

That's a lot of things you can turn on and off about the Start menu and taskbar. But, as they say on late night TV, that's not all. The Group Policy Editor also includes settings for the Control Panel, desktop, network, shared folders, system, and Windows components. If you're an inveterate tweaker, there's a lot here to play with—go at it!

The Bottom Line

The Windows Start menu is the gateway to just about everything that's stored on your computer. You can configure the Start menu your way, by selecting various options in the Taskbar and Start Menu Properties dialog box. In particular, you can choose which items are pinned permanently to the top of the left pane, as well as which system folders and utilities are displayed in the right pane—and whether they open a submenu or a new window when clicked.

6

Customizing Windows Explorer

Working with Windows, more often than not, means working with files and folders. And working with files and folders in Windows means working with Windows Explorer.

As often as you use Windows Explorer, wouldn't it be nice to personalize it just a tad, make it a little easier to work with? Well, your wish is granted, as there are lots of ways to make Windows Explorer look and feel your way.

Read on to learn more.

Understanding Windows Explorer

Windows Explorer is an application that displays the contents of hard drives and folders. You use it to navigate all the folders and files on your computer.

This makes Windows Explorer a file manager application. In fact, Explorer replaced Windows' self-named File Manager application, which ruled the roost from Windows 3.0 (1990) to Windows 95. Since that 1995 introduction, Windows Explorer has gone through quite a few permutations. In fact, there was time when it really wasn't called Windows Explorer.

That time was 2001, and the release of Windows XP. With XP, Microsoft decided to make Explorer more "discoverable" and task based. So instead of launching Windows Explorer as a separate folder, you opened the My Documents or My Music or My Whatever folder. Each of these folders was really Windows Explorer, pointing to a distinct folder on your hard drive, even if it wasn't called that.

So when you opened the Start menu and clicked My Documents, you launched Windows Explorer pointing to the My Documents folder.

With Windows 7, the name Windows Explorer is back in vogue. Yes, you can still open the Documents folder, but you can also launch Windows Explorer in and of itself. In fact, Windows Explorer is one of the default icons in the new taskbar, as you can see in Figure 6.1; click the taskbar icon to open Windows Explorer. (You can also launch Explorer by opening the Start menu and selecting All Programs, Accessories, Windows Explorer.)

Windows Explorer icon

FIGURE 6.1

Open Windows Explorer from the Windows 7 taskbar.

tip

If you right-click Explorer's taskbar icon, you also see a list of the most recently visited folders; click a folder to return to that location.

When you launch Windows Explorer, it opens to the new Library view— that is, a view of Windows 7's four default libraries (Documents, Music, Pictures, and Videos). As you can see in Figure 6.2, the Win7 version of Explorer also features a revamped navigation pane on the left, with five major sections: Favorites, Libraries, Homegroup, Computer, and Network.

note

Learn more about libraries in Chapter 7, "Extending File and Folder Management."

The easiest ways to navigate with Windows Explorer are to use the Favorites and Computer sections in the navigation pane. The Favorites section lets you go directly to your favorite folders (by default, these include Recently Changed, Public, Desktop, Downloads, Network, and Recent Places, although you can customize this favorites list), while the Computer section lets you drill down through all the drives and folders and subfolders on your computer system. Click an arrow next to a selection to expand that selection in the navigation pane; click any item to display the contents of that device or folder in the details pane of the Explorer window.

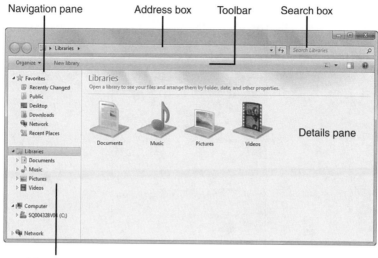

Navigation pane   Address box   Toolbar   Search box

Details pane

Library pane

FIGURE 6.2

Welcome to Windows Explorer.

Above the navigation and details panes is a context-sensitive toolbar. The contents of the toolbar change depending on what you have selected in the navigation pane. For example, select Computer in the navigation pane and the toolbar displays options for Organize, System Properties, Uninstall or Change a Program, Map Network Drive, and Open Control Panel; select the Documents item and the toolbar displays options for Organize, Share With, Burn, and New Folder.

The one constant in the toolbar is the Organize button. Click this button to display the Organize menu, shown in Figure 6.3. This menu features all manner of file-related operations, such as Cut, Copy, Paste, Delete, and so on.

At the very top of the Explorer window are back and forward buttons and two boxes. The bigger box is the address box, although Microsoft likes to call it the *breadcrumbs bar*. This box displays the folder path, but you can go backward through the path (like following a trail of breadcrumbs) by clicking any folder in the path; click a right arrow next to a folder and you see all the subfolders branching out from that folder. It's really a nice way to navigate, once you get the hang of it.

The second box at the top of the Explorer window is the search box. As you might suspect, you use this box to search for files and folders on your system; just enter the file or folder name (or part thereof) and press Enter; Explorer then returns a list of items that match your search, as shown in Figure 6.4. It works pretty well.

FIGURE 6.3

Windows Explorer's Organize menu.

Search results   Search box

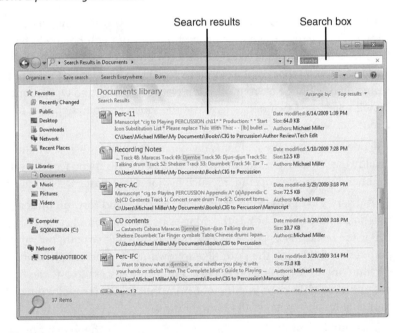

FIGURE 6.4

The results of a Windows Explorer search.

Displaying—or Hiding—Different Panes

There are quite a few things you can customize about Windows Explorer. Let's start with the Explorer window itself—and the various panes that are displayed.

By default, Explorer displays the navigation and details panes, as well as a small library pane, above the details pane, that displays information about the current folder or library. You can also opt to display a preview pane, to the right of the details pane, that displays a preview of any file you select in the details pane, as shown in Figure 6.5. It's kind of useful, but cuts down on the available real estate for navigation and browsing, which is probably why it's turned off by default.

The preview pane is not enabled by default.

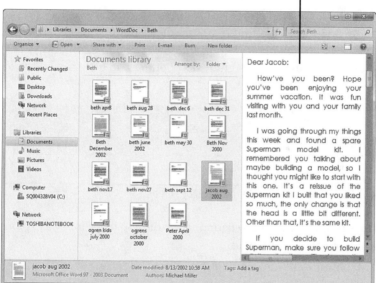

FIGURE 6.5

The Explorer window with the preview pane displayed.

To select which panes are displayed in the Explorer window, follow these steps:

1. From within Windows Explorer, select Organize, Layout.
2. Check those panes you want to display.
3. Uncheck those panes you don't want to see.

Pretty easy.

> **tip**
> You can also display the preview pane by clicking the Show the Preview Pane button on the far right of the Explorer toolbar. Click the button again to hide the preview pane.

Displaying the Menu Bar

There's one more screen element you might choose to display—especially if you're an old-timer, like me. You see, even though Microsoft does a good job placing context-sensitive operations on the Explorer toolbar, I still prefer the old-school pull-down menu bar that used to be part and parcel of just about every window in Windows. Well, Microsoft is doing away with menu bars, but still offers that option if you want to work at it. I do.

I simply find it easier to find things on the traditional menu bar, shown in Figure 6.6. For example, I know that file operations can always be found on the File menu, and that view options can be found on the View menu. Very little guessing involved.

FIGURE 6.6
The Windows Explorer menu bar—not displayed by default.

To that end, you can opt to permanently display the Windows Explorer menu bar. Follow these steps:

1. From within Windows Explorer, select Organize, Layout.

2. Check the Menu Bar option.

> **tip**
> You can also temporarily call up the menu bar at any time by pressing the Alt key on your computer keyboard. Press Alt again to hide the menu bar.

Changing Views

How do you like to see your files and folders displayed? Well, Windows Explorer offers a lot of different view options, including the following:

- Content, shown in Figure 6.7, which displays one item per line with information about that item—including date modified, size, author, or type.

- Tiles, shown in Figure 6.8, which is a grid of small icons for each item, with filename and size beside each file icon.

- Details, shown in Figure 6.9, a line listing of each item with columns for name, date modified, type, and size. The nice thing about Details view is that you can sort folder contents by any column; just click the column header to do the sort. You can also rearrange the columns, by clicking and dragging any column head to a new position. You can even customize the columns displayed by right-clicking the column header row and checking or unchecking file attributes in the resulting pop-up menu. A very versatile view.

- List, shown in Figure 6.10, which lists the contents of the folder, no other details displayed, using as many columns as necessary. This is probably the most economical view.

- Icons—individual icons for each file or folder, sized from small (Figure 6.11) to extra large (Figure 6.12).

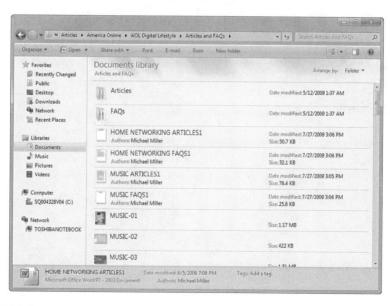

FIGURE 6.7

Content view.

FIGURE 6.8

Tiles view.

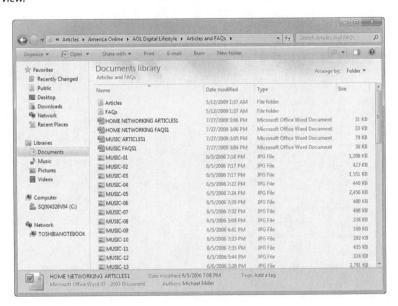

FIGURE 6.9

Details view.

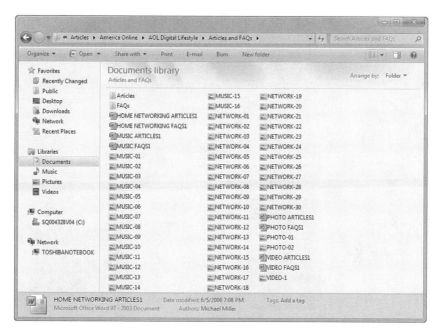

FIGURE 6.10

List view.

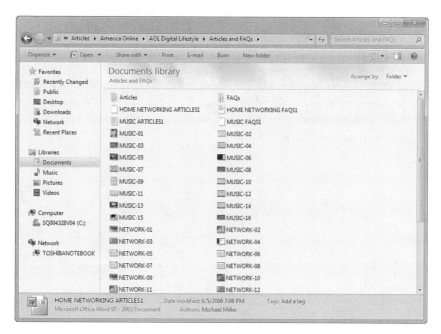

FIGURE 6.11

Small icon view.

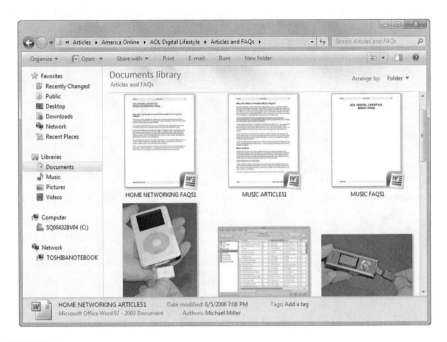

FIGURE 6.12

Extra large icon view.

> **note**
>
> In most views, file icons display a thumbnail preview of the file contents.

To switch views, simply click the Views button on the toolbar and select the view you want, as shown in Figure 6.13. For the icons views, use the slider to change icon size; the size is variable, so you aren't limited to a stock two or three sizes.

FIGURE 6.13

Changing Windows Explorer views.

---

caution

Useful as they are, displaying thumbnail views can slow down your PC's performance, especially when viewing photos (and folders containing photos). If you find your system getting sluggish, change to a non-thumbnail view.

Arranging and Sorting Files and Folders

No matter which view you select, you're still faced with the best way to organize folder contents—especially in crowded folders. Fortunately, you have several options.

Arranging Folder Contents

You can change how folder contents are arranged. By default, all contents are arranged by folder; in this arrangement, every file and folder appears as a separate item in the Explorer window. But there are several other options available, including the following:

- Author, where contents are stacked by who created them, as shown in Figure 6.14; double-click a stack to see all the files in that folder created by that author.

- Date modified, where contents are grouped by the date they were last modified, as shown in Figure 6.15.

- Tag, where contents are stacked by any tags assigned to the files. Since most files are not tagged by default, this is a less than useful view for most users.

- Type, where files are stacked by file type, as shown in Figure 6.16; double-click any stack to view all files of that type.

- Name, which lists files and folders in alphabetical order. (This is identical to Details view, but with files and folders mixed together.)

To change how folder contents are arranged, make sure the library pane is displayed; then click the Arrange By button and make a selection, as shown in Figure 6.17.

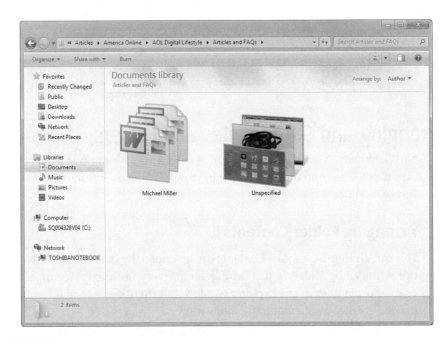

FIGURE 6.14
Arranging files by author.

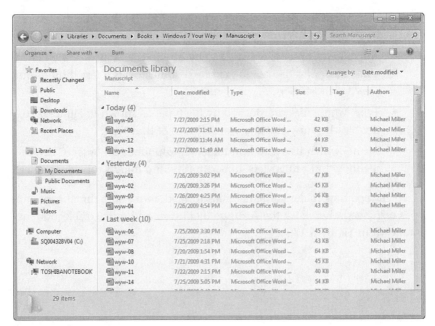

FIGURE 6.15
Arranging files by date modified.

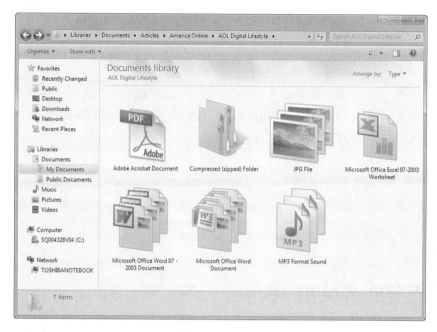

FIGURE 6.16

Arranging files by type.

FIGURE 6.17

Arranging folder contents.

Sorting Folder Contents

Arranging folder contents is different from sorting those contents. You may want to sort a folder's contents by filename, file type, file size, or the date the file was modified. Whatever view you're in, you can sort a folder's contents by following these steps:

1. Right-click in an open area of the details pane and select Sort By from the pop-up menu.

2. Select how you want to sort: Name, Date Modified, Type, or Size.

3. Select whether you want the contents sorted in Ascending or Descending order.

---

tip

For more sort options, select More from the pop-up menu to display the Choose Details dialog box. Check those details you want to display, and then click OK. You can then sort by one of the new details by repeating the steps just listed; the new details should show up in the Sort By list.

Displaying More Details

Let's return for a moment to the Details view, which displays several columns of details about your files. By default, the details displayed are name, date modified, type, and size. But Windows lets you display a lot more different details, which can help you better manage your files.

To display more details in additional columns, right-click the column header row and select one of the details listed in the pop-up menu, or click More. This displays the Choose Details dialog box, shown in Figure 6.18. This dialog box gives you a huge array of details you can display about items in this folder, everything from 35mm focal length (for digital photos) to language to word count. Check those details you want to display, and then click OK.

This is a really great feature, one that most users don't delve into, that lets you drill down into specific details about your files. Want to display f-stop and exposure information about your digital photos? How about manufacturer and model information about product files? Bitrate and contributing artists for music files? Parental ratings? Vertical resolution? Closed captioning? These are all details you can display—and that help you figure out what's what on your hard disk.

FIGURE 6.18
Displaying additional file details.

Customizing the Navigation Pane

There's one last part of the Windows Explorer window to personalize, and that's the navigation pane. There are two things you can customize about this pane—which folders are displayed and which items are shown in the Favorites section.

Displaying More Folders

By default, the navigation pane displays five sections: Favorites, Libraries, Homegroup, Computer, and Network. There are other folders that could be displayed, however, including Desktop, your main user folder, and the Recycle Bin. To display these items, follow these steps:

1. From within Windows Explorer, select Organize, Folder and Search Options. (Alternately, open the Control Panel and select Folder Options.)

2. When the Folder Options dialog box appears, select the General tab, shown in Figure 6.19.

3. In the Navigation Pane section, check the Show All Folders option.

4. Click OK.

FIGURE 6.19

Adding more items to the navigation pane.

Adding Items to the Favorites Section

And what about the Favorites section of the navigation pane, where your supposed "favorite" folders are displayed? What if these really aren't your favorites? What if you want to always show more folders here?

It's actually quite easy to add items to the Favorites section. All you have to do is follow these steps:

1. From within Windows Explorer, navigate to and open the folder you want to display in the Favorites list.

2. Right-click the Favorites item in the navigation pane and select Add Current Location to Favorites.

tip

To delete an item from the Favorites list, right-click it and select Remove.

I like having a few particular folders present in the navigation pane whenever I open Windows Explorer. Adding those folders to the Favorites list makes this happen.

Adding Items to the New Menu

You may or may not be familiar with Windows Explorer's New menu. You only see it when you right-click an empty space in the Explorer window;

the resulting pop-up menu has a New option. As you can see in Figure 6.20, select the New option and you have the option of creating new files of various types. It's a great way to quickly create new documents directly from Windows Explorer.

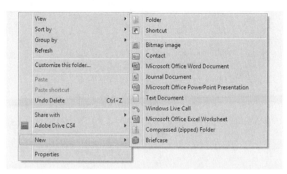

FIGURE 6.20
Windows Explorer's New menu.

Many applications add items to the New menu when the applications are installed. For example, Microsoft Office adds New items for its document types—Microsoft Office Word Document, Microsoft Office PowerPoint Presentation, Microsoft Office Excel Worksheet, and so forth.

You can add even more document types to the New menu, if you don't mind tweaking the Windows Registry a bit. This lets you easily create new documents of the types you work with most often.

note

Learn more about working with the Windows Registry in Chapter 27, "Tweaking the Windows Registry."

To add more options to the New menu, follow these steps:

1. Open the Start menu, enter **regedit** into the search box, and then press Enter.

2. When the Registry Editor window appears, open the **HKEY_CLASSES_ROOT** key, as shown in Figure 6.21.

3. Right-click the key for the file extension you want to add to the New menu and select New, Key. Name the new key **ShellNew**.

4. Right-click the new **ShellNew** subkey and select New, String Value. Name the new value **NullFile**.

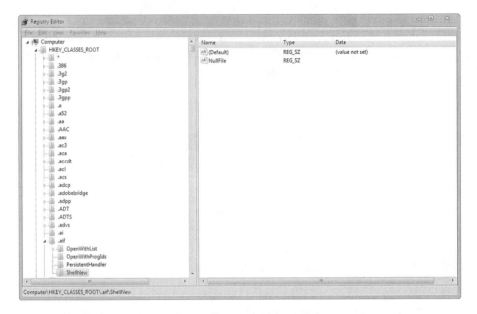

FIGURE 6.21

Using the Registry Editor to add a new file type to the New menu.

note

File types already present on the New menu already have a ShellNew subkey.

The next time you open Windows Explorer, when you right-click and select New you'll see the option for the file type you just added.

tip

You can also use the Registry Editor to remove file types from the New menu. Just navigate to the key for that file extension in the **HKEY_CLASSES_ROOT** key, and then right-click the **ShellNew** subkey and select Delete.

The Bottom Line

If you're like most Windows users, you use Windows Explorer a lot. How you use it, however, depends on how you have things configured. Fortunately, there's a lot of configuration possible—so you can use Windows Explorer to display files and folders your way.

7

Extending File and Folder Management

In the previous chapter we talked about how to configure Windows Explorer your way. Now it's time to examine the files and folders that you manage with Windows Explorer—and how to personalize that file and folder management in Windows 7.

Viewing File Extensions

Here's something I've not understood about the last few versions of Windows. Every file stored on your computer is of a given type, and that type is specified by the file's extension—the three characters after the "dot" at the end of the filename. You know what type of file you're dealing with by viewing the extension. But Windows does not, by default, display file extensions; when you view a file in Windows Explorer, all you see is the main file name, with the extension hidden.

That's not a good thing, in my opinion, especially when you're trying to protect against viruses that lurk in certain types of files. Fortunately, you can reconfigure Windows to display file extensions. Here's how you do it:

1. Open the Control Panel and select Folder Options.
2. When the Folder Options dialog box appears, select the View tab, shown in Figure 7.1.
3. Uncheck the Hide Extensions for Known File Types option.
4. Click OK.

Thus configured, Windows Explorer will now show extensions for all files.

FIGURE 7.1

Configuring Windows' folder options.

Viewing Hidden and System Files

Here's something else that Windows hides by default: system files. These are files that are essential to the operation of Windows. As such, these files should never be edited or deleted; by hiding them, Microsoft tries to ensure that they remain thus untouched.

---

note

Not all hidden files are system files. While most files are visible by default, any file or folder can be configured to be hidden. To configure a file as hidden, right-click the file in Windows Explorer, select Properties from the pop-up menu, and when the Properties dialog box appears, check the Hidden attribute.

There may be times, however, where you want to view these hidden files. To do so, you have to reconfigure Windows as follows:

1. Open the Control Panel and select Folder Options.

2. When the Folder Options dialog box appears, select the View tab.

3. Scroll to the Hidden Files and Folders section and check the Show Hidden Files, Folders, and Drives option.

4. Scroll down further and uncheck the Hide Protected Operating System Files option.

5. When prompted, answer Yes to continue.

6. Click OK.

caution

Avoid moving or deleting hidden system files. You could cause Windows not to run.

Changing Other Advanced Folder Settings

As you've probably noticed, there are a lot of other settings available in the Folder Options dialog box. Here's what they do:

- **Always Show Icons, Never Thumbnails.** By default, Windows Explorer shows thumbnails of a file's contents wherever possible. Check this option if you don't want to display these thumbnails, and instead display generic icons. (Displaying thumbnails takes some degree of graphics horsepower; you can speed up your system by displaying stock icons instead of the thumbnails.)

- **Always Show Menus.** Starting with Windows Vista, the pull-down menu bar was no longer displayed in Windows Explorer and other applications. The menus are still there, however, and you can show them by checking this option.

- **Display File Icon on Thumbnails.** This option, enabled by default, displays a small icon specific to a file type on top of all file/folder thumbnail images. If this little icon bothers you, uncheck this option.

- **Display File Size Information in Folder Tips.** Hover over a file or folder in Windows Explorer and you see a "folder tip," with information about that file or folder. By default, the size of the item is included as part of the tip. However, it takes some amount of processing power to calculate the size of all the files in a folder; speed up your system (slightly) by unchecking this option.

- **Display the Full Path in the Title Bar.** This is a holdover from Windows XP, where the path for a file or folder was displayed in the Explorer title bar. You can pretty much ignore this option.

- **Hide Empty Drives in the Computer Folder.** By default, Windows doesn't display in the Computer folder any drives connected to your

PC that are empty. If you'd rather see even empty drives, uncheck this option.

- **Launch Folder Windows in a Separate Process.** By default, when you open a folder in Windows Explorer, that folder opens in the same Explorer window. If you'd rather open each folder in a new window, check this option.

- **Show Drive Letters.** By default, drives connected to your computer are listed both by name and by letter in the Computer window. Uncheck this option to hide the drive letters.

- **Show Encrypted or Compressed NTFS Files in Color.** If you have any encrypted files on your system, they'll display in color by default. If you'd rather skip the color display, uncheck this option.

- **Show Pop-Up Description for Folder and Desktop Items.** By default, any item you hover over (in Explorer or on the desktop) displays an informative description, like the one shown in Figure 7.2. (This setting also lets you hover over a compressed/zipped folder and see the contents, without actually unzipping the folder.) To turn off these pop-up tips and file listings, uncheck this option.

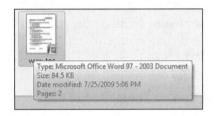

FIGURE 7.2

A pop-up tip displayed by default.

- **Show Preview Handlers in Preview Pane.** A preview handler is a utility that enables the preview of certain types of documents in Explorer's preview pane. If you'd rather not preview any files, uncheck this option.

- **Use Check Boxes to Select Items.** This is kind of a neat one. Not enabled by default, checking this option displays an empty check box next to any item you hover over in Windows Explorer. Select an item and the check box gets checked, as shown in Figure 7.3. It's good visual feedback for a selection process that confuses some users.

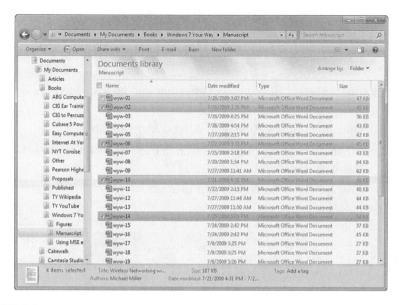

FIGURE 7.3

Check boxes enabled in Windows Explorer

- **Use Sharing Wizard.** By default, Windows makes it relatively easy to share a file with other users, by displaying a Share With button on the Explorer toolbar. If you'd rather hide this file sharing button, uncheck this option.

- **When Typing into List View (Automatically Type into the Search Box or Select the Typed Item in the View).** Here's kind of a hidden feature. When you're displaying Windows Explorer in List view, you can select a file by typing the first few letters of its filename. To turn off this feature (and have your typing go directly into Explorer's search box), check the Automatically Type into the Search Box option.

Configuring File Search

Windows 7 incorporates a fairly effective file search feature, dubbed Instant Search. Instant Search indexes all the files stored on your hard disk (including email messages) by type, title, and contents. So you can search for a file by extension, filename, or keywords within the document. You can then search for files that contain specific information by entering one or more keywords into the search box at the top of the Windows Explorer window.

tip

You can also search for files from the Instant Search box on the Windows Start menu.

You can, however, tell Windows both what and how to search. Follow these steps:

1. Open the Control Panel and select Folder Options.

2. When the Folder Options dialog box appears, select the Search tab, shown in Figure 7.4.

3. Check those options you want to apply.

4. Click OK.

FIGURE 7.4

Configuring search options.

And what of these search options? Here's what you can configure:

- **What to Search.** Choose to search filenames and contents in indexed locations but filenames only in locations that aren't indexed, or filenames and contents in all locations (indexed and non-indexed). This last option is much slower.

- **How to Search.** Choose to include subfolders in search results, find partial matches, use natural language search, or search for system files without using the index.

- **When Searching Non-Indexed Locations.** Choose to include system directories and/or compressed files.

You can get a slightly more complete search (but at a speed cost) by searching filenames and contents in all locations, but beyond that you probably want to stick with the default settings for these options.

Creating Libraries of Virtual Files

You're familiar with the way Windows uses folders and subfolders to organize files on your hard disk. A file physically resides within a given folder; open the folder to view its actual contents.

That might not be the best way to manage large volumes of data, however; you end up with similar files strewn across multiple folders. Microsoft recognizes this issue, and in Windows 7 introduced the concept of *libraries*.

Understanding Libraries

A Windows library is a kind of a virtual folder; it doesn't physically exist on your hard disk, but instead points to the subfolders and files you place within it. That is, the files contained within a given library are listed in the library but physically remain in their original folders. The library contains pointers to these files, rather than the files themselves. Think of it as a collection of shortcuts to files stored elsewhere.

If you've opened Windows Explorer, you've already seen four libraries. That's because the Documents, Music, Pictures, and Videos icons you see in Figure 7.5 don't represent specific folders, but rather libraries of files of a given type, wherever they're located on your hard disk. That's right, double-clicking doesn't open the Documents folder itself (although that folder does exist); it opens a virtual collection of documents.

Let's work through this, using the four default libraries:

- **Documents.** This library contains documents of various types—Word documents, Excel spreadsheets, PowerPoint presentations, you name it.
- **Music.** This library contains all the digital music files on your system.
- **Pictures.** This library contains all the digital photos on your system.
- **Videos.** This library contains all the digital video files on your system.

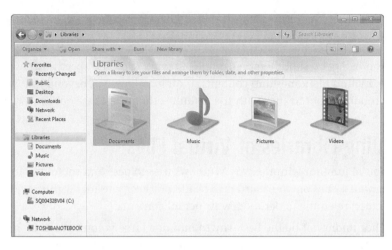

FIGURE 7.5
Windows 7's four default libraries.

Creating a New Library

In addition to these four default libraries, you can create your own libraries to virtually organize files from any folder on your hard disk. For example, you could create a library for a business project that has Word documents stored in one folder, Excel spreadsheets in another, and photos in still another; the library is then used to organize shortcuts to all these related files in one place.

To create a new library, follow these steps:

1. From within Windows Explorer, select the Libraries item in the navigation pane.

2. Click the New Library button on the Windows Explorer toolbar.

3. When the new library icon appears, type a name for the new library and press Enter.

note

The new library icon also appears in the Libraries section of the navigation pane.

4. Double-click the icon for the new library.

5. When the next screen appears, as shown in Figure 7.6, click the Include a Folder button.

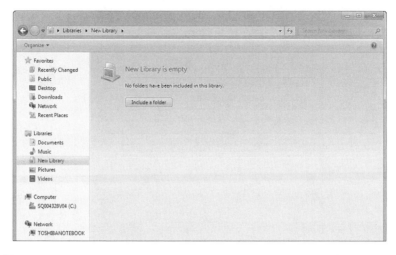

FIGURE 7.6
Getting ready to add the first folder to your library.

6. When the Include Folder dialog box appears, navigate to and click the folder you want to include in the library; then click the Include Folder button.

7. This adds the first folder to your library and displays that folder in the Explorer window, as shown in Figure 7.7. To add additional folders to this library, click the 1 Location link near the top of the details pane.

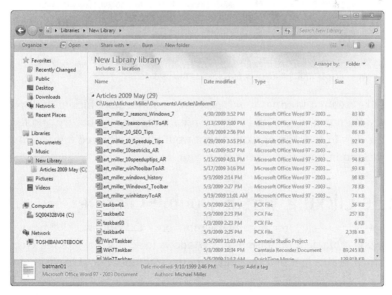

FIGURE 7.7
The folder(s) included in your library.

8. When the New Library Locations window appears, as shown in Figure 7.8, click the Add button.

FIGURE 7.8

Adding more folders to the library.

9. When the Include Folder dialog box appears, navigate to and click the folder you want to include in the library; then click the Include Folder button.

10. Repeat steps 7 to 9 to add even more folders to this library.

note

Libraries work by watching specific folders, not file types. You can't specify file types across multiple folders, only folders themselves.

I like creating libraries to monitor projects that store files in multiple folders. With a double-click of my mouse I can open the library and find all the files I need—an operation that would have required a lot of double-clicking in various folders before.

Single-Clicking Versus Double-Clicking

Speaking of clicking, if you remember back to Windows XP, Microsoft made a big deal about making Windows look and feel like the Web. In practice, this meant switching from the traditional double-clicking to being able to open files with a single click, much the way you'd click on a link on a web page.

Users didn't embrace the new paradigm, however, and in Windows Vista, Microsoft switched back to double-clicking as the default action. The single-click option is still there, however, if you prefer to work that way. Here's how to switch:

1. Open the Control Panel and select Folder Options.

2. When the Folder Options dialog box appears, select the General tab.

3. Check the Single-Click to Open an Item option.

4. Select whether you want to Underline Icon Titles Consistent with My Browser (i.e., titles are always underlined) or Underline Icon Titles Only When I Point at Them.

5. Click OK.

Naturally, you can return to double-click operation by repeating these steps and selecting Double-Click to Open an Item instead.

Stop Delete Confirmations

One of things you do most often in Windows is delete things. By default, when you try to delete a folder or file from Windows Explorer, Windows displays the "Are you sure you want to move this file to the Recycle Bin?" dialog box, shown in Figure 7.9. Delete enough items, and this little warning becomes quite annoying.

note

You only see the warning dialog box if you delete a file by pressing the Delete key or select Delete from the Organize menu or right-click menu. If you drag an item from Windows Explorer into the Recycle Bin, you don't get prompted.

If you want to do away with the annoying delete warning, follow these steps:

1. Right-click the Recycle Bin icon on the desktop and select Properties.

2. When the Properties dialog box appears, as shown in Figure 7.10, uncheck the Display Delete Confirmation Dialog option.

3. Click OK.

FIGURE 7.9

The annoying delete confirmation dialog box.

FIGURE 7.10

Disabling the delete confirmation dialog box.

The Bottom Line

Managing your files and folders can be a chore, but it helps if you can configure the way Windows handles things to be a little more to your liking. Fortunately, you can do this—including creating virtual libraries of files from various folders.

8

Managing Media Storage and Playback

These days, you use your PC just as much or more for media management than you do for writing letters and checking email. Today's personal computer is a high-powered digital media storage and playback device, used to organize digital photos, music, and videos.

Of course, when it comes to digital media, not everybody has the same needs. You want to customize Windows to manage media your way—to handle your particular mix of photos, music, and videos. Well, that's what this chapter is about, so read on.

Working with Media Libraries and Folders

Windows 7 stores your media files in three virtual libraries—Pictures, Music, and Videos. These libraries consolidate media files stored in various files across your hard disk.

> **note**
>
> Learn more about libraries in Chapter 7, "Extending File and Folder Management."

Table 8.1 indicates which folders are watched for each of these three libraries; the default folder for new file storage is shown in bold:

Table 8.1   Media Libraries

Library	Watched Folders
Pictures	**c:\users*username*\Pictures** c:\users\public\Pictures
Music	**c:\users*username*\Music** c:\users\public\Music\
Videos	**c:\users*username*\Videos** c:\users\public\Videos

Adding More Folders to a Library

You may want to store media files in folders other than the default Pictures/Music/Videos folders watched in the respective libraries. If you do so, you'll want to add those folders to the appropriate library. Follow these steps:

1. Open Windows Explorer and open the library to which you want to add the folder.

2. When the library window opens, click the Locations link at the top of the window, as shown in Figure 8.1.

3. When the Library Locations window opens, as shown in Figure 8.2, click the Add button.

4. When the Include Folder dialog box appears, navigate to and select the folder to add; then click the Include Folder button.

5. Click OK to close the Library Locations window.

FIGURE 8.1

Click the Locations link to add folders to the library.

> **tip**
>
> To remove a folder from a given library, open the Library Locations window, select the folder, and click the Remove button.

FIGURE 8.2

Adding folders to a library.

Changing the Default Folder

By default, new media files are saved in your My Pictures, My Music, and My Videos folders—that is, the Pictures, Music, and Videos subfolders in the c:\users*username*\folder. If you'd rather save new files in a different location, you can change the default folder for each of these three media types. Here's how to do it:

1. Open Windows Explorer and select the library you want to change.

2. When the library window opens, click the Locations link at the top of the window.

3. When the Library Locations window opens, right-click the folder you want as your new default, and then select Set as Default Save Location from the pop-up menu.

Managing the Pictures Library

The Pictures library is where Windows 7 consolidates all your digital photo files. These files may be physically stored in the My Pictures or Public Pictures folders, or in any subfolders within these folders.

As you can see in Figure 8.3, the Pictures library looks pretty much like any other Windows Explorer folder. The big difference is that individual photo files are displayed as thumbnails of the photos themselves. For this reason, it's better to display the Pictures library in one of the larger icon views; the larger the icons, the bigger the thumbnails. You can also view information about a file at the bottom of the Explorer window by clicking the file icon.

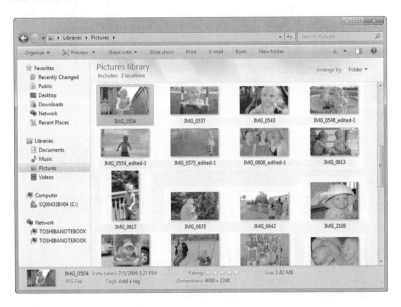

FIGURE 8.3

The Pictures library.

Previewing Pictures

One thing that a lot of users like to do is display a preview of each selected picture. To do this, you have to activate the preview pane, by clicking the Show the Preview Pane button on the Explorer taskbar. This displays a much larger version of the selected picture, as shown in Figure 8.4.

Managing Photo Properties

Windows 7 lets you sort your pictures by various file details, such as date taken, camera model, exposure time, f-stop, and the like. Some digital cameras add these attributes—called *metadata*—directly to the photo files, which Windows can then read. You can also manually enter metadata about a given photo, by following these steps:

FIGURE 8.4

Displaying a picture preview in Windows Explorer.

1. From within Windows Explorer, navigate to and right-click the file you want to edit.

2. Select Properties from the pop-up menu.

3. When the Properties dialog box appears, select the Details tab, shown in Figure 8.5.

4. Select a given property and enter a value.

5. Click OK.

note

Learn more about displaying details and sorting by these details in Chapter 6, "Customizing Windows Explorer."

There are a lot of photo properties available, if you want to take the time to enter them. Table 8.2 details the options.

Table 8.2   Available Photo Properties

Type of Property	Properties Available
Description	Title, Subject, Rating, Tags, Comments
Origin	Authors, Date Taken, Program Name, Date Acquired, Copyright
Image	Image ID, Dimensions, Width, Height, Horizontal Resolution, Vertical Resolution, Bit Depth, Compression, Resolution Unit, Color Representation, Compressed Bits/Pixel

Table 8.2   Continued

Type of Property	Properties Available
Camera	Camera Maker, Camera Model, F-Stop, Exposure Time, ISO Speed, Exposure Bias, Focal Length, Max Aperture, Metering Mode, Subject Distance, Flash Mode, Flash Energy, 35mm Focal Length
Advanced Photo	Lens Maker, Lens Model, Flash Maker, Flash Model, Camera Serial Number, Contrast, Brightness, Light Source, Exposure Program, Saturation, Sharpness, White Balance, Photometric Interpretation, Digital Zoom, EXIF Version
File	Name, Item Type, Folder Path, Date Created, Date Modified, Size, Attributes, Offline Availability, Offline Status, Shared With, Owner, Computer

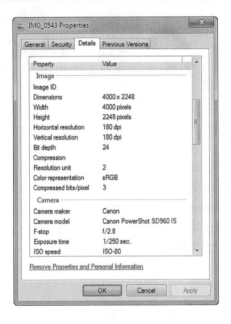

FIGURE 8.5

Editing photo properties.

If you're a serious photographer, you'll find this capability quite useful, for a couple of reasons. First, it's good to know exactly how a given picture was taken—the camera used, exposure, f-stop, and the like. Second, you can now sort and find pictures that meet specific criteria, such as all pictures taken with a specific lens, or all pictures of a given size or resolution. But remember, if your camera doesn't embed this information automatically, you'll have to enter it manually—which can be a chore.

Understanding Other Picture Options

You can do more than just browse through files in the Pictures library, however. For example, you can run a photo slideshow directly from this library—or from any folder or subfolder within the library. Just click the Slide Show button on the toolbar and you get a nice full-screen slideshow.

Select a picture file and you get even more options:

- Preview the file in a photo editing program by clicking the Preview button and then choosing one of the listed programs.

- Print a copy of the selected file by clicking the Print button. This opens the Print Pictures window, shown in Figure 8.6; select the layout in the right pane, as well as the number of copies to print; then click the Print button.

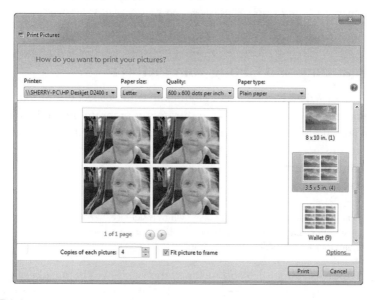

FIGURE 8.6

Printing pictures from the Pictures library.

- Email a copy of the selected file by clicking the E-mail button; this opens the Attach Files dialog box, shown in Figure 8.7. Select the size of the picture you want to send (in general, resizing smaller makes it easier to both send and receive), and then Windows will open your default email program with a new message with attachment open.

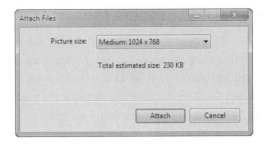

FIGURE 8.7

Emailing a picture.

> **tip**
>
> To view larger versions of each picture in the Pictures library, click the View but-
> ton on the Windows Explorer toolbar and move the slider up to the Large or
> Extra Large Icons view.

Organizing and Editing Your Pictures

Windows 7 does a good job of organizing small collections of photos, but
if you have a larger collection, a third-party program might do a better
job. You'll also need to use a third-party program to edit your photos
when they need editing; that capability is not built into the Windows
operating system.

> **note**
>
> Windows 7 does include the Paint utility, which is significantly revamped in this
> version. But Paint is a rudimentary editor at best, not a program I can recom-
> mend for even occasional photo editing.

In Windows Vista, Microsoft included the Windows Photo Gallery application for both organizing and editing digital photos. That app isn't bundled with Windows 7, although you can download the latest version,
Windows Live Photo Gallery, for free from download.live.com. It's a good
basic editing program, and the price is definitely right.

> **note**
>
> Learn more about downloading Windows Live Photo Gallery and changing
> default programs in Chapter 2, "Setting Default Programs."

If your needs exceed Photo Gallery's capabilities, you should probably
investigate a more fully featured photo editing program, such as one of
the following:

- Adobe Photoshop Elements (www.adobe.com), $99.99

- Paint Shop Pro Photo (www.corel.com), $99.99

- Picasa (www.picasa.com), free

- Ulead PhotoImpact (www.ulead.com), $69.99

These are relatively low-cost programs, good for casual and hobbyist photographers. For more serious and professional photographers, there's always Adobe Photoshop CS4 (www.adobe.com), which runs $699 but offers very advanced editing capabilities.

Whichever program you choose, you'll probably want to configure Windows' default programs so that this program opens when you double-click a photo file on your hard drive. Refer back to Chapter 2 for full instructions.

Managing the Videos Library

We now move from still pictures to moving pictures, in the form of digital videos. In Windows 7, digital video files are consolidated in the Videos library, and physically stored in the My Videos and Public Videos folders.

As you can see in Figure 8.8, video files are displayed as "filmstrip" icons, with thumbnails from each video as part of the icon. Click a file to view information about that file at the bottom of the Explorer window.

FIGURE 8.8

Viewing the Videos library.

Playing Videos

There aren't a whole lot of unique options in the Videos library. You can play any individual video by double-clicking the file icon, of course. You can also play all the videos in the library (or in any folder or subfolder) by clicking the Play All button in the Explorer toolbar.

Managing Video Properties

Windows 7 lets you sort your videos by various file details, such as name, date taken, tags, size, rating, and length. You can also sort by additional details, including frame rate, genre, director, and the like. Some camcorders add this metadata directly to the video files, or you can manually enter attributes by following these steps:

1. From within Windows Explorer, navigate to and right-click the file you want to edit.

2. Select Properties from the pop-up menu.

3. When the Properties dialog box appears, select the Details tab, shown in Figure 8.9.

4. Select a given property and enter a value.

5. Click OK.

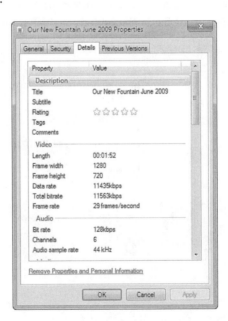

FIGURE 8.9

Editing video properties.

As with photo properties, there are a lot of video properties available. Table 8.3 details the options.

Table 8.3   Available Video Properties

Type of Property	Properties Available
Description	Title, Subtitle, Rating, Tags, Comments
Video	Length, Frame Width, Frame Height, Data Rate, Total Bitrate, Frame Rate
Audio	Bit Rate, Channels, Audio Sample Rate
Media	Contributing Artists, Year, Genre
Origin	Directors, Producers, Writers, Publisher, Content Provider, Media Created, Encoded By, Author URL, Promotion URL, Copyright
Content	Parental Rating, Parental Rating Reason, Composers, Conductors, Period, Mood, Part of Set, Initial Key, Beats-per-Minute, Protected
File	Name, Item Type, Folder Path, Size, Date Created, Date Modified, Attributes, Offline Availability, Offline Status, Shared With, Owner, Computer

Managing the Music Library

The Music library is where Windows 7 consolidates all your digital music files. These files may be stored in the My Music or Public Music folders, or in any subfolders within these folders. (For example, if you're an iPod/iPhone user, you'll find most of your music stored in the iTunes subfolder within the My Music folder.)

Individual music tracks are typically stored in folders for the corresponding album. Album folders are stored in folders for the performing artist. It goes like this: Music folder > Artist folder > Album folder > Track files.

Changing Album Artwork

Within each album folder are the individual tracks for that album, of course, but also several hidden system files that provide the artwork for those tracks. As you can see in Figure 8.10, the master artwork file is labeled Folder.jpg and is the image displayed when you play any of these tracks in Windows Media Player or other media player program. WMP also creates a file dubbed AlbumArtSmall and a few other oddly named AlbumArt files, which are resized versions of the Folder.jpg file used in various parts of the WMP display.

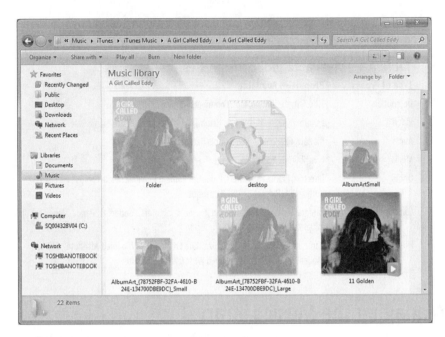

FIGURE 8.10

The contents of an album folder, including the Folder.jpg file.

> **note**
>
> Learn how to display these hidden files in Chapter 7.

If you want to use different album art for an album, you'll first need to delete the existing Folder.jpg and other artwork files. You can then copy the new artwork to that album's folder and rename the artwork file Folder.jpg.

Likewise, if an album didn't automatically have art downloaded, you can add the album art by copying the appropriate image file to the album folder. Make sure you rename the image file Folder.jpg, of course.

> **tip**
>
> One good place to search for album art is on Amazon.com. When you find the artwork for the album you want, right-click the image on the Amazon page, select Save Image As, and save the image to the album folder on your hard drive.

You can also embed artwork in individual music tracks. While this isn't necessary (and, in fact, increases the size of each file), it's something a lot of hard-core users like to do, just to make sure that the right artwork is displayed in every possible music player or device. You can't do this from within Windows, however; you have to use a third-party tag-editing program to do the job. The most popular of these tag editors include the following:

- Jaikoz Audio Tagger (www.jthink.net/jaikoz/), $25
- Mp3tag (www.mp3tag.de/en/), free
- TagTuner (www.tagtuner.com), $29.95

These programs will also edit other music file attributes—such as those we'll discuss next.

Managing Music Properties

Windows 7 lets you sort your music files by various file details, such as name, contributing artists, album, track number (#), and title. You can also sort by a slew of additional properties, including year, genre, length, composer, and even beats-per-minute (great if you want to string together a bunch of same-tempo songs for a dance mix).

Most of this information is added automatically by your music player program when you rip a CD, or included with the files you download from online music stores. You can, however, edit this information or enter additional information manually, using either a tag editor program (discussed previously) or from within Windows.

If you want to edit tracks within Windows, you have to do each file individually. Here's how it works:

1. From within Windows Explorer, navigate to and right-click the track you want to edit.
2. Select Properties from the pop-up menu.
3. When the Properties dialog box appears, select the Details tab, shown in Figure 8.11.
4. Select a given property and enter a value.
5. Click OK.

FIGURE 8.11

Editing music properties.

There are a lot of different music properties available, most of them quite useful, as detailed in Table 8.4.

Table 8.4   Available Music Properties

Type of Property	Properties Available
Description	Title, Subtitle, Rating, Comments
Media	Contributing Artists, Album Artist, Album, Year, # (track number), Genre, Length
Audio	Bit rate
Origin	Publisher, Encoded By, Author URL, Copyright
Content	Parental Rating Reason, Composers, Conductors, Group Description, Mood, Part of Set, Initial Key, Beats-per-Minute, Protected
File	Name, Item Type, Folder Path, Date Created, Date Modified, Size, Attributes, Offline Availability, Offline Status, Shared With, Owner, Computer

These attributes are used by your music player program (and portable music player devices) to organize music, create playlists, and the like. For example, you can easily sort your music in Windows Media Player by artist, album, genre, and year. So if you want to play only tracks by Bruce Springsteen, or music released in the year 2005, or blues tracks, you can do so—as long as those attributes are included in your music files.

Choosing Music File Formats

When you're working with your digital music in Windows, it helps to know a little bit about the various music file formats available. That's because when you're ripping tracks from a CD, you have a choice as to what file format and bit rate to use—and these choices affect not only the size of the resulting file, but the audio quality as well.

How Digital Sampling Works

To better understand digital music formats, let's start at the beginning of the process—in the recording studio. All digital recordings are made by creating digital samples of the original sound. The way it works is that special software "listens" to the music and takes a digital snapshot of the music at a particular point in time. The length of that snapshot (measured in *bits*) and the number of snapshots per second (called the *sampling rate*) determine the quality of the reproduction. The more samples per second, the more accurate the resulting "picture" of the original music.

For example, compact discs sample music at a 44.1kHz rate—in other words, the music is sampled, digitally, 44,100 times per second. Each sample is 16 bits long. When you multiply the sampling rate by the sample size and the number of channels (two for stereo), you end up with a *bit rate*. For CDs, you multiply 44,100 X 16 X 2, and end up with 1,400,000 bits per second—or 1,400Kbps.

All these bits are converted into data that is then copied onto some sort of storage medium. In the case of CDs, the storage medium is the compact disc itself; you can also store this digital audio data on hard disk drives, or in computer memory.

The space taken up by these bits can add up quickly. If you take a typical three-minute song recorded at 44.1KHz, you end up using 32MB of disk space. While that song can easily fit on a 700MB CD, it's much too large to download over a standard Internet connection, or to store on a portable music player.

This is where audio compression comes in. By taking selected bits out of the original audio file, the file size is compressed. If the right bits are excised, you'll never miss them.

Lossy Compressed Formats

When you rip or copy a digital audio file, you can either copy the file exactly (in non-compressed format) or you can use some sort of compression to reduce the otherwise-huge file sizes. If you choose a compressed format, you can opt for formats that use either *lossy* or *lossless* compression. Lossy compression loses some of the original audio information to create a smaller file, resulting in music that isn't quite as good-sounding as the original. Lossless compression doesn't affect the original sound quality, but results in larger files sizes—although not nearly as big as non-compressed files.

Lossy compression works by sampling the original file and removing those ranges of sounds that the average listener can't hear. A lossless encoder uses complex algorithms to determine what sounds a human is able to hear, based on accepted psychoacoustic models, and chops off those sounds outside this range. You can control the sound quality and the size of the resulting file by selecting different sampling rates for the data. The less sampling going on, the smaller the file size—and the lower the sound quality.

The problem with shrinking files to this degree, of course, is that by making a smaller file, you've dramatically reduced the sampling rate of the music. This results in music that sounds compressed; it won't have the high-frequency response or the dynamic range (the difference between soft and loud passages) of the original recording. To many users, the sound of the compressed file will be acceptable, much like listening to an FM radio station. To other users, however, the compression presents an unacceptable alternative to high-fidelity reproduction.

The most popular lossy compressed format today is the MP3 format, although there are many other formats that work in the same fashion. Here's a list of available lossy formats:

- **Advanced Audio Coding (AAC, M4A).** Also known as MPEG-4 AAC, this is the audio format used by Apple's iTunes and iPod. AAC offers slightly better sound quality than MP3 files; AAC files can also be subject to digital rights management protection. While older versions of Windows Media Player couldn't play the AAC format, Windows Media Player 12 (included with Windows 7) is fully compatible with both AAC and M4A format files—as long as the files don't have DRM encoding.

- **MP3 (MP3).** Short for MPEG-1 Level 3, the MP3 format is the most widely used digital audio format today, with a decent compromise between small file size and sound quality. The primary advantage of MP3 is its universality; unlike most other file formats, just about every digital music player and player program (including Windows Media Player) can handle MP3-format music.

- **OGG Vorbis (OGG).** An open-source encoding technology originally known as "Squish," OGG Vorbis was designed as a substitute for MP3 and WMA. It uses variable bit rate compression, which encodes different parts of a song with higher or lower compression, to produce better quality when needed.

- **RealAudio Media (RA, RM, RMA).** Proprietary format used by Real Networks, designed particularly for real-time streaming audio feeds.

- **Windows Media Audio (WMA).** Microsoft's digital audio format is promoted as an MP3 alternative with similar audio quality at half the file size. That may be stretching it a bit, but WMA does typically offer a slightly better compromise between compression and quality than you find with MP3 files. The iPod, however, cannot play WMA format files—nor can the iTunes music player.

Lossless Compressed Formats

If you care about audio fidelity, lossy compression just doesn't cut it. No matter how high the sampling rate or how good the compression algorithm, lossy files don't sound quite as good as the originals. (Remember that word "lossy"—you lose something in the translation!)

If you want to create a high-fidelity digital archive, a better solution is to use a lossless compression format. These formats work more or less like ZIP file compression; redundant bits are taken out to create the compressed file, which is then uncompressed for playback. So what you hear has exact fidelity to the original, while still being stored in a smaller-sized file.

Of course, a lossless compressed file isn't nearly as small as a file with lossy compression. While an MP3 file might be 10% the size of the original, uncompressed file, a file with lossless compression is typically about 50% the original's size. This is why lossless compression isn't recommended for portable music players like the iPod, where storage space is limited. If you're storing your CD collection on hard disk, however, it works just fine—especially with today's cheap hard disk prices. You can easily store 1,000 CDs on a 300GB hard disk, using any lossless compression format.

What formats can you choose from? The list isn't as long as with lossy compression, nor or the formats as well known. Here's a short list:

- **Apple Lossless Audio Codec (ALAC, M4A).** A lossless version of the AAC format, available for use with Apple's iTunes and iPod. (WMP12 can now play back this format, too.)

- **Free Lossless Codec (FLAC).** An open-source lossless format, embraced by many consumer electronics manufacturers and usable with all major operating systems, including both Windows and Linux.

- **Windows Media Audio Lossless (WMA).** Microsoft's lossless compression format—probably the best option for lossless compression today. Uses the same WMA file extension as normal Windows Media Audio files.

Non-Compressed Formats

Compressed audio is the way to go when you're ripping your own music to create a digital media archive. But the original digital music files you find on a CD are uncompressed, as are the digital sounds used by the Windows operating system. If you insist on archiving your music in its original unaltered form, you'll want to use one of the following uncompressed digital audio formats:

- **Audio Interchange Format (AIF, AIFF).** File format for Macintosh system sounds, similar to Windows' WAV format. You won't find this one used on Windows computers.

- **Compact Disc Digital Audio (CDA).** This format is used for encoding music on all commercial compact discs. If you buy a CD from a store, the music on that CD is stored in CDA format. Unfortunately, your computer can't store files in CDA format, so you still have to convert CDA files to another format to store on your hard disk.

- **Waveform Sound Files (WAV).** This format (pronounced "wave") produces an exact copy of the original recording, with zero compression. The result is perfect fidelity but with very large file sizes—the same size as the original, in fact. It's not a good choice for portable use, because it takes up too much storage space, but it's the preferred format for uncompressed archiving.

---

note

There's one last digital audio format that you should be aware of, even though it's not used for recording music from CDs. The MIDI format (short for Musical Instrument Digital Interface) is used by professional musicians to reproduce instrumental music in very compact files. MIDI doesn't record an actual performance; instead, it creates a kind of roadmap for frequencies and rhythms that can be fed to synthesizers and other musical instruments for playback.

Choosing the Right Bit Rate

Besides compressing the data in an audio file, all compressed file formats also let you choose the rate at which the original music is sampled. The lower the sampling rate, the smaller the file size; the higher the sampling rate, the better the sound quality. It's a trade-off.

For example, if you choose to encode an MP3 file at a 128Kbps bit rate, a three-minute song that takes up 32MB in uncompressed format will compress to just 3MB of storage. That's small enough to download easily, or to send via email.

note

Sound quality is highly subjective, as you can imagine—some "golden-eared" audiophiles find it difficult to listen to any audio files created with lossy compression—no matter what the bit rate.

Both Apple's iTunes software and Windows Media Player let you rip songs at a variety of bit rates, from 16Kbps to 320Kbps. Obviously, the lower bit rates are appropriate only for spoken word or low-fidelity recordings; the higher bit rates are more appropriate for higher-fidelity recordings.

The default bit rate in both iTunes and WMP is 128Kbps, which is a decent compromise between sound quality and file size. Know, however, that while some refer to this bit rate as "CD quality," it really isn't; the quality is more like that of a good FM radio station—which, as I said, is good enough for most listeners but not necessarily for audiophiles.

Which File Format Should You Use?

When it comes to ripping music from a CD to your computer's hard drive, you have to choose which file format and bit rate to use. As you've just discovered, there are a lot of choices.

Of the compressed formats, the MP3 format is the oldest and most universal; almost every music player program and portable music player is MP3-compatible. You can play MP3 files on an Apple iPod or iPhone, and with both the iTunes and Windows Media Player programs. That makes it a very good choice for most users.

The two other primary compressed formats present some compatibility issues. The WMA format was developed by Microsoft and is used by most commercial online music stores (except for the iTunes Store); it's compatible with all music player programs except Apple's iTunes, and with all portable music players except Apple's iPod. Obviously, this is the default format used in Microsoft's Windows Media Player program.

The AAC format is used by both iTunes and the iPod and iPhone; however, it's not compatible with many other music player programs and portable music players. That said, DRM-free AAC files *can* be played in Windows Media Player 12, and they show up in WMP's default Music library.

> **note**
>
> Previous versions of WMP could *not* play AAC files. AAC compatibility is a new feature of WMP 12—which for many users is reason enough to upgrade.

If you're downloading music from an online music store, you probably don't have a choice of formats; you have to take the music in the format that it's in. Practically, that means if you have an iPod or iPhone and use the iTunes Store, you'll get your music in AAC format. If you have any other type of player (such as the Microsoft Zune or Creative Zen) and get your music from any other online music store (such as Napster or the Zune Marketplace), you'll get your music in either WMA or MP3 format.

When you're copying files from your CD to your PC, however, you have your choice of format. For compatibility with all portable music players (including the iPod), use the MP3 format. If you have an iPod and don't care about playing your music on other portable music players, you can use the better-sounding AAC format. Or if you have a non-Apple player and never want to play your music on an iPod, you can use the equally good sounding WMA format.

And here's another consideration: What if you want to play your digital music not on a PC or portable audio player, but rather on your home audio system? Neither the AAC, MP3, nor WMA formats have good-enough audio quality to sound good when played through a quality home system. In this instance, you can save your files in WAV format, although that will take a lot of disc space—about 650MB per CD. A better alternative is to use a format that incorporates lossless compression, such as WMA Lossless (for Windows PCs) or AAC Lossless (for compatibility with the iPod). These formats reproduce the exact sound of the original, with no deterioration in audio quality, but at a smaller file size than the noncompressed WAV format. (Lossless files are larger than compressed AAC, MP3, or WMA files, however.)

note

Learn more about playing digital music on a home audio system in Chapter 9, "Extending Windows Media."

Dealing with DRM

Until recently, most music you downloaded from online music stores was encoded with *digital rights management* (DRM) technology. DRM was designed to prevent the unlawful distribution, copying, and sharing of copyrighted music. If a track you downloaded is protected with DRM, you're limited as to how you can copy and listen to that song.

DRM works by encoding the audio file in a type of wrapper file format. This wrapper file includes a user key, which is used to decode and play the track—under specified conditions. For example, a DRM license might dictate how many different PCs or portable music players the track can be copied to, whether it can be burned to CD, and so on. If you try to use the song in a way not permitted by the license, the DRM protection keeps it from playing.

note

While DRM technology can be applied to audio files in the AAC and WMA formats, it cannot be applied to MP3 files. This is why most online music stores encode their music as either AAC or WMA formats, to facilitate DRM.

Recently, however, the trend has been away from DRM to selling DRM-free tracks, most often in the MP3 format. (Apple iTunes is an exception to this, selling its DRM-free tracks in its own AAC format.) The benefit to DRM-free music is that once you purchase it, you can use it however you want; you can play it on any number of PCs or portable music players, and burn it onto an unlimited number of custom CDs. It's a much more listener-friendly solution, which is why many online music stores are now offering DRM-free music.

tip

Check with the individual online music store to see if it encodes its tracks with DRM—and if so, what the terms of its DRM license are.

Customizing Windows Media Player

When it comes to music and movies (or videos of any kind), Windows uses the Windows Media Player (WMP) program to manage and play back these types of media files. Windows 7 features the latest and greatest version 12 of the program, and you can tweak it a bit to do what you want to do.

note

With WMP 12, all your iPod music should automatically appear in your Music library. (Older versions of WMP could not play AAC files, and such files would not appear in the WMP library.)

Customizing the Full Display

Windows Media Player provides several different display options. Not only can you resize the WMP window, as you can any Windows application, but you also can display it in the compact Now Playing mode—or as a Mini Player on the Windows taskbar.

The default display mode for WMP is the full or library mode. You have the library pane on the left, the contents pane in the middle, and the list pane on the right. Items in the contents pane can be displayed in three views: Details view, with columns for title, length, contributing artist, and the like; Icon view, with album covers displayed; and Tile view, shown in Figure 8.12, with album covers and key information (title, artist, genre, year, and rating) displayed. You switch views by clicking the View Options button on the toolbar; you can then sort the contents of your music library by artist, album, and genre, by clicking the appropriate option in the Music section of the library pane.

Switching to Now Playing Mode

If you'd rather display the player without all the extraneous controls and library listings, you can switch to the Now Playing mode, shown in Figure 8.13. This is a smaller and simpler playback window, new to WMP12, that takes up a lot less desk space than the normal WMP window; it's just a media player, pure and simple. To switch to Now Playing mode, click the Switch to Now Playing button at the lower-right corner of the main WMP window. (To switch from the Now Playing window to the larger Windows Media Player window, click the Switch to Library button in the upper-right corner.)

FIGURE 8.12
Windows Media Player with library contents displayed in Tile view.

note

When you play an audio CD, WMP starts in Now Playing mode by default.

FIGURE 8.13
WMP's Now Playing window.

Changing Skins

Then there's the option of changing the Now Playing windows' "skin." A skin is a customized interface for the mini player, and there are several available. To switch to Skin mode in the Now Playing window, press the Alt button to display the hidden pop-up menu (similar to the hidden menu bar in the main player window), and then select View, Skin.

To give you an idea of how different skins can change the way WMP looks and feels, check out Figures 8.14 and 8.15. Changing skins is a great way to put your personal stamp on your media player.

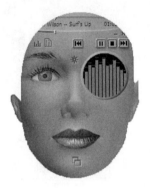

FIGURE 8.14

WMP with the Cerulean skin.

FIGURE 8.15

WMP with the Radio skin.

To change skins, follow these steps:

1. From within the Now Playing window, press the Alt button and select View, Skin Chooser.

2. When the Skin Chooser window appears, as shown in Figure 8.16, select a skin from the left-side list. The skin you choose will be previewed in the right-side window.

3. Click the Apply Skin button. WMP now switches to Skin mode with the new skin applied.

Windows Media Player includes a fair selection of skins built-in, but there are a lot more skins available online. Just go to the Skin Chooser window and click the More Skins button, and WMP launches Internet Explorer and connects to the Skins page on the Windows Media website. Pick a new skin and follow the onscreen instructions to download it to your system.

FIGURE 8.16

Choosing a new skin for Windows Media Player.

note

Previous versions of WMP offered an additional display mode, the Mini player that docked to the Windows Taskbar. The Mini player is not offered as a feature in WMP 12.

Viewing Visualizations

When you're playing music in WMP's Now Playing window, you have a choice of what you see in the window. By default, the window displays album art for the currently playing song. But you can also display *visualizations*, splashes of color and shapes that move to the beat of the music, like the one shown in Figure 8.17.

FIGURE 8.17

Viewing a visualization in the Now Playing window.

---

note

In previous versions of WMP you could view visualizations in the full player window; this is not an option in WMP 12.

WMP includes a slew of visualizations you can watch while you're listening to music. The visualizations are grouped into collections based on specific themes. You can pick a specific visualization to watch, and even (for some visualizations) configure individual visualization properties.

To select a visualization, right-click anywhere in the Now Playing window and select Visualizations. You can now choose a collection (Alchemy, Bars and Waves, or Battery) and then select an individual visualization from within that collection. To switch back to the album art display, select Album Art from the Visualizations menu.

As you might suspect, additional visualizations are available from the Internet. Just right-click the Now Playing window and select Visualizations, Download Visualizations. This opens a web browser window and takes you to the Windows Media website, where you can browse for and download new visualizations.

Searching for Media Files

Once your music and video libraries reach a certain size, it may become difficult to browse to individual media files from within WMP. An easier way to find a specific song or video is to search for it, using WMP's Instant Search feature.

Instant Search is accessed from the search box at the top of the library window. Just enter a few keywords (from the song title, movie name, artist, or whatever) into the search box. You don't even have to press the Enter key; the results of your search appear in the Library tab as you type, as shown in Figure 8.18, and are updated as you enter each new letter of your search query.

For example, enter the letters **ste** and you might get 3 results for artists, 24 for albums, and 279 for songs; enter a fourth letter (**stew**) and your results might be fine-tuned to just 1 artist, 12 albums, and 131 songs. Keep entering your query to further fine-tune your results.

You can also fine-tune your media search, using a variety of search criteria. Here are some tips for smarter searching:

- To find an item with a specific title or artist, enclose the exact phrase in quotation marks. For example, to search for the group Black Eyed Peas, search for the entire phrase like this: **"black eyed peas"**.

FIGURE 8.18

Searching for files in WMP.

- To search for a specific album by a given artist, use the AND operator. For example, to search for the Beatles' *White Album* (and nothing else), search for **beatles AND "white album"**.

- If you only want to see certain albums by an artist, you can exclude albums from an artist search by using the NOT operator. For example, to search for all albums by the Beatles except *Abbey Road*, search for **beatles NOT "abbey road"**.

- To search for multiple songs or artists, use the OR operator. For example, to search for tracks from either Paul McCartney or John Lennon, enter **mccartney OR lennon**.

You can also restrict your search to specific fields within a music file's metadata. For example, you search only within the album title field, or within the composer field, or within the genre field. Just enter the appropriate search operator, followed by a colon, followed by the appropriate keywords. Table 8.5 lists all the search modifiers available when searching your music library.

Table 8.5 WMP Search Modifiers

Modifier	Searches For	Example
Album:	Album name	album:"abbey road"
AlbumArtist:	Primary album artist (artist on an entire album)	AlbumArtist:usher

Table 8.5 **Continued**

Modifier	Searches For	Example
Artist:	Either the primary or contributing artist	Artist:"elton john"
Composer:	Music composer	Composer:"jimmy webb"
Conductor:	Orchestra conductor	Conductor:"georg solti"
ContentProvider:	Content provider	ContentProvider:urge
ContributingArtist	Contributing artist (artist on a single track)	ContributingArtist:"bonnie raitt"
DateReleased	Album release date	DateReleased:2006
Genre:	Genre	Genre:rock
Length:	Length of track (in seconds)	Length:200
Protected:	Digital rights management (DRM) protection (yes/no)	Protected:yes
Rating:	1-5 star rating	Rating:5
Title:	Song title	Title:"born to run"

Adding or Changing Album Art

When you rip a track from a CD, WMP goes to an online database to retrieve song information and album art. Sometimes, however, there is no album art available for that CD, as shown in Figure 8.19. Sometimes the database has the wrong album art for the CD. Sometimes the album art is correct, but isn't that great looking—too light, too dark, whatever.

FIGURE 8.19

An album listed in the WMP library without any album art.

Whatever the reasons, there will be instances when you want to change the album art associated with a CD you've ripped to your hard disk. The good news is that you can easily add or change album art from within WMP.

All you have to do is locate the right album art, preferably in JPG format, and copy it. That art can be stored on your PC's hard drive, or located somewhere on the Web. Just right-click the JPG file and select Copy. Then move to Windows Media Player, navigate to that album, right-click on the existing album art (or the blank art placeholder), and select Paste Album Art. The new album art now appears in Windows Media Player. Just like that.

Setting the Audio File Format and Bit Rate

As noted earlier in this chapter, when you rip music from audio CD to your hard drive, which you can use WMP to do, you first have to determine what format you want to use for your ripped files, as well as the bit rate to use for the recording. This is typically a one-time configuration, although you can change the format and bit rate at any time. Follow these steps:

1. From the full WMP window, click the Organize button on the toolbar and select Options.

2. When the Options dialog box appears, select the Rip Music tab, shown in Figure 8.20.

3. Pull down the Format list and select the desired format.

4. Use the Audio Quality slider to select the desired bit rate.

5. Click OK.

FIGURE 8.20

Configuring rip settings.

> **note**
>
> The WAV, WMA Lossless, and WMA Variable Bit Rate formats do not have accom-
> panying bit rate settings, as the bit rate is preset for all these file formats.

Change the Location for Ripped Files

By default, music you rip from CD will be saved in your My Music folder
(location c:\users*username*\Music\). If you'd rather store ripped music in
another folder, follow these steps:

1. From the full WMP window, click the Organize button on the toolbar
   and select Options.

2. When the Options dialog box appears, select the Rip Music tab.

3. In the Rip Music to This Location section, click the Change button.

4. When the Browse for Folder dialog box appears, navigate to and
   select a new folder; then click OK.

5. Back in the Options dialog box, click OK.

Playing DVDs and Videos

Of course, Windows Media Player isn't just for music. You can also use
WMP to play back movies on DVD, videos you've downloaded from the
Internet, or TV programs you've recorded to your PC's hard disk.

When you insert a DVD in your PC's DVD drive, playback should start
automatically in the Now Playing window. Your system should sense the
presence of the DVD, launch Windows Media Player, and start playing
the movie.

Playing a video file you've stored on your PC's hard drive is very similar
to playing back a DVD. All you have to do is click the Videos option in
the navigation pane; this displays all the video files you have stored in
your Videos library, as shown in Figure 8.21. To begin playback, double-
click a video clip—or select the clip and click the Play button.

If you have a TV tuner card in your PC, you can also use Windows Media
Player to play back television programs you've recorded. Selecting a
recorded program for playback is just like selecting a video clip. Begin by
clicking the Recorded TV option in the navigation pane, then double-click
the program you want to watch.

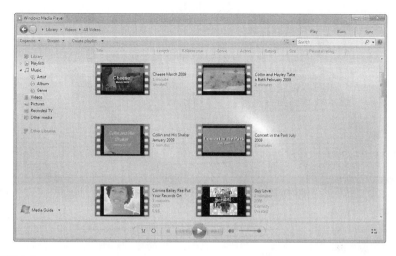

FIGURE 8.21
Selecting a video file for playback.

You can watch movies and videos within the main WMP window or in the Now Playing window—which expands to the size of the video. If you'd prefer to view the video on the full computer screen (with all remnants of Windows—including the taskbar—hidden), click the View Full Screen button in the bottom right corner of the Now Playing window. Press Esc to return to normal viewing mode.

Enhancing Audio and Video Playback

When you're playing music and movies in Windows Media Player, you have the ability to change the player's audio and video playback settings. These settings are generically referred to as *enhancements*, and you access them from the Now Playing window. Just right-click within the window, select Enhancements, and then click the enhancement you want to configure. This opens a separate Enhancements pane, shown in Figure 8.22; you can cycle through the various enhancements by clicking the blue left and right arrows.

What enhancements are available? Table 8.6 details the options.

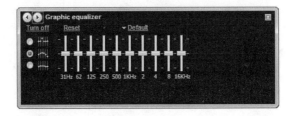

FIGURE 8.22

Enhancing playback via the Enhancements pane.

Table 8.6   Audio/Video Enhancements

Enhancement	Details
Graphic Equalizer	Boost or minimize specific frequency ranges.
Play Speed Settings	Plays back music and videos at faster or slower than normal speeds.
Quiet Mode	Minimizes the difference between loud and soft sounds; useful when playing music at a reduced volume level.
SRS WOW Effects	Enhances the sound from small computer speakers; includes TruBass (changes bass level), WOW Effect (widens or collapses stereo effect), and Speaker selection (optimize enhancements for large speakers, normal speakers, and headphones).
Video Settings	Adjusts the hue, saturation, brightness, and color of videos.
Dolby Digital Settings	Three settings for playback of Dolby Digital content: Normal (reduces audio range for quieter listening); Night (reduces music levels and increases voice levels); Theater (provides full range listening experience).
Crossfading and Auto Volume Leveling	Crossfading creates smooth transitions between songs during playback; auto volume leveling reduces the volume differences between songs.

Adding More Functionality with Plug-Ins

You can add extra functionality to Windows Media Player by downloading and installing a variety of different plug-ins. A plug-in is a utility that attaches to WMP and provides additional features, such as audio and video effects, or the ability to play new file formats.

To download new plug-ins, follow these steps:

1. Press the Alt button to display the hidden menu bar.

2. Select Tools, Plug-Ins, Download Plug-Ins.

3. This opens your web browser to Microsoft's Plug-ins for Windows Media Player page. Here you can find Microsoft-endorsed plug-ins of various types, all available for free download.

Switching to Another Media Player Program

I actually like the Windows Media Player and use it for most of my music playback on my desktop PC. Most of my playback, but not all; Apple's iTunes player is necessary for synching with and managing music from my iPhone and iPod libraries, and is a decent music player, to boot.

If you want to make iTunes (or any other program) the default media player program in Windows 7, you can do it. The default program, of course, is the one that launches when you double-click a music or video file in Windows Explorer. To make the switch, follow the instructions given back in Chapter 2; everything you need to know is there.

The Bottom Line

There's a lot you can customize in regards to digital pictures, music, and videos in Windows 7. Not only can you change the default location for files (and which folders are monitored in the corresponding media libraries), you can also configure Windows Media Player in all sorts of ways and choose the file type and bit rate for music you rip from your favorite CDs. If you're a music lover, this is all good stuff—and there's even more to come in the next chapter, if you're into whole-house audio.

9

Extending Windows Media

Windows media—music, videos, even photos—don't have to be limited to viewing and playback on your desktop or notebook computer. With the right tools, you can play music, watch movies, and view photos on other computers connected via your network or the Internet, or on television sets in your living room or around your house. It's a matter of extending Windows media—your way.

Using Windows Media Center in the Living Room

When you want to extend Windows media for viewing on your living room TV—and on other TVs in other rooms—you use something called Windows Media Center. This is a special "10-foot interface" to Windows media, included with most versions of Microsoft Windows 7.

Configuring a Living Room System

Why would you want a PC in your living room? There are quite a few things you can do with a living room PC, including the following:

- **Play CDs and DVDs.** The first thing a personal computer can do is play audio CDs and movie DVDs. Now, I'll admit that this isn't a real impressive function; after all, you can buy a $30 DVD player from Wal-Mart that does just this. However, if you're looking to cut down on the number of devices in your home audio/video system, it's nice to consolidate CD/DVD playback in your PC.

- **Burn CDs and DVDs.** This is a function not available on that $30 DVD player; it's something you find in almost all PCs today, but it's unusual to do in your living room.

- **Play digital music.** Listening to music is one of my favorite activities, and with Windows Media Center I can access my entire music library on my main audio/video system. It's like having a really big iPod in the living room—and listening through a big speaker system sounds a lot better than playing music on your PC's speakers.

- **View digital photographs.** Here's another fun one. While you're listening to music, you can access all the digital photos on your PC in a big-screen slideshow. My family spends lots of evenings revisiting our old and new photos in just this fashion.

- **View home movies.** If you take a lot of home movies with a digital camcorder, transfer those movies to your computer and watch them anytime you want on your living room TV. No extra cables to connect; everything you want to watch is right there on your hard disk.

- **Watch and record TV.** When you purchase a computer with a built-in TV tuner—or add an external tuner to an existing PC—you get the option of recording television shows directly to your PC's hard drive for future playback. Plus you get a neat electronic program guide to help you determine what to view—and what to record.

Any or all of this sound like something you'd like to do? Then you need to connect your PC to your living room TV and use Windows Media Center to view and play all your digital media.

Getting to Know the 10-Foot Interface

Operating a computer in your living is a much different experience than operating a computer in your office. In your office, you're sitting 10 inches away from the computer screen; everything you see is small and compact yet still visible from the 10-inch level. In your living room, you're sitting 10 *feet* away from the television screen; all the onscreen icons and buttons need to be big enough to be seen from the extended distance. It's the difference between a 10-inch interface and a 10-foot interface.

In Windows 7, the 10-foot interface is dubbed Windows Media Center, which runs on top of the main Windows 7 operating system. Windows Media Center is designed as a 10-foot interface that lets you use your computer as a home entertainment server in the living room environment.

The Media Center interface lets you perform most common home enter-tainment operations with the click of a button on the optional remote control unit. It's not designed for desktop applications; there's no built-in web browser, word processor, or email client. If you want to do office work, shut down the Media Center interface and revert to plain old Windows. But if you want to listen to music, watch DVDs, record televi-sion programs, or view your favorite digital photos, Media Center is the perfect interface. It's simple, intuitive, and easy to read from across the room; it's a computer interface that doesn't look like a computer interface. And you don't need to take a training course to learn how to use it. It's easy enough to use that your parents (or grandparents!) can probably fig-ure it out.

That doesn't mean that Windows Media Center is limited in functionality. There's a lot of fancy stuff you can do from the comfort of your couch, even if you have to hunt around for some of it.

Operating Media Center

You launch Windows Media Center from the Windows Start menu. What you see next is the start menu, which you can navigate using your com-puter's keyboard or mouse, or a Media Center remote control. You scroll down or up through the menu options until you find the one you want; then you scroll right or left through the available operations and click what you want to do.

When you're using Media Center in your living room, you probably don't want to string a keyboard or mouse across the floor; remote control opera-tion is definitely the way to go. A Media Center remote, like the one shown in Figure 9.1, is fairly intuitive. Use the up, down, right, and left arrow buttons to move around the screen, and the big OK button to select an option.

Probably the most important button on the remote is the big green button in the middle, called—appropriately enough—the Green Button. (The Green Button is sometimes referred to as the *Start button*, for obvious rea-sons.) When you press the Green Button, you're taken straight to the Media Center start menu. It doesn't matter what you're doing or where you are in the Media Center menu system, the Green Button takes you home.

FIGURE 9.1

Keyspan's ER-V2 Windows Media Center remote control. (Photo courtesy Keyspan, by Tripp-Lite.)

Also important are the Back and More Info buttons. The Back button simply takes you back a step, returning you to the page previous to the one you're on now. The More Info button displays more information about selected items onscreen, or (in some cases) additional menu options; in many ways, it functions like right-clicking an item with your mouse in Windows.

Where do you get a Media Center remote? Some new computers come with one; otherwise, you'll have to purchase a unit from Microsoft, Keyspan, MediaGate, Pinnacle, or another manufacturer. The remote should come with the transmitter (that's the unit you operate) and a receiver, which connects to your computer via USB. Like most remotes, the Media Center remote operates via infrared technology, so you'll have to have a clear line of sight between the remote and the receiver.

tip

Once you've connected the Media Center remote's infrared receiver to your PC, you can program most universal remotes to operate your Media Center PC.

Navigating the Menus

Media Center's start page (which you get to by pressing the Green Button on the remote) is shown in Figure 9.2. This is a lot different from the traditional Windows desktop; it's much more streamlined, with only a handful of important options. It's also designed to be seen from clear across the living room, of course.

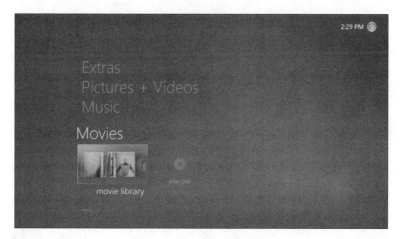

FIGURE 9.2

The Media Center start menu.

Media Center's menus are scrolling menus; you can scroll up or down through the menu, using your remote's up and down directional buttons. There are a handful of main menu items, with association operations under each main item. You scroll up or down to the main item, and then right or left to the specific operation.

For example, if you want to listen to music from your Windows Music library, scroll up or down to the Music item, and then right or left to the Music Library item. Click OK on Music Library and Media Center displays all your music onscreen, as shown in Figure 9.3. Sort your music library by album, artist, genre, and the like; then click an album to play it. You can even play playlists and entire genres!

It's just as easy to view your digital photos in Media Center. Just scroll to the Pictures & Videos section of the start menu, and then select Picture Library. From there you can navigate to individual folders in your Picture library, as shown in Figure 9.4; click a picture to view it full-screen, or click Play Slide Show to start a slideshow of all the pictures in the current folder.

FIGURE 9.3

Accessing your music library in Windows Media Center.

FIGURE 9.4

Viewing pictures in Windows Media Center.

Those are only two of the operations present in Windows Media Center. Table 9.1 details each of the main menu items and the individual operations therein.

Table 9.1   Windows Media Center Menus and Operations

Menu	Operations
Pictures + Videos	Picture Library
	Play Favorites
	Video Library
Music	Music Library
	Play Favorites
	Radio
	Search
Now Playing	Current song or video
Movies	Movie Library
	Play DVD
TV	Recorded TV
	Guide
	Live TV Setup
Sports	Scores
	Players
	Leagues
Tasks	Shut Down
	Settings
	Learn More
	Burn CD/DVD
	Sync
	Add Extender
	Media Only
Extras	Extras Library
	Explore
	Internet TV
	News
	Learn How
	New Extenders

note

Some applications and utilities may install their own items on the Media Center menu, typically in the Extras menu.

I won't go through all the various things you can do with Media Center; suffice to say, it's a great way to listen to music, play movies, and view photos on a big screen. That means, of course, that you need to connect your computer to your living room TV—which we'll discuss next.

Connecting Your Computer in the Living Room

You can connect any computer to your living room audio/video system. While some manufacturers make dedicated Media Center PCs (designed to look more like an audio component than a traditional PC), any desktop or notebook PC has the requisite output jacks to connect to your audio/video equipment.

Let's start with the video connection—that is, connecting your computer to your TV. The type of video connection you make depends on three factors: the types of video *output* jacks available on your PC; the types of video *input* jacks available on your TV set; and whether you're using your PC to view DVDs, standard-definition analog television, or high-definition digital television.

The first two items need little explanation; the third item, however, bears discussion. It's like this. If you're not using your Media Center PC to view television or DVDs, you don't need to use a high-quality connection. If you are viewing TVs or DVDs, you need a high-quality connection. And if you're viewing high-definition television, you need the highest-quality connection possible.

Table 9.2 provides a quick overview on what types of connections to use for which purposes; Figure 9.5 shows you what each of these connectors looks like.

Table 9.2 Preferred Video Connections

Video Connection	HDTV	DVD	SDTV	Basic Media Center Display
HDMI	Yes	Yes	Yes	Yes
DVI	Yes	Yes	Yes	Yes
Component video	Yes	Maybe (may not work with some copy-protected DVDs)	Yes	Yes
S-Video	No	Yes (480i only)	Yes	Yes
Composite video	No	Yes (480i only)	Yes	Yes

As you can see, HDMI and DVI connections will handle anything you throw at them. Component video (three connectors—red, green, and blue) is almost as good, but has some trouble playing some copy-protected DVDs. S-Video and composite video are poor choices for playing DVDs (they transmit only the standard-definition interlaced signal, not the higher-quality progressive scan signal), and won't transmit HDTV signals at all. You should use S-Video and composite video connections only as a last resort, or if you're using your Media Center PC strictly to listen to music—and thus need to display only the Media Center interface on your TV.

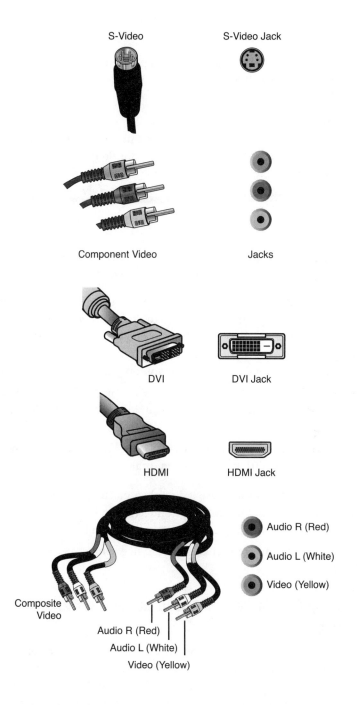

FIGURE 9.5

Different types of video connections.

caution

Most computers have a VGA video output, typically used to connect to a computer monitor. Unfortunately, not all TVs have a VGA input, so this may not be a viable means of connecting your PC to your TV.

If you want to be future-safe, you'd connect your computer to your TV using either an HDMI or DVI connector. But here's the complicating factor: Not all PCs have HDMI connections, nor do all TVs have DVI connections. So if your computer has a DVI output and your TV has an HDMI input, you'll have to purchase a DVI-to-HDMI converter cable—or use one of the other connector types.

tip

You can connect your computer directly to your television set, or to an audio/video receiver that is then connected to your TV.

If you connect via HDMI (not via DVI), you don't have to worry about audio, since HDMI carries both video and audio signals. Any other type of video connection, however, carries only the video signal—which means you need to make a separate audio connection between your PC and TV or audio/video receiver. Fortunately, you only have a few options here:

- If you're using your Media Center PC to watch TV or DVDs with surround sound, use an optical or coaxial digital connection (either will work fine).

- If you're using your Media Center PC solely to listen to stereo music, use the stereo (right/left) analog audio connection.

You can also, if you want, use a digital connection to listen to stereo audio—but you can't use a stereo connection to listen to surround sound. If in doubt, just use a digital connection, and you'll be good for anything.

When you get it all connected, it should like something like the system in Figure 9.6

Starting Media Center Automatically When You Turn On Your PC

When you're using Media Center on a normal desktop or notebook PC, you launch Media Center manually from the Windows Start menu. But when you're using your computer as part of your home audio/video system, you don't want to deal with regular Windows at all; you want to work exclusively in the Media Center interface.

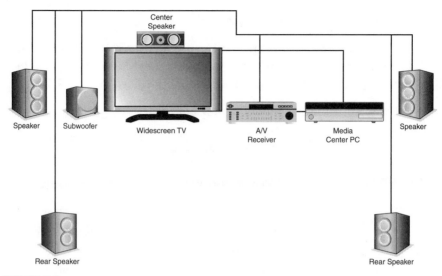

FIGURE 9.6

A living room digital home entertainment system.

Fortunately, you can configure Windows to launch Media Center automatically whenever your PC is turned on. You do this configuration from within Media Center, by following these steps:

1. From the Media Center start menu, select Tasks, Settings, General, Startup and Window Behavior.

2. When the Startup and Window Behavior page appears, as shown in Figure 9.7, check the Start Windows Media Center When Windows Starts option.

3. Click Save.

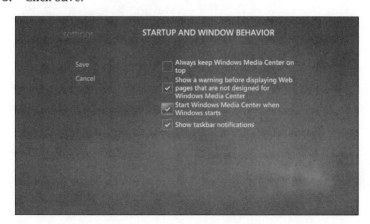

FIGURE 9.7

Configuring Media Center to launch when you first turn on your PC.

Configuring Other Settings

You can configure Media Center in a number of ways. To access the configuration settings, go to the start menu and select Tasks, Settings; on the resulting Settings screen, you find the options detailed in Table 9.3.

Table 9.3   Windows Media Center Settings

Menu	Settings
General	Startup and Window Behavior
	Visual and Sound Effects
	Windows Media Center Setup
	Parental Controls
	Automatic Download Options
	Optimization
	About Windows Media Center
	Privacy
TV	Set Up TV Signal
	Configure Your TV or Monitor
	Language
	Audio
	Closed Captioning
Pictures	Slide Shows
	Slide Show Screen Saver
	Favorite Pictures
	Ratings
Music	Favorite Music
	Ratings
	Visualizations
	Now Playing
DVD	Language
	Audio
	Subtitle
	Remote Control Options
Start Menu and Extras	Start Menu
	Extras Library Options
	Extras Library
	Clear List of Trusted Applications
Extender	Manage Connected Media Center Extenders
Media Libraries	Manage Music, Pictures, Videos, Recorded TV, and Movies Libraries

---

tip

The first time you start Media Center, Windows should have launched the Setup Wizard, which walks you through Media Center's basic setup. You can rerun the Setup Wizard at any time by going to the Media Center start page and selecting Tasks, Settings, General, Windows Media Center Setup, Run Setup Again.

Configuring the Display

If you're lucky, Media Center correctly determined the size and resolution of your television display, and configured itself accordingly. If you're not lucky, Media Center is displayed in a little box in the middle of your television screen—or, even worse, you see only part of the screen. If this happens to you, you need to reconfigure Media Center for your particular display.

You can also, if you want, use Media Center to fine-tune your television display. These aren't adjustments within Media Center itself, but rather a series of patterns and tests that you can reference when adjusting the picture controls on your television set.

This display configuration is part of the Setup Wizard, or you can access it separately, as we'll discuss here. Just follow these steps:

1. From the Media Center start page, select Tasks, Settings, TV, Configure Your TV or Monitor.

2. When the Display Configuration page appears, click Next.

---

note

If you're running Media Center in a window on your computer's desktop, the Display Setup dialog box appears and prompts you to display Media Center in full-screen mode. Click Yes to continue.

---

3. If you're viewing Media Center on your main display, select Yes and then click Next.

4. On the Identify Your Display Type page, shown in Figure 9.8, select the type of television display you have—monitor (traditional CRT computer monitor) built-in display (for notebook PCs), flat panel (such as LCD or plasma), television (traditional CRT display), or projector. Click Next when done.

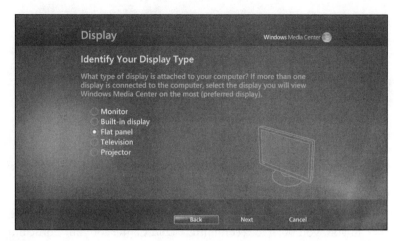

FIGURE 9.8

Select the type of television display you're using.

5. On the Connection Type page, select the type of video connection you're using—composite or S-Video; DVI, VGA, or DisplayPort; HDMI; or component (three-cable) connection. Click Next when done.

tip

To best display Media Center on a widescreen TV, you might also need to adjust the display size settings for your PC's video card. (For example, my NVIDIA video card lets me fine-tune the video for specific display resolutions.) This means exiting Media Center and adjusting the video display settings from within the standard Windows interface, as directed by your video card or computer manufacturer.

6. The Display Width screen asks you whether you have a standard 4:3 display or a widescreen 16:9 display. Make the correct choice, and then click Next.

7. The next screen details the current resolution settings for the screen display. If this resolution is correct, click Yes. If not, click No and follow the onscreen instructions to change the resolution.

note

If you're connecting to an older TV with the 4:3 standard aspect ratio, the screen resolution is 640 x 480 pixels. If you're running a 720p high definition display, the screen resolution is 1280 x 720. If you're running a 1080i or 1080p high resolution display, the screen resolution is 1920 x 1080.

8. When the Adjust the Display Settings page appears, select Adjust Display Controls if you want to adjust your television's picture display, and then click Next. (If you don't want to adjust your television set, select Finish This Wizard instead.)

9. When the next screen appears, click Next.

10. You can now choose from a number of different display calibration options: Onscreen Centering and Sizing; Aspect Ratio (Shape); Brightness (Black & Shadow); Contrast (White); and RGB Color Balance. Select which option you want to adjust and follow the onscreen instructions from there.

11. When you're finished making adjustments, click the Next button.

12. When the You Are Done! page appears, click Finish.

Configuring Audio Settings

Your Media Center PC has to be configured for the type of sound system you're using—traditional stereo, 5.1-channel surround sound, or 7.1-channel surround sound. It's likely that the factory default settings work just fine for your system, but it's also possible that they don't, and you'll have to adjust them manually. Unfortunately or not, these audio settings are not part of the Setup Wizard, which means you have to access them from the Media Center Settings page.

Follow these steps:

1. From the Media Center start page, select Tasks, Settings, General, Windows Media Center Setup, Set Up Your Speakers.

2. When the welcome screen appears, click Next.

3. On the Speaker Connection Type page, select the type of cable that you use to connect your speakers or audio receiver to your PC.

4. On the Number of Speakers page, shown in Figure 9.9, select the option that best describes your audio system: 2 speakers, 5.1 surround speakers, or 7.1 surround speakers. Click Next to proceed.

5. Media Center now displays a test page. Click the Test button to make sure that you're receiving sound from each of your speakers. If everything is working properly, check I Heard Sound from All of My Speakers, and then click Next. (If you don't hear a sound, you need to troubleshoot your audio setup—from the Media Center configuration all the way to the individual speaker connections.)

6. Click Finish to complete the setup.

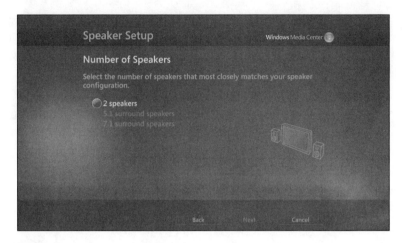

FIGURE 9.9

Configuring Media Center for your specific speaker setup.

tip

You might also need to configure individual settings for your PC's sound card. You have to do this outside of Media Center, from the standard Windows interface; see your manufacturer's manual for instructions.

Changing Media Center's Color Scheme

The default Media Center interface has a soothing blue background. But there are two other color schemes available: High Contrast White (shown in Figure 9.10) and High Contrast Black (shown in Figure 9.11). To switch to one of the other color schemes, follow these steps:

1. From the Media Center start page, select Tasks, Settings, General, Visual and Sound Effects.

2. On the Visual and Sound Effects page, select a new color scheme.

3. Click Save.

Configuring Slideshow Options

As I've said previously, my family likes looking at pictures on the big-screen TV in our living room, via Windows Media Center. It's relatively easy to start a slideshow of our favorite pictures, but Media Center offers several options for how these slideshows display.

Follow these steps to configure Media Center's slideshow options:

FIGURE 9.10

Media Center in High Contrast White.

FIGURE 9.11

Media Center in High Contrast Black.

1. From the Media Center start page, select Tasks, Settings, Pictures, Slide Shows.

2. When the Slide Shows page appears, as shown in Figure 9.12, check the Show Pictures in Random Order option. (Unless you want to show your pictures in the order in which they were saved to the Pictures folder, that is.)

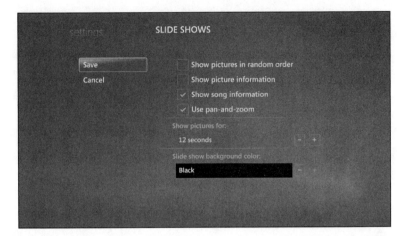

FIGURE 9.12

Configuring slideshow options.

3. If you want to display information about each picture onscreen, check the Show Picture Information option.

4. If you want to show information about the currently playing song while watching a slideshow (at the beginning and end of the song only), check the Show Song Information option.

5. If you want to transition between pictures using a fancy "Ken Burns"-like effect, check the Use Pan-and-Zoom option.

6. Use the + and - controls in the Show Pictures For section to determine how long each picture is displayed.

7. For pictures that don't fill the whole screen, select a background color from the Slide Show Background Color control.

8. Click the Save button.

Customizing the Music Interface

One part of Media Center that you can configure your way is the Music interface—how your music library is displayed and what you see when you're playing music.

Let's deal with the music library first—in particular, how you browse for music. Along the top of the library list is a series of filter options: Albums,

Artists, Genres, Songs, Playlists, Composers, Years, Album Artists, and Shared. Select one of these filters to display your library in this fashion. For example, when you select Genres, the library display changes to display the available genres (Classical, Country, Folk, and so on) shown in Figure 9.13. Select a genre to view the music within.

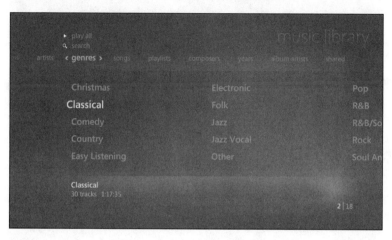

FIGURE 9.13

Viewing your music library by genre.

When you're viewing music within a genre or playlist or whatever, by default you view all the albums within—or more accurately, the album covers. If you'd rather view a text list of songs, select Songs at the top of the page.

You can also change how the albums are displayed. Press the Info button on your remote or right-click your mouse on the page, and you see the pop-up menu shown in Figure 9.14. To display smaller album covers, select View Small; to display a text list of albums instead, select View List. Return to the default album view by selecting View Large.

When you play an album, you see the album cover and song information on top of a kind of collage of other album covers, as shown in Figure 9.15. If you'd rather view a collage of your own pictures in the background, press Esc and then select Play Pictures from the left-hand menu. You can also display typical Windows Media Player visualizations in the background by selecting Visualize from the menu.

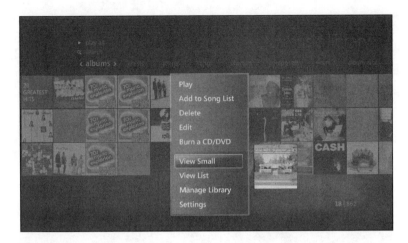

FIGURE 9.14

Changing the default library view.

FIGURE 9.15

Viewing a background collage of album covers.

Alternately, you can play a proper photo slideshow while you're listening to music, using pictures from whatever folder you select. Just start your music playback, and then press the green or menu button to return to the start menu. With the music still playing, select Pictures + Videos, Picture Library, and then navigate to your folder of choice and select Play Slide Show.

Starting Media Center Your Way

Previously, we discussed how to launch Media Center automatically whenever Windows starts. There are more options available for how Media Center starts, however; applying these options involves editing the Media Center shortcut to append one or more "switches" to the launch command.

Here's how to edit the Media Center shortcut:

1. Open the Windows Start menu and navigate to All Programs, Media Center.

2. Right-click the Media Center icon and select Properties from the pop-up menu.

3. When the Properties dialog box opens, select the Shortcut tab.

4. The command in the Target box should look something like this: **%windir%\ehome\ehshell.exe**. Append the desired switch to the *end* of this command, leaving a space between the "ehshell.exe" and the backslash at the start of the switch.

5. Click OK to close the dialog box.

So, for example, if you wanted to launch Media Center with no startup animation and with your favorite music playing, the Target command would look like this:

```
%windir%\ehome\ehshell.exe /nostartupanimation /playfavmusic
```

Table 9.4 details all the available startup options.

Table 9.4   Media Center Startup Switches

Switch	Effect
/nostartupanimation	Launches Media Center with none of the typical startup animation and sounds
/mediamode	Launches Media Center in so-called *media mode*, with no close/minimize/optimize options in the top right corner
/widescreen	Forces Media Center to display in widescreen mode, even on 4:3 aspect ratio displays
/nochrome	When in windowed mode, displays Media Center without the window frame ("chrome")
/noshutdownui	Removes the "shutdown" item from the Tasks menu
/playallmusic	Automatically starts playing all music in the Music library
/playfavmusic	Automatically starts playing your favorite music
/playslideshow	Automatically starts playing all your photo slideshows

Table 9.4   Continued

Switch	Effect
/playfavslideshow	Automatically starts playing your favorite slideshows
/playslideshowwithmusic	Automatically starts playing all your slideshows with background music
/playfavslideshowwithmusic	Automatically starts playing your favorite slideshows with background music
/screensaver	Starts the Media Center screen saver
/configures	Launches Media Center and displays the Configure Slidesaver screen

Finding and Using Other Media Center Applications

By default, Media Center plays CDs and DVDs, video files, and music files; displays digital photographs; and, if you have a TV tuner connected to your PC, plays and records television programs. That's not all Media Center can do, however; dozens of software developers have developed a number of add-on programs that let you perform all manner of interesting tasks, right from the Media Center interface.

Some of these Media Center add-ons are free. Some have a free trial period, but then require payment. Some require payment up front. Most can be downloaded from the Web, so you don't have to get in your car and go shopping for them. Almost all have a similar look and feel to what you're used to with Media Center.

For example, I really like the mceWeather program (www.scendix.com), shown in Figure 9.16. It installs directly in the Media Center start menu (under a new Weather menu item) and displays weather maps, current conditions, and weather forecasts for any number of locations. It's nice to get the weather forecast while I'm listening to my favorite music in my living room.

Where do you find Media Center add-on programs? Unfortunately, there's no central repository for these programs, but you can find a good list of plug-ins and applications at The Green Button (www.thegreenbutton.com), itself a valuable resource for all Media Center users.

note

Plug-ins written for the Windows Vista version of Media Center should be compatible with Windows 7 Media Center.

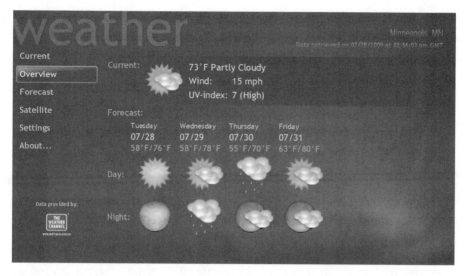

FIGURE 9.16

The mceWeather application for Windows Media Center.

Configuring a Whole House Audio/Video System

If you have all your music and videos stored on your main computer, you can listen to that music and view those videos on any TV in your house. All you need to do is (1) have Windows Media Center running on your main PC, (2) have a wireless home network, and (3) connect a Media Center Extender or Xbox 360 to your other TVs in the house. Media Center then streams your media over your home network to the Media Center Extenders or Xbox units, providing similar functionality to every connected TV.

Understanding Media Center Extenders

A Media Center Extender is a simple device, really; it's a set-top box that connects to any television or audio system anywhere in your house. An Extender also connects to your home network (via either wired Ethernet or wireless Wi-Fi), and thus to your main Media Center PC, on which all your media files are stored.

You control the Media Center Extender through its own remote control unit; the interface on the secondary TV is practically identical to the regular Media Center interface, which means you can choose what music, videos, or photos you want to watch and listen to on your secondary TV.

You can watch one thing on your main Media Center PC and another thing on each Media Center Extender you have installed. And you can use up to five Media Center Extenders simultaneously.

note

Media Center Extenders are not PCs, and (with the exception of the Xbox 360) do not include hard disk drives. An Extender is a network device that connects to your main PC; it doesn't store any data itself.

Different Types of Extenders

Most Media Center Extenders are small boxes that can sit on top of any TV, or alongside other audio/video components. For example, the D-Link DSM-750 Wireless N HD Media Center Extender, shown in Figure 9.17, looks like a small DVD player, but without a DVD slot. Its faceplate is rather plain; all the functions are controlled via remote control. Pricing is typically in the $250-$300 range.

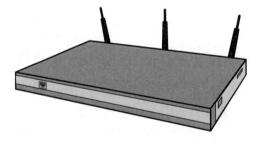

FIGURE 9.17

D-Link's DSM-750 Media Center Extender. (Photo courtesy D-Link.)

In addition, if you have a Microsoft Xbox 360 video game console, shown in Figure 9.18, you can use it as a Media Center Extender, as it has Extender capabilities built in. For game players, this is a great way to add Media Center functionality to their main TV—without placing a bulky Media Center PC in their living room. Just use your desktop PC to store your music and video files; the Xbox connects to the PC via your home network and plays back your audio/video programming via the Media Center interface.

Both types of Extenders—the standard type and the type built into the Xbox console—feature some sort of network connection on the back. This might be a wired Ethernet connection, or a wireless Wi-Fi connection.

FIGURE 9.18

Microsoft's Xbox 360, with built-in Media Center Extender technology. (Photo courtesy Microsoft.)

> **tip**
>
> A wireless connection is fine for listening to music and for viewing digital photos on a Media Center Extender, but not always fast enough to stream television and video programming. If you want to use your Extender for video, it's best to use the faster Ethernet connection.

Connecting Your System

To implement a whole house entertainment system, you need one main computer (typically connected to your main audio/video system) and a Media Center Extender for each room you want to include. The main PC, of course, should be connected to your living room TV and audio/video system, and to your home network (via Ethernet or Wi-Fi). Each Extender must be connected to a television display and (optionally) an audio system. The entire system should look something like the one in Figure 9.19.

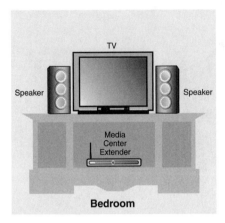
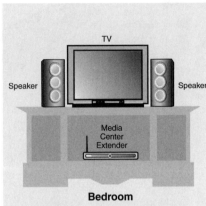
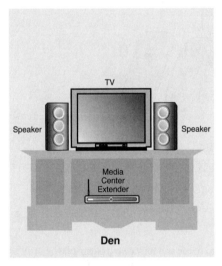
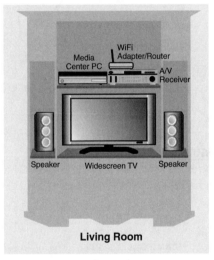

FIGURE 9.19

Using multiple Media Center Extenders in a whole house entertainment system.

How you connect an Extender to your TV depends on what connections are available on each device. If your Extender has an HDMI output and your TV has an HDMI input, go with that. If your Extender has a three-cable component video output instead, then use that along with a digital audio or R/L analog audio connection.

Using a Media Center Extender

After everything is connected, using your Media Center Extender is pretty much identical to using a regular Media Center PC. The Extender uses the same Media Center interface that you have on the PC, minus the Play DVD menu—an omission dictated by our old pal, digital rights management (DRM), which won't let you stream DVD content across a home network. DVD playback aside, just scroll through the onscreen menus using the Extender's remote control unit and make your selections as you would normally.

Remember, whatever you select to play on your Media Center Extender is completely independent from what's playing on your main Media Center PC—or on other Extenders. Each device operates independently from the others, so you could have up to six different songs or programs playing on five separate Extenders plus the main PC. It's a great way to share all those songs you've downloaded from the Internet or ripped from CD—and all the television programs you've recorded.

Accessing Your Media from Other Computers—At Home or Away

You don't have to use a Media Center Extender to share your media across your home network. There's another way to stream music, videos, and pictures from your main PC to any connected computer—even computers outside your home. As long as both computers are running Windows 7 and connected either to your network or to the Internet, you can play and view all your media in real time.

Sharing Media on Your Local Network

When you configure your host computer for media sharing, all the media on that computer can now be played and viewed by other computers on your network. It all starts by turning on Windows 7's media streaming feature on your host computer, via Windows Media Player. Here's how you do it:

1. From Windows Media Player, click the Stream button and then select Turn On Media Streaming. (If you don't see the Turn On Media Streaming option, then media streaming is already enabled; select More Media Streaming Options instead and proceed directly to Step 3.)

2. When the Media Streaming Options window opens, click the Turn On Media Streaming button.

3. You now see the window shown in Figure 9.20. Make sure that Local Network is selected in the Show Devices On list.

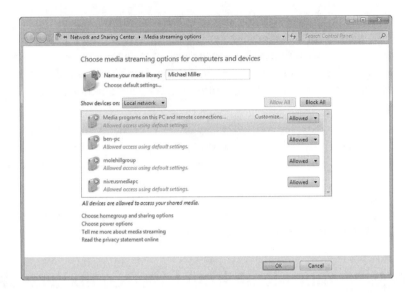

FIGURE 9.20

Configuring media streaming.

4. In the main Media Programs on this PC item, make sure that the Allowed option is selected.

5. If you want to stream only selected files, click the Customize link to display the Customize Media Streaming Settings window, shown in Figure 9.21. From here you can choose to stream only files with a high star rating, or only files with a specific parental rating. Click OK to save your choices.

6. Back in the Media Streaming Options window, click OK.

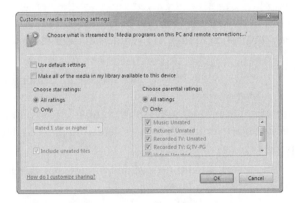

FIGURE 9.21

Customizing the types of files you share.

Thus configured, your host computer will show up as a media sharing device on your network. When other computers access the network, they'll see this device in their Network window, as shown in Figure 9.22. (Shared media devices appear with a small filmstrip and musical note overlaid on the normal icon.) Double-clicking this device on the remote PC opens Windows Media Player and displays the media libraries from your host computer. The remote user can now play or view any file, just as if it were located on the remote PC.

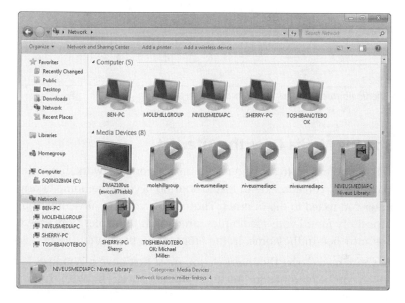

FIGURE 9.22

Remote media libraries shown in the Network window.

Remote media libraries also display in Windows Media Player's navigation pane, as shown in Figure 9.23. Select the media library for a given computer and you see and can play all the media files stored on that PC.

caution

You can only stream unprotected media files—which means you can't stream DRM-protected music or movies purchased from some online media stores.

FIGURE 9.23

Remote media libraries shown in WMP's navigation pane.

Sharing Media Over the Internet

You're not limited to sharing media on your own network, however. With Windows 7, you can extend media sharing beyond the home to any computer connected to the Internet. That means you can have one single depository for all your media files, and access those files from wherever you may be—in the home, in the office, or on the road.

To share media over the Internet, you must first have a Windows Live ID, which can be obtained for free from windows.live.com. With that in hand, follow these steps:

> **note**
>
> If you have a Hotmail, Messenger, or Xbox Live account, you can use that ID as your Windows Live ID.

1. From Windows Media Player, click the Stream button and then select Allow Internet Access to Home Media.

2. When you see the Internet Home Media Access window, shown in Figure 9.24, click Link an Online ID.

3. When the Link Online IDs window appears, click Add an Online ID Provider.

4. A new page now opens in your web browser; click the Windows Live icon.

FIGURE 9.24

Setting up media streaming.

5. You are see a page that talks about Windows Live ID Sign-in Assistant. You need to download and install this software, so scroll down to the Files in This Download section and click the appropriate Download button. (Use the wllogin_32.msi file if you're running 32-bit Windows; use the wllogin_64.msi file if you're running 64-bit Windows.)

6. When prompted, opt to run the file.

7. Once the file is downloaded, you should see the Windows Live ID Sign-in Assistant Setup Wizard; follow the instructions to install and set up the software.

8. When the wizard is complete, return to the Link Online IDs window, shown in Figure 9.25, and click Link Online ID in the WindowsLiveID section.

9. When the Window Live Sign In window appears, enter your Windows Live ID and password; then click Sign In.

10. Once you've signed in, return to the Link Online IDs window and click OK.

11. Return to the Internet Home Media Access window and click Allow Internet Access to Home Media.

12. When you receive the User Account Control prompt, click OK.

13. You now see a confirmation dialog box. Click OK.

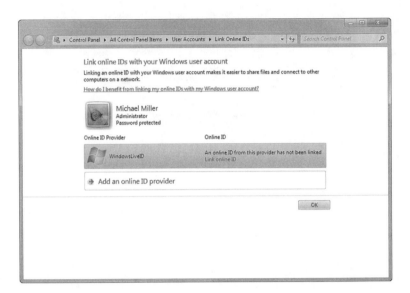

FIGURE 9.25

Linking to an online ID.

You'll need to complete this process for your host PC and for any remote PC you want to use to access your host media library.

caution

Remote media access only works with computers running Windows 7. You can't use a machine running an older version of Windows to either host or access media over the Internet.

To access media stored on your host PC, make sure the remote PC is connected to the Internet and configured for remote access, as just described. When you launch Windows Media Player, click Other Libraries in the navigation pane; you should now see the media libraries on your host PC. Click through to display the desired media and start streaming!

Playing to Other Devices

There's one more remote media feature new to Windows 7 that's worth examining. The Play To feature lets you play media on your PC on other PCs and devices, essentially turning the other units into remote media players.

To use Play To, you first have to enable media streaming on both the host and remote PCs, as previously described. Then go to the remote PC and follow these steps:

1. From Windows Media Player, click the Stream button and then select Allow Remote Control of My Player.

2. When the Allow Remote Control window appears, click Allow Remote Control on This Network.

That's all you have to do in terms of configuration. Using Play To, however, is a bit more complex.

First, both PCs have to be running Windows 7. They also have to be connected to the same HomeGroup, they both have to have media streaming enabled, and they both have to have Windows Media Player running. Those preliminaries out of the way, you begin the Play To function on the host PC by navigating to and selecting an album, track, or playlist in WMP. Right-click the item and select Play To from the pop-up menu; then select the remote PC. This starts playback on the remote PC as well as opens the Play To window, shown in Figure 9.26, on the host PC. You can then use the Play To window to control playback on the remote PC.

FIGURE 9.26

Using the Play To feature to stream media to a remote PC.

The Bottom Line

You can a lot do with media in Windows 7. You can play media on your living room TV using Windows Media Center; you can play media throughout your house using Media Player Extenders; you can stream media to other PCs over your home network; you can stream media to other PCs over the Internet; and you can control playback of media on remote PCs using the Play To feature on your host computer. That's a full menu of media options—all available your way with Windows 7.

10

Managing User Accounts

Now that we've got the fun media stuff out of the way, it's time to turn to more mundane—but equally important—user and network configuration items. We start in this chapter by examining user accounts—Windows' way of letting different people use the same PC. By creating different accounts, each user gets to use the PC in his or her own way, with his own desktop theme, folders and libraries, and the like.

Adding New Users to Your PC

Unless you're a hermit or dedicated bachelor, chances are you live in a house full of other people. In fact, you probably have more people than you have PCs—kids, a spouse, roommates, you name it. Fortunately, you can configure Windows so that different people using your computer sign on with their own custom settings—and access their own personal files.

Rather than multiple people logging in under the same name, it's good form to assign each user in your household his own password-protected *user account*. A user account is simply a name (called a *user name*) by which a given user is known to a computer. Most often the user must also supply a password to log on to the computer; the logon procedure consists of entering the user name and password, which are then recognized (or not) by the host computer.

Creating different user accounts is both a convenience and a security feature. Anyone trying to access another user's account and files without the required password will then be denied access.

Different Types of Accounts

You can create two types of user accounts—administrator and standard. A person with a standard account can perform most general computing tasks, such as running programs, opening documents, and the like. A standard-level account can't make any changes that might affect other users or the security of the computer or network, such as installing new programs or deleting important files. He can change his own account picture and password, but can't change his account type or edit others' accounts; he can still, however, store and edit files in his own personal folders. In other words, a standard user can only use the PC, not modify it.

A person with an administrator account, on the other hand, has permission by Windows to perform any function, including installing programs and modifying or deleting files. Administrators have complete access to the computer and can make changes that might affect other users—as well as the PC's security. He can access all system files, create and delete user accounts, and create passwords for other user accounts.

note

In addition to these two primary user account types, Windows also hosts a Guest account. This is a third account type, available only for this one account, intended for temporary users who don't have a user account on this computer. The Guest account has no password, so guests can log on quickly to browse the Internet, launch programs, and the like. Users of the Guest account can only run software already installed on a machine and cannot install any new software.

When you first configured Windows on your PC, you were set up as an administrator. (You need at least one administrator on the PC, after all.) The other members of your household should be set up with standard accounts; they'll be able to use the computer and access their own files but won't be able to install software or mess up the main settings.

tip

You can have more than one administrator account per PC, so you might want to set up your spouse with an administrator account, too. Or not, depending on your relationship.

Creating a New Account

Only the computer administrator can add a new user to your system. To set up a new account in Windows 7, follow these steps:

1. Open the Control Panel and select User Accounts.

2. When the User Accounts window opens, as shown in Figure 10.1, click Manage Another Account.

3. When the Manage Accounts window opens, click Create a New Account.

4. When the next window appears, as shown in Figure 10.2, enter a name for the new account.

5. Select either Standard User or Administrator status for this account.

6. Click the Create Account button.

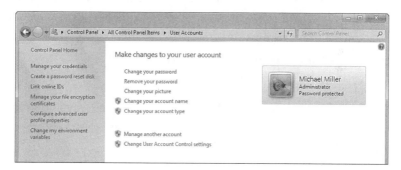

FIGURE 10.1

The User Accounts window.

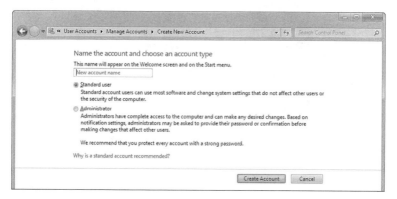

FIGURE 10.2

Creating a new user account.

Windows now creates the new account and randomly assigns a picture that will appear next to the user name. Windows does *not* automatically assign a password to this account; read on to learn how to do this.

Adding a Password to an Account

As just noted, no password is assigned to any new account you create. If you want to assign a password to an account, follow these steps:

1. Open the Control Panel and select User Accounts.

2. When the User Accounts window opens, click Manage Another Account.

3. When the Manage Accounts window opens, as shown in Figure 10.3, select the account to which you want to add a password.

4. When the user account window appears, click Create a Password.

5. When the next window appears, as shown in Figure 10.4, enter and confirm the new password.

6. If you want, enter a hint into the Type a Password Hint box.

7. Click the Create Password button.

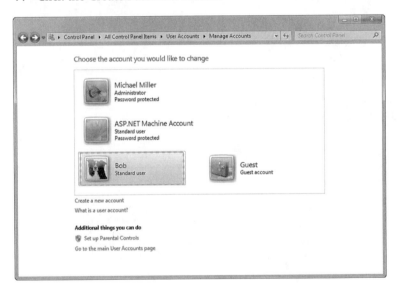

FIGURE 10.3

Managing user accounts.

---

caution

If you create a password for your account, you better remember it. You won't be able to access Windows—or any of your applications and documents—if you forget the password. (If another user forgets his password, however, you as the administrator can reset that password.)

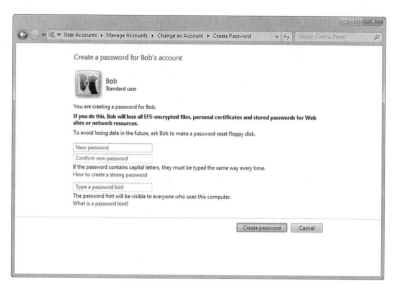

FIGURE 10.4

Creating a new password.

Changing Account Details

Once you've set up a user account, you can change some of the details of that account—including the picture that Windows uses for that account.

Changing Your Account Picture

Windows assigns a small picture to each user account. This picture is displayed not only on the Windows logon screen, but also at the top of the Start menu, as shown in Figure 10.5.

If you don't like the picture assigned to an account, you can change this picture at any time. Windows supplies a number of stock photos you can use for this purpose.

To change your account picture, follow these steps:

1. Open the Control Panel and select User Accounts.

2. When the User Accounts window opens, click Change Your Picture.

3. When the Change Your Picture window, shown in Figure 10.6, appears, click the picture you want to use for your profile.

4. Click the Change Picture button.

FIGURE 10.5

The user account picture at the top of the Windows Start menu.

FIGURE 10.6

Changing your account picture.

Changing Your Account Picture—To Your Own Picture

Windows' stock profile pictures are fine, but do you really want to be a soccer ball or a kitty cat? Wouldn't it be better to use your own photo for your Windows profile picture, the same way you do on Facebook and MySpace?

Most users don't know this, but you can choose *any* picture on your hard drive as your profile picture. For example, I use a publicity photo of myself as my user account photo—this way I know who I am when I'm using my computer!

How do you choose a non-stock picture as your account picture? It's easy—just follow these steps:

1. Open the Control Panel and select User Accounts.
2. When the User Accounts window opens, click Change Your Picture.
3. When the Change Your Picture window appears, click Browse for More Pictures.
4. When the Open dialog box appears, navigate to and select the picture you want, and then click Open.
5. Back in the Change Your Picture window, click the Change Picture button.

It's that easy!

Changing Your Account Name

Don't like the user name you chose for your account? Then change it! Just follow these steps:

1. Open the Control Panel and select User Accounts.
2. When the User Accounts window opens, click Change Your Account Name.
3. When the Change Your Name window appears, shown in Figure 10.7, enter a new account name.
4. Click the Change Name button.

FIGURE 10.7

Changing your account name.

Changing Your Password

Likewise, you can change the password assigned to your account. To do so, however, you have to know your existing password. (Of course, you need to know that to sign into your account in the first place, don't you?) Follow these steps:

1. Open the Control Panel and select User Accounts.

2. When the User Accounts window opens, click Change Your Password.

3. When the Change Your Password window appears, shown in Figure 10.8, enter your old password into the first box.

4. Enter and confirm your new password into the next two boxes.

5. If you want, enter a password hint.

6. Click the Change Password button.

You can also remove the password from your account. Just go to the User Accounts window and click Remove Your Password; when prompted, enter your current password, and then click the Remove Password button.

---

caution

Removing a password is only a good idea if you're the only user on this PC, and you don't want to be bothered with entering a password every time you turn the machine on.

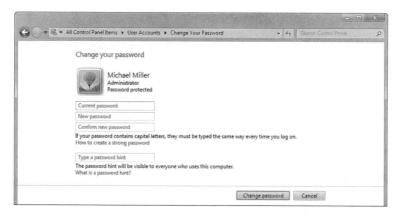

FIGURE 10.8

Resetting your password.

Changing and Deleting Accounts

As an administrator, you have the ability to change other accounts from standard to administrator status (and back again), or completely remove user accounts from your system. Read on to learn more.

Changing an Account Type

If you want to promote a standard user to administrator status, or demote an administrator to standard status, you first have to log on with your own administrator account. Then follow these steps:

1. Open the Control Panel and select User Accounts.

2. When the User Accounts window opens, click Manage Another Account.

3. When the Manage Accounts window appears, select the account you want to change.

4. When the Change an Account window appears, click Change the Account type.

5. When the Change Account Type window appears, select a different account type.

6. Click the Change Account Type button.

Deleting an Account

Likewise, you can remove any user account from your computer. This is a good thing to do if a person no longer uses this computer, or if you want to keep a person from using the PC. As with changing a password, you first have to log on with your own administrator account. Then follow these steps:

1. Open the Control Panel and select User Accounts.
2. When the User Accounts window opens, click Manage Another Account.
3. When the Manage Accounts window appears, select the account you want to change.
4. When the Change an Account window appears, click Delete the Account.
5. When the Delete Account window appears, select whether you want to keep that user's files on the PC (Keep Files) or delete all of that person's files (Delete Files).
6. You now see the Confirm Deletion window. Click the Delete Account button.

Disabling—Not Deleting—An Account

What if you want to temporarily disable an account—without completely deleting it? This is possible, but you have to use Windows 7's Administrative Tools. Here's how it works:

note

Administrative Tools are utilities typically used by IT staff to manage computers and user accounts over a network.

1. Open the Control Panel and select Administrative Tools.
2. When the Administrative Tools window opens, double-click Computer Management.
3. When the Computer Management window opens, as shown in Figure 10.9, go to the navigation pane and select System Tools, Local Users and Groups, Users.
4. In the contents pane, double-click the user account you want to disable.
5. When that account's Properties dialog box appears, as shown in Figure 10.10, make sure the General tab is selected.

FIGURE 10.9

Using Windows' Administrative Tools.

6. Check the Account is Disabled option.
7. Click OK.

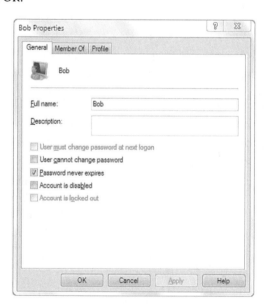

FIGURE 10.10

Disabling an account with Administrative Tools.

tip

You can also use Administrative Tools to change the name, password, and level of any account—although doing so from this utility is more cumbersome than using Windows' standard user account options.

Managing Parental Controls

There's one more thing you may want to configure on one or more user accounts. If you have children using your PC, you may want to enable Windows' parental controls feature.

To configure parental controls for an account, follow these steps:

1. Open the Control Panel and select Parental Controls.

2. When the Parental Controls window opens, select the account you want to change.

3. When the User Controls window appears, select the On, Enforce Current Settings option.

4. To control when this user can use the computer, click Time Limits. When the Time Restrictions window appears, as shown in Figure 10.11, drag your cursor to select what hours you want this user blocked, and then click OK.

5. To control what types of games this user can play, click Games. When the Game Controls window appears, as shown in Figure 10.12, click No if you don't want the user playing any games; click Set Game Ratings to select which ratings (Teen, Mature, and so on) are OK for this user to play; and click Block or Allow Specific Games to select which individual games this user can or can't play. Click OK when done.

6. To keep this user from running certain applications, click Allow and Block Specific Programs. When the Application Restrictions window appears, as shown in Figure 10.13, check Can Only Use the Programs I Allow; then check the programs that are OK for this user to use. Click Ok when done.

7. Back in the User Controls window, click OK.

tip

More parental controls are available from Windows Live (download.live.com). Learn more in Chapter 2,"Setting Default Programs."

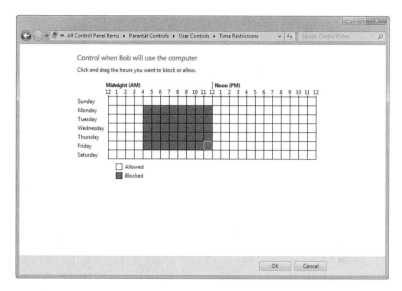

FIGURE 10.11

Select when this user can use the computer.

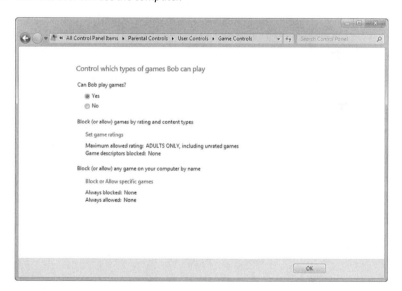

FIGURE 10.12

Select which types of games this user can play.

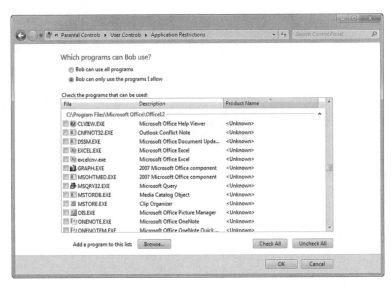

FIGURE 10.13

Select which programs this user can use.

The Bottom Line

When you have more than one person using a computer, set up different accounts in Windows for each user. Each user can then configure Windows his way, and access his own individual desktops and folders when he logs on to Windows. For additional security, protect each account with a password—and, if children are using the computer, use parental controls to manage what they do and when.

11

Configuring User Account Control

Keeping your system safe is an admirable goal. So is making your system easy to use. When one of these goals conflicts with the other, you compromise either security or usability—or both. This is what happened in Windows Vista, with its then-new User Account Control feature, which was well-intentioned but overly intrusive. Well, Microsoft redesigned User Account Control in Windows 7, so it's now something you can configure your way—and strike the right balance between security and usability.

Understanding User Account Control

As the world's most-used computer operating system, Windows has always been subject to attack from computer hackers, malicious techies looking for some sort of "hole" that would let them access other computers and use them for their own nefarious means. This sort of system breach was made easier when a hacker could obtain administrative level access to a machine; as you learned in the previous chapter, administrators can do all sorts of stuff that regular users can't.

With the release of Windows Vista, Microsoft directly addressed this problem with something called User Account Control (UAC).

How UAC Works

As you might suspect, User Account Control is tied into the concept of user accounts and enhances the security of the Windows operating system. UAC is designed to prevent unauthorized people and processes from taking control of a computer and then installing and running malicious programs.

Prior to the implementation of UAC in Windows Vista, all users were automatically assigned administrator status. (Although you could manually choose to create a new limited account, the administrator level was the default.) This resulted in rampant security problems because users could inadvertently install malicious software and spyware on their system—and that software could then take control of the PC, using the original user's administrator privileges.

---

note

Learn more about user levels in Chapter 10, "Managing User Accounts."

With UAC, new users are automatically assigned standard-level access, not administrator access. (You can manually choose to create a new administrator account, of course.) This blocks the average user from executing tasks that could damage the system—and improves system security.

More important, with UAC activated, Windows doesn't automatically accede to all administrator-level requests. When any user—even an administrator—attempts to perform an administrative-level task (such as installing a new software program, changing system settings, or deleting a system file), UAC dims the screen and presents a dialog box that says Windows needs your permission to continue. The task will not be executed until the user clicks Continue.

In addition, UAC doesn't give Administrator status to software programs, as older versions of Windows with UAC did. In older versions of Windows, any program could launch another program or make system-level changes without the user ever knowing it. With UAC, you're asked to approve any such changes made by software programs—which should cut down on spyware and viruses trying to take over your computer system.

Unintended Consequences

Theoretically, this combination of fewer administrators and the double-checking of task authorization should improve system security, in the form of fewer virus infections and spyware intrusions. The likelihood of having your computer remote-controlled for zombie attacks should also be reduced.

If all works as planned, that is.

As you can see, Microsoft implemented UAC with the best of intentions. But as the old saying goes, the road to hell is paved with good intentions. In Windows Vista, UAC definitely illustrated the law of unintended consequences—and led to a hellish experience for many users.

One of the things that most users, me included, despised about the Windows Vista version of UAC was that it got in the way too often. The constant nagging to approve mundane actions caused most users to either approve everything by default (just say "yes") or turn off UAC. That's right, the thing was so danged annoying that it was better to do without than to suffer through the constant prompting process.

The unintentional result, then, was *decreased* system security—the exact opposite of what UAC was intended to achieve.

UAC in Windows 7: New and Improved

Well, Windows 7 provided Microsoft an opportunity for a "do-over" in terms of how UAC works. Hearing our complaints, Microsoft rejigged UAC in Windows 7 to be much less intrusive. In fact, you'll hardly know it's there; about the only confirmation dialogs you'll see are when you're installing new hardware or software on your system. Some critics are saying that this makes Win7 less secure than Vista, but I think it makes it more usable. Less nagging is a good thing.

What's changed in Windows 7? A few things:

- UAC at its default level no longer prompts you when you install a new program or make a system-level change. Instead, you only get nagged if a program attempts to make these sorts of changes.

- Standard users can run more tasks without prompting than they could in Windows Vista. No longer are you prompted for every little thing you do (like copying files!).

- Dialog boxes generated by Windows 7 UAC are a bit more informative than the generic ones in Windows Vista. By providing context-sensitive feedback, users can make more intelligent decisions about whether or not to approve specific actions.

- Windows 7 now lets you adjust the "comfort level" of UAC. Windows Vista had only two options for UAC—on or off. In Windows 7, you can adjust just how strongly UAC works—and how much nagging you get.

Changing User Account Control Settings

The key to making UAC both unobtrusive and protective is the new UAC level feature. That is, you can fine-tune the degree to which UAC works; you can make it more secure (and thus more intrusive) or less intrusive (and thus slightly less secure). It's UAC your way.

How do you adjust the amount of UAC you see in Windows? Follow these steps:

1. Open the Control Panel and select User Accounts.
2. When the User Accounts window appears, click Change User Account Control Settings.
3. When the User Account Control Settings window appears, as shown in Figure 11.1, adjust the slider to the level you prefer.
4. Click OK.
5. When prompted by UAC to confirm your changes, click OK.

What UAC levels are available? Table 11.1 details the options.

Table 11.1 User Account Control Levels

Level	Prompts When Programs Try to Install Other Programs	Prompts When Programs Try to Make Changes to Windows Settings	Prompts When You Make Changes to Windows Settings
Always Notify (top)	Yes	Yes	Yes
Default (second from top)	Yes	Yes	No
Notify Me (second from bottom)	Yes (doesn't dim desktop)	Yes (doesn't dim desktop)	No
Never Notify (bottom)	No	No	No

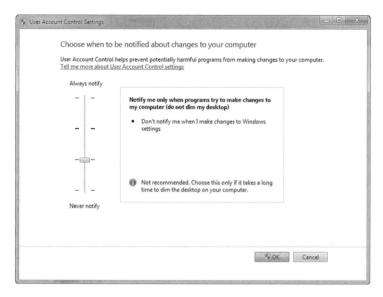

FIGURE 11.1

Configuring User Account Control in Windows 7.

So what level should you select? The default level is probably best; it protects you from malicious programs without nagging you about tasks you yourself perform. If you're worried that others on your system might try to make unauthorized changes or install unwanted software, select the strictest level, but be prepared for a Vista-like level of nagging. But you should avoid the Never Notify level, as it unnecessarily opens up your system to attack.

---

tip

The level below the default works similarly to the default level, but without dimming the Windows desktop when a UAC prompt is displayed. This is a good option if your computer has slow graphics performance and takes too long to restore the screen after a dimming.

The Bottom Line

User Account Control is a good thing—when done right. In Windows 7, UAC is a lot more usable (and thus more protective) than it was in Windows Vista, because it doesn't nag you as much. Even better, you can configure the amount of control it asserts, just by sliding a control up or down. It's easy to find the right compromise between security and usability.

12

Managing Network Connections

With each version of Windows, Microsoft makes it easier and easier
to connect multiple computers in a network. In Windows 7, networking for most users is no more difficult than connecting an
Ethernet cable or selecting an existing wireless network from a list;
just about everything else is handled automatically.

That said, there are still some things you can configure to make
your network work your way. That's what this chapter is about.

Configuring Windows for Network Use

Let's assume that you've already set up your home or small business
network. That is, you've connected a network router, run the appropriate Ethernet cable, or set up your router's wireless capability.
What you haven't done is configure your computer to work with
your network.

In Windows 7, this is a painless and practically transparent process.
In fact, if you're connecting via Ethernet, you don't have to do a
thing; Windows will recognize your new network and start using it,
automatically.

If you're connecting via a wireless connection, configuration is only
slightly more involved. Just follow these steps:

1. Click the Network icon in the notification area of the taskbar.

2. When the Jump List of available networks appears, as shown
   in Figure 12.1, select your network from the list.

3.   Click the Connect button.

4.   When prompted to select a network location, select Home.

That's all there is to it.

FIGURE 12.1
A Jump List of available wireless networks.

note

When configuring a wireless network, you should enable some form of wireless security to protect against unauthorized users. Learn more in Chapter 20, "Managing System Security."

Configuring a Network Workgroup

In Windows, just connecting to an existing network isn't enough. You also have to make sure that all your computers are connected to the same *workgroup*—what Microsoft calls a typical peer-to-peer network. If different computers are configured for different named workgroups, they won't be able to share files or devices.

By default, both Windows 7 and Windows Vista assign your network the workgroup name "WORKGROUP." This may not be the same workgroup name used by other computers on your network; for example, Windows XP assigned the workgroup name "MSHOME" by default.

caution

Because of the workgroup name disparity, you may not see older PCs on your Windows 7 network—unless you change the workgroup name on one of the computers.

tip

What is the name of your current workgroup? To find out, open the Control Panel and select System. The workgroup name is displayed in the resulting System window.

You need to assign the same workgroup name to all computers on your network. So if all your computers are in the MSHOME workgroup except your Windows 7 PC (which is assigned to the WORKGROUP workgroup, if you recall), you should change the workgroup name on your Windows 7 PC to MSHOME. Or you could change the workgroup for *all* your PCs to something a little less generic, such as BOBGROUP or MYWORKGROUP or whatever.

If you want or need to change the workgroup for a given computer, follow these steps:

1. Open the Control Panel and select System.

2. When the System window appears, shown in Figure 12.2, scroll to the Computer Name, Domain, and Workgroup Settings section and click Change Settings.

3. When the System Properties dialog box appears, select the Computer Name tab.

4. Click the Change button.

5. When the Computer Name/Domain Changes dialog box appears, as shown in Figure 12.3, enter a new name for your workgroup into the Workgroup field, and then click OK.

6. When you see the "welcome" message box, click OK.

7. When prompted to restart your computer, click OK.

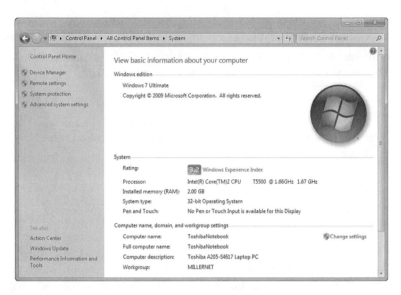

FIGURE 12.2

Viewing system information—and your current workgroup name—in the System window.

FIGURE 12.3

Changing the name of your Windows workgroup.

Adding Your Computer to a HomeGroup

Workgroups were the way that Microsoft handled networks prior to Windows 7. While workgroups are still present, Windows 7 adds a new *HomeGroup* feature that purportedly makes it easier to network together multiple home computers. A HomeGroup is kind of a simplified network that consists of other computers running Windows 7. All computers connected to the HomeGroup can automatically share files and printers.

caution

Only PCs running Windows 7 can be part of a HomeGroup. PCs running older versions of Windows do not have the HomeGroup feature, and must use the normal networking functions instead. For that reason, it makes sense to enable HomeGroups only on networks consisting solely of Windows 7 computers.

I'll be honest: I find HomeGroups fairly useless and almost totally duplicative of the existing workgroups feature, especially on a mixed network—one that includes a mix of computers running Windows 7 and other versions of Windows. HomeGroups only works with Windows 7 computers, and few people I know have an all Win7 environment. That said, if all your computers are running Win7, HomeGroups makes setting up your network and sharing files and devices a little easier than the traditional workgroup method of Windows networking.

In any case, let's walk through the process of creating a new HomeGroup. Here's what you need to do:

1. Open the Control Panel and select Network and Sharing Center. (Alternately, click the Network icon in the taskbar notification area and select Open Network and Sharing Center.)

2. From the Network and Sharing Center, click Choose HomeGroup and Sharing Options.

3. When the HomeGroup window appears, click Create a HomeGroup.

4. On the next screen, shown in Figure 12.4, check those types of items you want to share across your network: Pictures, Music, Videos, Documents, or Printers, and then Click Next.

5. Click Create Now.

6. Write down the HomeGroup password so that you can enter it when configuring other computers on the network.

7. Click Finish.

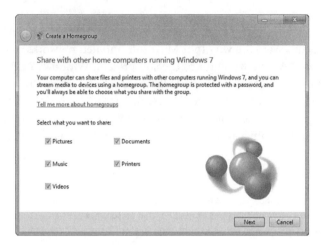

FIGURE 12.4

Creating a new HomeGroup.

Managing Your Network

In Windows 7, all network functions are monitored and managed via the Network and Sharing Center. To open the Network and Sharing Center, open the Control Panel and select Network and Sharing Center. Alternately, you can click the Network button on the taskbar and then click Open Network and Sharing Center.

As you can see in Figure 12.5, the Network and Sharing Center displays a simplified map of your current network, along with a variety of configuration settings. We'll discuss these settings next.

Viewing a Larger Network Map

The network map displayed in the Network and Sharing Center is a basic map that shows only the immediate connections for the current computer. To view a larger and more complete map of your entire network, click the See Full Map link in the Network and Sharing Center window.

The resulting Network Map window displays all your connected network devices. To open any network computer or device shown on the map, simply double-click its icon.

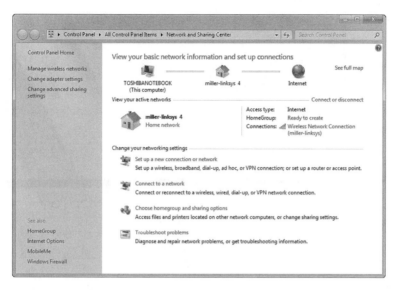

FIGURE 12.5

Managing your network with the Network and Sharing Center.

caution

Computers running Windows XP or older operating systems may not automatically appear in the network map, instead appearing by themselves below the map. That's because the map displays only those computers that have Link-Layer Topology Discovery (LLTD) installed. If you have a Windows XP computer that doesn't appear on the network map, you can download LLTD for that computer from support.microsoft.com/kb/922120.

Changing the Type of Network Location

When you first connect your computer to the network, you are prompted to set your type of network location—Home, Work, or Public. You can later change the network location type for a given network connection by following these steps:

1. While logged on to the network, open the Network and Sharing Center.

2. Click the Location link beneath the name of your current network in the View Your Active Networks section.

3. When the Set Network Location window appears, as shown in Figure 12.6, select Home Network, Work Network, or Public Network.

4. When the next window appears, click the Close button.

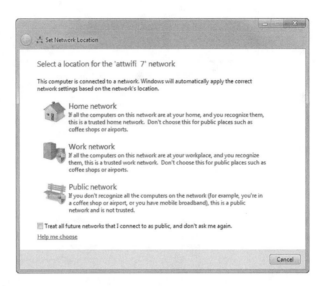

FIGURE 12.6

Changing network location settings.

Configuring Network Sharing and Discovery

The Network and Sharing Center offers easy access to most key network configuration settings. These settings determine how your computer appears on the network, as well as how it shares files and devices.

To configure your network in this manner, open the Network and Sharing Center and click Change Advanced Sharing Settings. This opens the Advanced Sharing Settings window, shown in Figure 12.7. From here you can configure the following settings:

- **Network Discovery.** Enables this computer to see other network computers, and vice versa.

- **File and Printer Sharing.** Enables other users on your network to access shared files and printers on this computer.

- **Public Folder Sharing.** Lets other users on the network either view or view, edit, and create files stored in this computer's Public folder.

- **Media Streaming.** Enables users and devices on the network to access shared music, videos, and pictures stored on this computer. Also lets this computer access shared media files on other computers connected to the network.

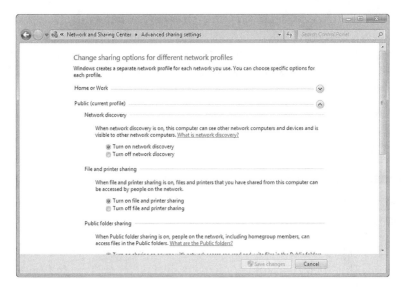

FIGURE 12.7

Configuring your network's sharing and discovery options.

- **File Sharing Connections.** Determines the degree of encryption used to protect file-sharing connections. The most secure option is 128-bit encryption, but you may need to select the 40- or 56-bit encryption option to maintain compatibility with all devices.

- **Password Protected Sharing.** When enabled, limits access to public folders to those users who have an account and password on this computer.

- **HomeGroup Connections.** By default, Windows manages HomeGroup connections; alternately, you can opt to manage your own connections with user names and passwords.

These settings are available separately for all three types of connections—Home, Work, and Public. To configure the settings for both Home and Work networks, click the down arrow next to Home or Work; to configure the settings for Public networks, click the down arrow next to Public.

Managing Network Connections

To view information about your current network connection—connection speed, amount of data transmitted, and the like—as well as to manage the connection itself, you use the Network Connections folder. To access this folder, open the Network and Sharing Center and click Change Adapter Settings.

As you can see in Figure 12.8, the Network Connections folder displays icons for each available network connection on this PC. Depending on your computer and available networks, there may be an icon for both a wired and a wireless network—and, if you have a Bluetooth keyboard or mouse connected, for a Bluetooth network.

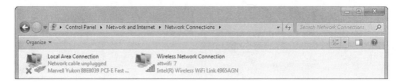

FIGURE 12.8
Managing your network connections.

To view and manage a given connection, double-click the connection's icon. This opens the Status dialog box, like the one shown in Figure 12.9. From here you can:

FIGURE 12.9
Viewing and editing information about a particular network connection.

- Click the Details button to view even more technical details about this connection, as shown in Figure 12.10.

- Click the Properties button to edit various technical properties for this connection, including the underlying TCP/IP protocols, as shown in Figure 12.11.

tip

You can also open the Properties dialog box by right-clicking a connection in the Network Connections folder and selecting Properties from the pop-up window.

- Click the Diagnose button if you're having network problems and need to troubleshoot.
- Click the Disable button to disable this particular connection.

FIGURE 12.10

Viewing more technical details about the connection.

tip

To rename a network connection, right-click the connection's icon in the Network Connections folder and select Rename. The connection's name is now highlighted; type a new name and then press Enter on your computer keyboard.

Changing IP Addresses

Okay, now for some technical stuff—which you probably won't ever need to use. (Still, it's good to know.)

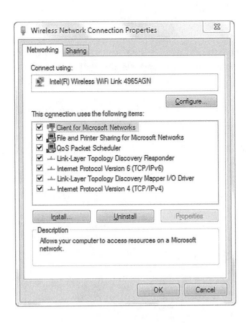

FIGURE 12.11

Editing a connection's technical properties.

Windows uses TCP/IP technology to enable network communication between multiple computers. By default, Windows uses the Dynamic Host Configuration Protocol (DHCP) to automatically assign each computer on your network its own unique Internet Protocol (IP) address; this means you don't have to bother with creating an address for each PC.

note

TCP/IP stands for Transmission Control Protocol/Internet Protocol, a combination of two similar protocols. The older and still current version of the IP protocol is IPv4; its successor, not yet widely implemented, is IPv6.

In some circumstances it may be necessary to assign one or more PCs on your network its own specific IP address. For example, some print servers require a specific address (or an address in a given range) for the host computer; without the specific address, the print server doesn't know which PC is hosting it. You may also need to assign a computer an IP address if your network has trouble recognizing that machine.

In most instances when assigning a manual IP address is necessary, the manufacturer of the given device will indicate what address or range of addresses you should use. That said, it's good to know how to do it if you need to do it. So if you need to manually assign a specific IP address to the current PC, follow these steps:

1. Open the Network and Sharing Center and select Change Adapter Settings.

2. When the Network Connections window opens, right-click the connection you want to change and select Properties from the pop-up menu.

3. When the Properties dialog box appears, select either Internet Protocol Version 4 or Internet Protocol Version 6; then click the Properties button.

4. If you selected IPv4, select the General tab, select Use the Following IP Address (shown in Figure 12.12), and enter the appropriate settings into the IP Address, Subnet Mask, and Default Gateway boxes.

5. If you selected IPv6, select Use the Following IPv6 Address (shown in Figure 12.13) and enter the appropriate settings into the IPv6 Address, Subnet Prefix Length, and Default Gateway boxes.

6. Click OK when finished.

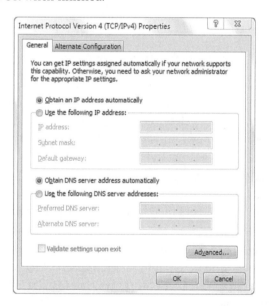

FIGURE 12.12

Manually entering an IPv4 address.

tip

In some instances you may need to indicate specific DNS server address settings to establish an Internet connection. If your Internet service provider supplies you with this information, open the IPv4 or IPv6 dialog box, check Use the Following DNS Server Addresses, and then enter the desired addresses into the Primary DNS Server and Alternate DNS Server boxes.

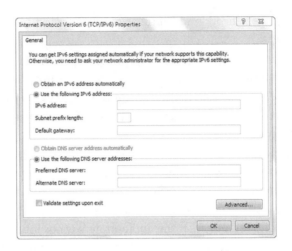

FIGURE 12.13

Manually entering an IPv6 address.

Managing Wireless Networks

If you have a notebook PC, you're probably used to connecting to WiFi hotspots when you're out and about. The problem is, you're often presented with multiple wireless networks to connect to. Assuming you know which one is which, how can you better manage the list of available networks?

Fortunately, Windows lets you control the order of wireless networks that your computer connects to. This way you'll connect to your favored network when available, and then go down the list of available networks in order of preference.

To manage the order of wireless networks on your computer, open the Network and Sharing Center and select Manage Wireless Networks; this opens the Manage Wireless Networks window. As you can see in Figure 12.14, all the wireless networks to which you've ever connected are listed here. Windows uses this list to determine which wireless network to connect to first.

To change the order of a given network, select it and then click either Move Up or Move Down to move it up or down the list. If you'd rather delete a network from this list, select it and click Remove.

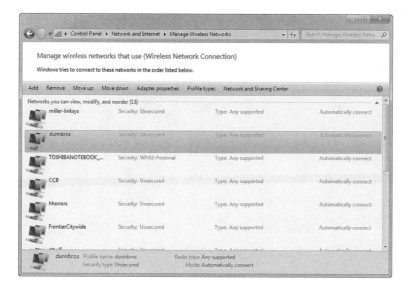

FIGURE 12.14

Changing the order of wireless networks.

tip

You probably want to place your own wireless network at the top of this list, to make sure you automatically connect to it rather than to a neighbor's network.

The Bottom Line

Connecting your Windows 7 computer for network use is easier than it's ever been. You can, however, configure your computer—and your network—your way, in terms of how you handle file sharing, printer sharing, network discovery, and so forth. Most everything is done from the Network and Sharing Center; just open it up and start clicking.

13

Sharing Files, Folders, and Devices

One of the important ways to have Windows your way involves
what files and devices you share with other users on your network.
You can choose to share with everyone or no one, or just with
selected users. Network sharing makes for more versatile computer
use—if you know how to do it.

Configuring File Sharing

When your computer is connected to a network, it's relatively easy
to copy or move files from one computer to another. It's also easy to
share a single network printer between multiple computers on your
network. To do all this, however, you first have to enable file and
printer sharing on each of your computers.

How File Sharing Works

Just because you have multiple PCs connected to your home network doesn't mean that the contents of each of the PCs will be automatically visible to each other. In fact, all of the contents of a PC
are hidden from other users by default—so you *can't* view or share
files. (It's a security thing.)

If you want other users on your network to be able to view or edit a
document on one of your computers, you must first enable file sharing for that computer. We'll discuss how to do this in a moment, so
hang tight.

After you've enabled file sharing in general, you can choose which
files and folders to share. There are two ways to do this.

If you want to share a single document, the easiest way to proceed is to save that document to the Public folder on your hard disk. This folder is, by default, accessible to every user on this computer, as well as every user on the network.

Windows also lets you configure any other folder or drive on a given computer as a shared folder/drive. That way another user could go directly to your Documents or Music folders, for example, without you first having to move the shared file to your Public folder.

After file sharing has been enabled for a given file or folder, all the other computers on your network can see the drive or folder you decided to share. (Unless, as we'll shortly discuss, you limit sharing to specific users.) When you open the Network Explorer on another computer, you'll see the shared drive/folder displayed.

Taking Precautions

Although it's great to share files across two or more PCs on your network, you should be cautious about enabling file sharing. When you let a folder or drive be shared, anyone accessing your network can access the contents of that folder or drive. (Unless you've limited sharing to selected users, of course.) Make sure that you share only those folders and drives you want to share, and keep the other folders on your computer private.

You should also make sure that you have a firewall installed on your network and that you've activated adequate wireless security (if you have a wireless network). This will keep unwanted intruders from hacking into your network—and gaining unauthorized access to your private files.

---

note

Learn more about securing your files and folders in Chapter 20, "Managing System Security."

Enabling File and Printer Sharing

With Windows 7, you enable both file and printer sharing in a single process. Here's what to do:

1. Open the Control Panel and select Network and Sharing Center. (Alternately, click the Network icon in the taskbar notification area and select Open Network and Sharing Center.)

2. From the Network and Sharing Center, click Choose Homegroup and Sharing Options.

3. In the next window, click Change Advanced Sharing Settings.

4. On the next screen, shown in Figure 13.1, click the down arrow next to Home or Work.

5. Scroll to the File and Printer Sharing section and click Turn On File and Printer Sharing.

6. Scroll to the Public Folder Sharing section and click Turn On Sharing So Anyone with Network Access Can Read and Write Files in the Public Folders.

7. If you want only users with a password to access your files (a nice security precaution), scroll to the Password Protected Sharing section and click Turn On Password Protected Sharing

8. Click Save Changes.

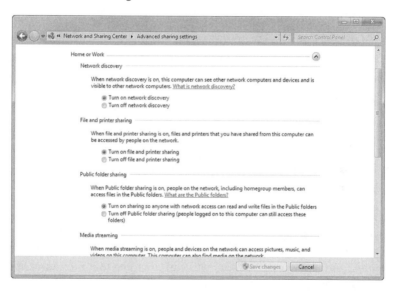

FIGURE 13.1

Enabling file and printer sharing.

If you don't enable password protected sharing, any user on your network can access your files. With password protected sharing enabled, a user must have a user account and password *on your computer* in order to share your files. Users of other computers who do not have an account on your machine will not be able to access your files.

Sharing Files and Folders

As we just discussed there are several ways to share files and folders on your PC with others on your network. We'll look at each option next.

Sharing the Public Folder

The easiest way to share files in Windows 7 is to move or copy the files you want to share into the Public folder. Other users across the network can then access the Public folder and all its contents as a shared folder.

---

caution

For public folder sharing to work, you need to enable public folder sharing for your entire computer, as described previously.

In Windows 7, the Public folder contains a number of relevant subfolders, each of which is shared with others on your network. Use these subfolders to organize your shared content:

- Public Documents
- Public Downloads
- Public Music
- Public Pictures
- Public Recorded TV
- Public Videos

You can also put files directly into the main Public folder, of course. To open the Public folder, open Windows Explorer and click Public in the Favorites section of the navigation pane. (If the Public folder doesn't appear in the Favorites section, you can navigate to it manually at c:\Users\Public\.)

Sharing Other Folders

Using the Public folder may be the easiest way to share files, but not the only way. It's a little more involved, but you can designate any folder in Windows as a shared folder; this lets other users on the network access any folder you specify, without having to move files into the Public folder.

---

caution

For individual folder sharing to work, you need to enable file sharing for your entire computer, as described previously.

---

1. Open Windows Explorer and navigate to (but don't open) the folder you want to share.

2. Right-click the folder you want to share and select Share With, Specific People.

3. The File Sharing window, shown in Figure 13.2, now appears and lists all the users on this machine in the pull-down Add list. Select one or more users from this list with whom you want to share this folder; then click the Add button to add them to your share list.

4. Pull down the Permission Level list next to each user and select either Read or Read/Write. The Read option enables users to only look at files, not edit them; the Read/Write option lets users fully edit files.

5. Click the Share button.

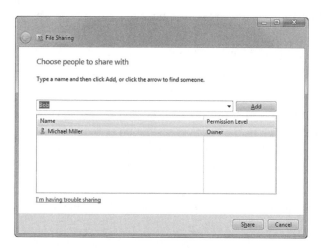

FIGURE 13.2

Selecting users with whom to share this folder.

If your computer is connected to a Windows 7 HomeGroup, you can opt to share this folder with all members of your HomeGroup. Right-click a folder in Windows Explorer and select Share With and then either Homegroup (read), to let others look at but not edit files, or Homegroup (Read/Write), to let others make changes to files.

Sharing Complete Drives

Windows also lets you share complete drives on your network computers. Before you can share a drive, however, you have to give the drive a distinct name; Windows won't let you name your share "C:", but it will let you name it "C" or "Drive C", if you can see that distinction.

> **caution**
>
> Sharing the complete contents of a drive—especially drive C, which contains your system files—can be risky. It's better to designate specific folders to share, rather than allow unfettered access to your entire drive.

Follow these steps to configure a drive for sharing:

1. From the Windows Start menu, select Computer.

2. When the Computer window opens, right-click the drive you want to share and select Share With, Advanced Sharing.

3. When the Properties dialog box appears, make sure the Sharing tab is selected.

4. Click the Advanced Sharing button.

5. When the Advanced Sharing dialog box appears, as shown in Figure 13.3, check the Share This Folder option.

6. Enter a name for the drive you want to share into the Share Name box.

7. To specify which users can access this drive, click the Permissions button. When the Permissions dialog box appears, as shown in Figure 13.4, select which users can access the drive and then check a permission level—Full Control, Change, or Read. Click OK when done.

8. Back in the Advanced Sharing dialog box, click OK.

FIGURE 13.3

Configuring a drive for sharing.

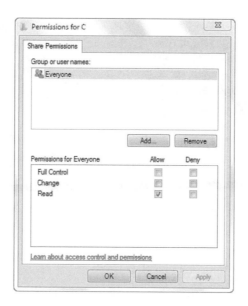

FIGURE 13.4

Configuring sharing permissions.

Sharing Files from Other Computers

Once you've got everything configured correctly, how do you access files from other computers across your network? It's a matter of knowing which folders to go to, as you'll soon learn.

Accessing Other Computers on Your Network

To access other computers on your network, follow these steps:

1. Open Windows Explorer and click Network in the navigation pane.

2. This displays all your network computers, as shown in Figure 13.5. Double-click any networked computer to view its shared folders and files.

4. You can then navigate through all the shared folders and printers on that PC, as shown in Figure 13.6, and then access or open individual files.

---

tip

On most systems, shared files are stored in the Public folder. Look in this folder first for the files you want.

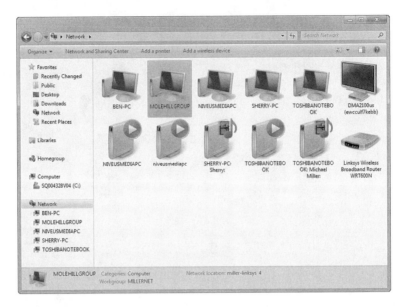

FIGURE 13.5
Viewing all the computers on your network.

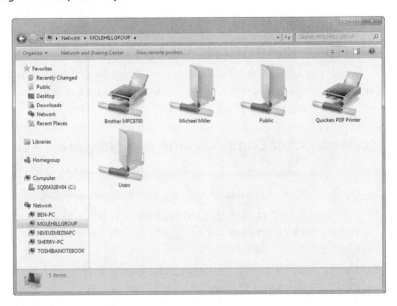

FIGURE 13.6
Viewing the shared contents of a networked computer.

Creating a Shortcut to a Shared Folder

By default, only computers are displayed in the top level of the Network folder. If you regularly access a particular shared *folder* on a given computer, you might find it easier to create a shortcut directly to that folder in Windows Explorer. You do this by assigning a virtual drive letter to the shared item; accessing this single drive letter is quicker and easier than navigating down to the folder on the remote computer.

Here's how to do it:

> **note**
>
> When you assign a drive letter to a shared folder or drive, this is called *mapping* the folder or drive.

1. Open the Windows Start menu and select Computer.

2. Click Map Network Drive from the toolbar.

3. When the Map Network Drive window appears, as shown in Figure 13.7, select an available drive letter. This is how you'll refer to the shared folder, and it doesn't have to correspond with the actual letter of the drive you're mapping; this, for all intents and purposes, is a *virtual* drive letter.)

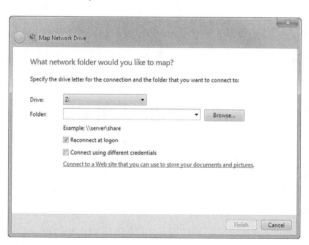

FIGURE 13.7

Getting ready to map a shared folder.

4. Click the Browse button.

5. When the Browse for Folder window appears, as shown in Figure 13.8, navigate to and select the desired computer and folder to share, then click OK.

6. Back in the Map Network Drive window, check the Reconnect at Logon option to connect to and show the shared item whenever Windows launches.

7. If you need to enter a user name and password to connect to the shared item, check the Connect Using Different Credentials option.

8. Click the Finish button.

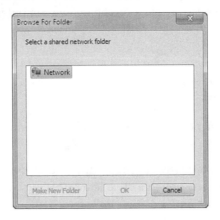

FIGURE 13.8

Selecting the shared folder to map.

This creates an icon for the shared folder in Windows Explorer. Double-click this icon to go directly to the folder, without having to click through all the network computers and drives to get there.

Installing a Network Printer on Other PCs

There's one last sharing option we need to address. That's sharing a printer over your network—a great way to save money. With printer sharing enabled, you don't have to buy separate printers for each computer on your network; instead, you can have all your computers share a single printer.

We previously discussed how to enable printer sharing, which you need to do on the computer to which the printer is connected. You then need to install that network printer on all the other computers on your network. In Windows 7, you do so by following these steps:

1. Click the Start button and select Devices and Printers.

2. When the Devices and Printers window opens, as shown in Figure 13.9, click Add a Printer from the toolbar.

3. When the Add a Printer window opens, click Add a Network, Wireless or Bluetooth Printer; then click Next.

4. When the next window appears, as shown in Figure 13.10, select your printer from the list; then click Next.

5. When the next screen appears, click Next.

6. If prompted to install a driver for this printer, select Yes.

7. If you want this printer to be your default printer, click Set as the Default Printer.

8. Click Finish.

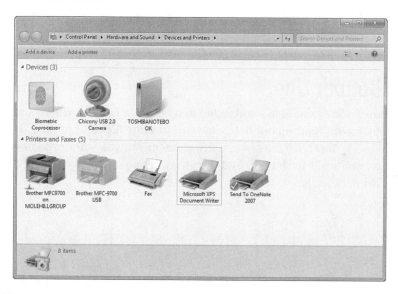

FIGURE 13.9

Getting ready to install a network printer on a remote PC.

After the network printer is installed, it should appear in the list of available printers whenever you choose to print a document or photo from this PC.

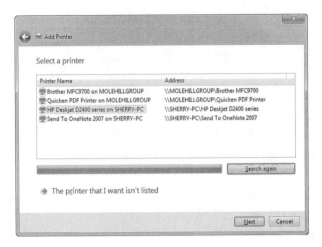

FIGURE 13.10

Selecting your network printer.

The Bottom Line

When your computer is connected to a network, having Windows your way means figuring out how you want to share files and printers over the network. You have a lot of options; choose what you want to share and how you want to share it, and then start taking advantage of everything your network has to offer.

14

Configuring and Customizing Internet Explorer

We now turn our attention to the Internet, and in this chapter, your web browser. In Windows 7, that means Internet Explorer 8, and there's a lot you can do with it to browse the Internet your way.

Personalizing Internet Explorer

Internet Explorer 8 (IE8) is a good-looking browser, much easier to use than previous versions. But that doesn't mean you have to accept the default interface; there are lots of things you can personalize, if you like. For example, you can add or delete buttons from the Command bar, add your own personal links to the Favorites bar, or add any number of new toolbars to the browser. Read on to learn more.

Customizing the Command Bar

Let's start with the main IE toolbar, technically called the Command bar, located to the right of the browser tabs. By default, you have the eight buttons shown in Figure 14.1: Home, RSS Feeds, Read Mail, Print, Page, Safety, Tools, and Help. You can, however, hide any of these buttons—or display additional ones.

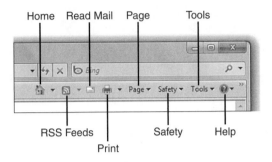

FIGURE 14.1

The IE8 Command bar.

To change the buttons on the Command bar, follow these steps:

1. Select Tools, Toolbars, Customize.

2. When the Customize Toolbar dialog box appears, as shown in Figure 14.2, select any existing button you want to delete from the Current Toolbar Buttons list and then click the Remove button.

3. To add a new button to the Command bar, select it from the Available Toolbar Buttons list and click the Add button.

4. To change the order of the Command bar buttons, select a button from the Current Toolbar Buttons list and click either the Move Up or Move Down button.

5. Click the Close button when done.

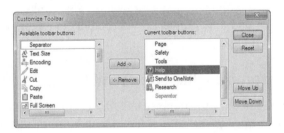

FIGURE 14.2

Customizing buttons on the Command bar.

---

tip

To return to the default Command bar setup, click the Reset button in the Customize Toolbar dialog box.

You can also change how the Command bar buttons are displayed. With IE8, you have the option of displaying selective text (the default view), large icons, text labels only, or icons only. To change the Command display, right-click the toolbar and select Customize from the pop-up menu; then click the appropriate option.

tip

You can also choose to place the stop and refresh buttons before the Address bar, instead of after. Just right-click the Command bar and select Customize, Show Stop and Refresh Buttons Before Address Bar.

Displaying Other Toolbars

The IE8 interface is relatively clean, not cluttered with lots of extraneous toolbars like previous versions tended to be. If you prefer the clutter, however, you can add all manner of other toolbars to IE8. This includes built-in toolbars, such as the Favorites bar, as well as toolbars from third parties, such as Google, Yahoo!, and eBay.

For example, the Google toolbar (available at toolbar.google.com), shown in Figure 14.3, features a search box and one-click access to Google News and other content. The Yahoo! toolbar (available at toolbar.yahoo.com), shown in Figure 14.4, is similar to the Google toolbar, but with a Yahoo! search box and buttons for Yahoo! content, instead. And the eBay toolbar (available at pages.ebay.com/ebay_toolbar/), shown in Figure 14.5, lets you search eBay auctions and view the status of your current bids.

FIGURE 14.3

The Google toolbar.

FIGURE 14.4

The Yahoo! toolbar.

FIGURE 14.5

The eBay toolbar.

caution

While toolbars from major websites are legitimate, some toolbars from lesser-known websites are actually a form of spyware, designed to report your browsing activity back to another site on the Web. As such, you may need to run an anti-spyware program to completely get rid of these malware toolbars.

To manage the toolbars installed in Internet Explorer, click the Tools button and select Toolbars. You can then check those toolbars you want displayed, or uncheck those you want to disable.

By the way, there are two toolbars that you don't want to uncheck. The Command bar is the main IE toolbar; hide it and you won't be able to access key commands. The Status bar is the space at the bottom of the browser window, shown in Figure 14.6, that displays the loading status of the current web page, along with zoom level and other info. It's useful to keep this bar displayed, as well.

FIGURE 14.6

The Status bar, at the bottom of the browser window.

tip

If you accidently uncheck the Command bar, you can restore it by right-clicking next to IE's tabs and checking Command Bar from the pop-up menu.

Adding Links to the Favorites Bar

Another one of IE's built-in toolbars is the Favorites bar, shown in Figure 14.7. This toolbar lets you put links to your favorite web pages right in front of your face—not hidden in the Favorites pane. (Which we'll discuss separately, in a few pages.) When you add a website to the Favorites bar, you can jump to that site with the click of a button.

FIGURE 14.7

The Favorites bar—with a few of the author's favorite sites

To display the Favorites bar, click the Tools button and select Toolbars, Favorites Bar. As you can see, it automatically displays to the right of the Favorites button, which then kicks the browser's tabs down one level.

tip

You can put more links on the Favorites bar than can be displayed in the width of the browser. To view these additional links, click the right-arrow at the far right of the Favorites bar.

To add a site to the Favorites bar, all you have to do is drag the site's icon from the Address bar onto the Links bar. You can rearrange buttons on the Links bar by dragging them from one position to another.

Adding a Menu Bar

Part of IE8's clean interface is due to its lack of a traditional pull-down menu bar. That said, many users still like this old-school approach. Fortunately, you can add back the menu bar, if you like.

To display the IE8 menu bar, shown in Figure 14.8, click the Tools button and select Toolbars, Menu Bar.

FIGURE 14.8

The Menu bar.

tip

If you only need to temporarily access the menu bar, press the Alt key on your computer keyboard. Press Alt again to hide the menu bar again, or just do anything on the page—it goes away automatically.

Moving the Toolbars

Okay, it's easy to go overboard and clutter up your browser with all sorts of toolbars. You can, however, rearrange the order of the toolbars—but first, you have to unlock them. Follow these steps:

1. Click the Tools button and select Toolbars; then uncheck the Lock the Toolbars option.

2. The toolbars are now unlocked, indicated by a dotted line at the left of each toolbar. To move a toolbar, grab the dotted line with your mouse and drag the bar to a new position.

3. When you're done moving toolbars, click the Tools button again, select Toolbars, and then check the Lock the Toolbars option.

You can stack toolbars on top of each other, or move them so that they share a single row. You also can resize a toolbar within a row, also by dragging the left side of the toolbar.

Displaying the Browser Full Screen

If you want to display a completely clean web page, with the minimal amount of browser interface, use IE's full-screen mode. Just press F11 (or select Tools, Full Screen), and your web page will be displayed full screen, with all toolbars hidden. You can display the toolbars by moving the cursor to the top of the screen; press F11 again to return to normal browser mode.

Playing with Tabs

Prior to Internet Explorer 7, the browser featured a single-document interface—that is, each browser window could contain only a single web page. Internet Explorer 7 and 8, in contrast, have a multidocument interface, with multiple web pages displayed in a single browser window via the use of tabs. This feature is called *tabbed browsing,* and it's proven very popular.

> **tip**
>
> The use of tabs within a single browser window lets you open multiple web pages simultaneously. This is great when you want to keep previous pages open for reference or want to run web-based applications in the background.

To open a web page on a new tab, just click the empty tab to the right of any open tabs, enter a URL into the Address box, and press Enter. You can also choose to open a link within a page in a new tab by right-clicking the link and selecting Open in New Tab.

> **tip**
>
> When you open more than one page from the same website in different tabs, those tabs are displayed in the same color.

You switch between tabs by clicking a tab with your mouse or by pressing Ctrl+Tab on your keyboard. You can also reorder your tabs by dragging and dropping them into a new position.

Even better, you can view the contents of all open tabs with IE's Quick Tabs feature. When you click the Quick Tab icon or press Ctrl+Q, all open web pages are displayed as thumbnails in a single window, as shown in Figure 14.9. Click any thumbnail to open that tab in the full window.

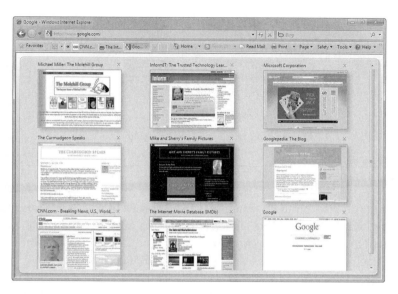

FIGURE 14.9

Viewing Quick Tabs.

> **tip**
>
> You can open a web page in a new tab by right-clicking any link to that web page, and then selecting Open in New Tab from the pop-up menu.

Creating a Home Page Tab Set

You're used to setting a single web page as the home page for your browser. Well, in IE8 you can designate a set of tabs as your "home page"—that is, all the tabs open to the assigned pages when you launch the browser or click the Home button.

To create what IE8 calls a *tab set* for your home page, follow these steps:

1. Open the necessary tabs and navigate to the desired pages on each tab.

2. Click the down arrow next to the Home button and select Add or Change Home Page.

3. When the Add or Change Home Page dialog box appears, as shown in Figure 14.10, select Use the Current Tab Set as Your Home Page.

4. Click Yes.

FIGURE 14.10

Selecting a tab set as your browser's "home page."

You can also manually enter URLs to be opened in your home page tab set. Select Tools, Internet Options to open the Internet Options dialog box, and then select the General tab. Enter the individual URLs into the Home Page box, each address on its own line, and then click OK.

Bookmarking Favorite Pages

We talked earlier about the Favorites bar, but that's not the only way to save your favorite pages in Internet Explorer. The more common approach is to add these pages to the Favorites list, which is then displayed in the Favorites pane, as shown in Figure 14.11.

FIGURE 14.11

Viewing your favorite web pages in IE8's Favorites pane.

note

Internet Explorer calls your favorite pages "favorites"; other browsers call them "bookmarks."

To add a page to your Favorites list, follow these steps:

1. Navigate to the web page and then click the Favorites button.

2. When the Favorites panel appears, click the Add to Favorites button.

3. When the Add a Favorite dialog box appears, as shown in Figure 14.12, confirm the page's name and select the folder where you want to place this link; then click OK.

FIGURE 14.12

Saving a web page in your Favorites list.

To display your Favorites, click the Favorites button. The Favorites pane now appears; select the Favorites tab to display your favorite sites. Click any folder to display the contents of that folder; click a favorite page to display that page in the browser window.

Displaying Explorer Bars

The Favorites pane is actually what Microsoft calls an *explorer bar*. There are several explorer bars in Internet Explorer:

- Favorites, which displays your favorite websites
- History, which displays the websites you've recently visited
- Feeds, which displays any RSS feeds to which you've subscribed
- Research, which lets you search various reference books

These explorer panes display on the left side of the browser window. To display a specific pane, click the Tools button, select Explorer Bars, and then check the bar you want to display.

---

note

Other applications may add other explorer bars. For example, some versions of Microsoft Office add a Discuss bar, which displays at the bottom of the browser window and lets you collaborate on Office documents via Internet Explorer.

Making Text and Pages Bigger—And Smaller

Once you start getting a little older, you find that some webmasters design their pages with text that's just a little too small to read. Fortunately, IE8 lets you enlarge the text on a page if need be. Just click the Page button, select Text Size, and then check one of the following options: Smallest, Smaller, Medium, Larger, Largest. (Medium is the default.) This change applies to all subsequent pages you visit, so you'll probably need to change it back sooner or later.

The Text Size option affects only the text on a page, not the graphics. If you want to enlarge the entire page, both text and graphics, IE has another option for you. In this instance, click the Page button, select Zoom, and then select a zoom option—anywhere from 50% to 400% of the original size. You can also opt to zoom in or out in increments, by selecting Zoom In or Zoom Out.

IE also places zoom controls in the Status bar in the lower right corner of the browser window, as shown in Figure 14.13. Click the big zoom button to zoom in one increment at a time, or click the down arrow to select a specific zoom level.

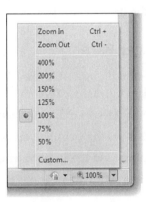

FIGURE 14.13

Adjusting zoom levels from the Status bar.

tip

In addition, you can zoom in by pressing **Ctrl +** on your keyboard, or zoom out by pressing **Ctrl -**.

Changing the Search Provider

There's one last personalization option we'll discuss, and it involves web searching. Normally, you search for information by going directly to a search site such as Google or Yahoo! In Internet Explorer 8, you don't have to visit the search site to perform a search; you can do all your searching from within the browser window by using the Instant Search box.

As you can see in Figure 14.14, the Instant Search box is located next to the Address box at the top right of the browser window. To conduct a search from within the browser, just enter your query into the Instant Search box and press the Enter key on your keyboard. Your query is sent via IE over the Internet to the selected search provider. The search site receives the query, searches its own previously compiled index of web pages, and returns a page of search results, which is displayed in the Internet Explorer window.

FIGURE 14.14

The Instant Search box.

By default, IE routes your search to Microsoft's Bing search engine. If you prefer to use another search engine for a given search, just click the down arrow next to the Instant Search box and select the desired search engine from the list.

If the search site you want isn't in this list, select Find More Providers from the pull-down menu. When the Search Providers web page appears, as shown in Figure 14.15, click the search engine you want to use. This adds the search engine to the list that appears when you click the down arrow.

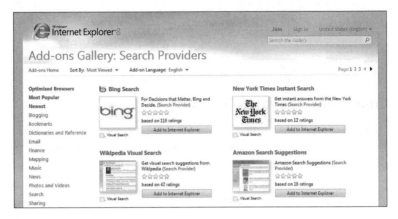

FIGURE 14.15

Looking for more search providers.

To change IE's default search engine, follow these steps:

1. Click the down arrow next to the Instant Search box and select Manage Search Providers.

2. When the Manage Add-Ons window appears, as shown in Figure 14.16, make sure that Search Providers is selected in the Add-On Types pane.

3. Select the search engine you want to use as your default.

4. Click the Set as Default button.

5. Click the Close button.

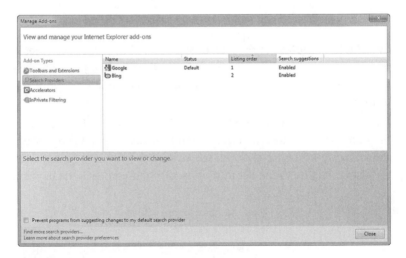

FIGURE 14.16

Setting IE's default search provider.

Configuring Internet Explorer

In addition to the personalization options just discussed, there are several other options available that can make Internet Explorer better suit your personal needs. For example, you may want to change the color of links you have visited—or the background color you see when visiting web pages.

You change all these options from the Internet Options/Properties dialog box. You display this dialog box by clicking the Tools button and selecting Internet Options. Alternately, you can open Control Panel and select Internet Options from there. (The dialog box is labeled Internet Options if you open it from within Internet Explorer, or Internet Properties if you open it from the Control Panel; it's the same dialog box, either way.)

The following sections examine the options you'll find.

General Options

The General tab in the Internet Options/Properties dialog box, shown in Figure 14.17, is probably the tab you'll use most often. Here is what you'll find on this tab:

FIGURE 14.17
Configuring general options in the Internet Options/Properties dialog box.

- **Home Page.** In this section, select which page (or pages) to use as IE's home page.

- **Browsing History.** Opt to manually delete your browsing history, automatically delete your history when exiting the browser, or click the Settings button to configure how long a history to keep and how to manage your browser's temporary files.

- **Search.** Click the Settings button to open the Manage Add-Ons window and manage IE8's search providers.

- **Tabs.** Click the Settings button to configure how tabs work.

- **Appearance.** Click the Color button to change your browser's text, background, and links colors. Click the Languages button to add new language sets to view foreign web pages. Click the Fonts button to select the default font displayed on web pages that don't indicate their own fonts. And click the Accessibility button to ignore fonts and colors specified on web pages—theoretically making them easier to read.

Security Options

The Security tab is where you manage the security settings for Internet Explorer, using so-called "content zones." You assign different security levels to different zones to ensure your system's security while you're browsing individual web pages.

note

Learn more about Internet Explorer's security and privacy options in Chapter 16, "Surfing Securely—And Secretly."

Privacy Options

The Privacy tab is where you set the privacy level for the sites you visit, by configuring how IE handles cookies from that site. This tab also enables you to turn off or on the Pop-up Blocker feature, which blocks annoying pop-up windows, and configures IE8's InPrivate anonymous browsing feature.

Content Options

The Content tab, shown in Figure 14.18, lets you manage the web content that can be viewed with your browser. Here is what you'll find on this tab:

- **Parental Controls.** Click the Parental Controls button to configure Windows' parental controls feature to restrict Internet usage for specific users of your computer.

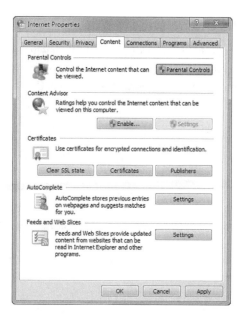

FIGURE 14.18

Configuring content options in the Internet Options/Properties dialog box.

note

Learn more about parental controls in Chapter 10, "Managing User Accounts."

- **Content Advisor.** When you enable the Content Advisor, you block access to certain types of websites—which is a good way to protect younger users from inappropriate content.

note

Learn more about the Content Advisor in Chapter 16.

- **Certificates.** This section lets you view and manage the security certificates used for encrypted identification and connections.
- **AutoComplete.** Click the Settings button to enable or disable IE's AutoComplete feature, which automatically lists possible matches for any entry you make in the address bar, website forms, and user name/password requests.
- **Feeds and Web Slices.** Click the Settings button to determine how frequently feeds and web slices are downloaded. (Learn more about web slices later in this chapter.)

Connections Options

The Connections tab, shown in Figure 14.19, is where you manage any dial-up and virtual private network (VPN) connections. You can change the settings for any existing connection, or click the Setup button to create new connections using the New Connection Wizard.

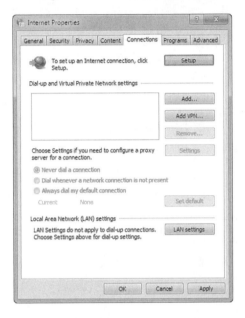

FIGURE 14.19

Configuring connections options in the Internet Options/Properties dialog box.

Programs Options

The Programs tab, shown in Figure 14.20, designates which "helper" programs are used for which Internet-related functions. It's also where you manage add-on programs (also discussed later in this chapter) and, if you like, make Internet Explorer your default web browser.

Advanced Options

The Advanced tab, shown in Figure 14.21, might be one you naturally shy away from—even though it contains some of IE's most useful configuration settings.

FIGURE 14.20
Configuring programs options in the Internet Options/Properties dialog box.

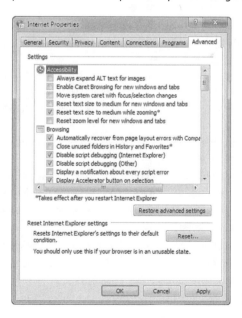

FIGURE 14.21
Configuring advanced options in the Internet Options/Properties dialog box.

Basically, this tab lists, using a tree structure, all manner of browser configuration settings. The options are too numerous to go into in detail, but you can view a summary of what's available in Table 14.1. If you can't find a particular option anyplace else, chances are it's somewhere on this tab!

Table 14.1   Internet Explorer Advanced Settings

Category	Setting	Description
Accessibility	Always expand ALT text for images	Expands the image size to fit all of the alternate text, when the image itself is not displayed. Ensures that the ALT text is not cut off on smaller images.
	Enable Caret Browsing for new windows and tabs	When enabled, you can move up, down, left, or right through a web page using the cursor keys; select text using Shift+ cursor keys; and copy text using Ctrl+ cursor keys.
	Move system caret with focus/selection changes	Automatically repositions the cursor when the focus or selection changes.
	Reset text size to medium while zooming	Automatically sets the text size to "medium" when using the zoom option.
	Reset zoom level for new windows and tabs	Automatically sets the zoom level to 100% when a new window or tab is opened, even if you're using a different zoom level in the current window/tab.
Browsing	Automatically recover from page errors with Compatibility View	When a page doesn't load properly, shifts to IE8's Compatibility View to display the page using older browser standards.
	Close unused folders in History and Favorites	Closes any unused folders in the History and Favorites lists. Keeps old pages and favorites from cluttering up these lists.
	Disable script debugging (Internet Explorer)	Does not display script debugging messages when page errors occur.
	Disable script debugging (other)	Similar to previous settings, but for scripts run in add-on programs.
	Display a notification about every script error	Displays a message when a feature on a web page doesn't work.
	Display Accelerator button on selection	Displays the Accelerator button when you select text or object on a web page.
	Enable automatic crash recovery	Forces IE8 to recover the previously viewed web page in the event of a crash.
	Enable FTP folder view (outside of Internet Explorer)	Displays traditional Windows folders/subfolders when browsing an FTP server.
	Enable page transitions	Creates a fade out/in effect when switching web pages.

Table 14.1 Continued

Category	Setting	Description
	Enable Suggested Sites	Enables IE8's Suggested Sites feature.
	Enable third-party browser extensions	Lets IE use Browser Help Objects (BHOs)—which can, unfortunately, introduce some kinds of malware.
	Enable visual styles on buttons and controls in web pages	Displays an enhanced graphical user interface for various controls on a web page.
	Enable websites to use the search pane	Enables the older Search sidebar, which is by default disabled in favor of the newer Search box.
	Force offscreen compositing even under Terminal Server	Enables one image to be overlaid on another when running Terminal Services. (Terminal Services enable you to connect to another computer and treat it as if it were your own.)
	Notify when downloads complete	Displays a dialog box informing you when a download from a web page is completed.
	Reuse windows for launching shortcuts (when tabbed browsing is off)	When enabled, clicking on a link opens the next web page in the same window. When disabled, clicking on a link opens the next web page in a new browser window.
	Show friendly HTTP error messages	When checked, shows a plain English message when a web page doesn't load. When unchecked, displays the hated "404: Page Not Found" message when an error is encounted.
	Underline links (always, hover, never)	When set to Always, links on a web page are always underlined. When set to Hover, links are only underlined when the cursor hovers over the link. When set to Never, links are never underlined.
	Use inline AutoComplete outside of Internet Explorer	When enabled, IE tries to complete partial URLs entered into the Address Bar.
	Use most recent order when switching tabs with Ctrl+Tab	When enabled, pressing Ctrl+Tab displays the last-viewed web page.
	Use Passive FTP (for firewall and DSL modem compatibility)	Defaults to the Passive FTP protocol when problems exist accessing FTP sites through a firewall or DSL modem.
	Use smooth scrolling	Enables automatic scrolling software and hardware to display content at a predetermined speed.
HTTP 1.1	Use HTTP 1.1	Uses the newer HTTP 1.1 standard instead of the older 1.0 standard.
	Use HTTP 1.1 through proxy connections	Enables use of the HTTP 1.1 standard if you're connecting to the Internet via a proxy connection.
International	Always show encoded addresses	IE can navigate to International Domain Names (IDN) written with Unicode characters from all the world's languages; when enabled, all IDN addresses are displayed in encoded form.

Table 14.1 Continued

Category	Setting	Description
	Send IDN server names	Enables IE to send IDN names for international web servers.
	Send IDN server names for Intranet addresses	Enables IE to send IDN names for addresses on an Intranet.
	Send UTF-8 URLs	Sends URLs in Unicode UTF-8 format, used for representing characters in multiple languages.
	Show Information Bar for encoded addresses	Displays an Information Bar with encoded IDN addresses.
	Use UTF-8 for mailto links	Uses the international UTF-8 standard for mailto: links.
Multimedia	Always use ClearType for HTML	Uses ClearType technology to smooth the edges of web page type.
	Enable automatic image resizing	Automatically resizes large images to fit the confines of your computer screen.
	Play animations in webpages	Enabled by default; turn off to not automatically run web page animations.
	Play sounds in webpages	Enabled by default; turn off to not automatically play web page sounds and music.
	Show image download pageholders	If an image on a web page is not available, displays the alternate text for that image.
	Show pictures	Enabled by default; turn off to not automatically display web page images.
	Smart image dithering	When enabled, produces better-looking results for resized pictures.
Printing	Print background colors and images	Turn on to print web page background images and colors when printing a web page; turn off to print page content on a plain white background.
Search from the Address bar	Do not submit unknown address to your auto-search provider	By default, IE submits any unknown URLs you enter as a search to your auto-search provider. Disable this option to not pass unknown addresses through as a search.
	Just display the results in the main window	Displays results from a Search bar query in the main IE window.
Security	Allow active content from CDs to run on My Computer	Enables web pages to access files from a CD inserted in your PC.
	Allow active content to run in files on My Computer	Enables web pages to access files stored on your PC's hard drive.
	Allow software to run or install even if the signature is invalid	Enables web-based software to install even if the publisher does not have a certificate.

Table 14.1 Continued

Category	Setting	Description
	Check for publisher's certificate revocation	Permits IE to check and see if a software publisher's certification has been revoked.
	Check for signatures on downloaded programs	Forces IE to check for digital signatures before downloading executable programs.
	Do not save encrypted pages to disk	Prevents IE from saving encrypted pages to disk that contain secure (HTTPS) information, such as passwords and credit card information.
	Empty Temporary Internet Files folder when browser is closed	When enabled, forces IE to delete the contents of the Temporary Internet Files folder when all browser windows are closed.
	Enable DOM storage	DOM technology is a way of storing personal data on a third-party website; disable this option for increased security.
	Enable Integrated Windows Authentication	Allows automatic log-in to some sites using authentication data stored in Windows.
	Enable memory protection to help mitigate online attacks	Activates Data Execution Protection (DEP) technology to guard against certain types of browser attacks.
	Enable native XMLHTTP support	XMLHTTP is the foundation of AJAX programming, enabling the object to send and receive XML information via the HTTP protocol. When enabled, this option makes it possible to create responsive web applications that do not require downloading the entire page to receive new data.
	Enable SmartScreen Filter	When enabled, every URL you visit is submitted to Microsoft to see if it's a known phishing site. If a phishing site is found, IE displays a red warning bar and corresponding message.
	Use SSL 2.0	Forces use of the older SSL 2.0 secure page protocol.
	Use SSL 3.0	Enables use of the newer SSL 3.0 secure page protocol.
	Use TLS 1.0	Forces IE to use older version of Transport Layer Security (TLS) security protocol.
	Use TLS 1.1	Forces IE to use older version of TLS protocol.
	Use TLS 1.2	Enables use of the latest version of TLS protocol.
	Warn about certificate address mismatch	Notifies you if a website's security certificate is used by a different address; guards against spoofing websites.
	Warn if changing between secure and not secure mode	Displays a warning when you switch between secure and non-secure websites.
	Warn if POST submittal is redirected to a zone that does not permit posts	Warns if a forms submittal is being redirected to another page. Helps secure against hijacking of your personal information.

Working with Browser Add-Ons

I promised we'd discuss IE's add-on programs, so here we are. An add-on (or plug-in) program is actually a small utility that works within Internet Explorer to help display certain types of web pages.

To manage IE's add-on programs, click the Tools button and select Manage Add-Ons; this displays the Manage Add-Ons window, shown in Figure 14.22. This window organizes all add-ons by type—toolbars and extensions, search providers, and accelerators, as well as InPrivate blocking lists and subscriptions. Select a tab to view all available add-ons of that type.

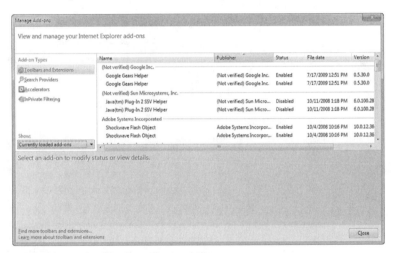

FIGURE 14.22

Managing browser add-ons in Internet Explorer 8.

You may need all of the add-ons currently running to view the variety of content currently available on the Web—or you may not. For example, you might find that a particular website has installed an add-on to view content on its site, but that add-on is not necessary when visiting other sites. Single-site add-ons of this type can drain resources and cause your browser to run slower than normal.

> **tip**
>
> Many users choose to strip their browsers of all but the most essential add-ons. To remove an add-on, select it from the Manage Add-Ons dialog box and then click the Disable button.

Determining which add-ons to keep and which to disable is mainly a matter of trial and error; there are no universal recommendations. One user might want to disable the Shockwave Flash add-on, used to display animations and videos, while another user might balk at not having any Flash animations display in his browser. The key is whether you frequently visit sites that use a particular add-on; if not, you can speed up your web browsing by disabling that add-on.

If you're unsure of what an add-on does, consult the Manage Add-Ons window. When you select an add-on, information about that program is displayed at the bottom of the window. Click the More Information link in the information pane for even more details.

Working with Suggested Sites

Internet Explorer 8 adds some new features not found in previous versions of the browser. One of these features is called Suggested Sites. When enabled, Suggested Sites uses your browsing history to suggest other websites you might like to visit.

To enable Suggested Sites, click the Tools button and select Suggested Sites. When prompted, click Yes.

Once enabled, you display a list of suggested sites by following these steps:

1. Click the Favorites button.

2. Click the See Suggested Sites link at the bottom of the Favorites pane.

You now see a Suggested Sites page; click any link to view a suggested site.

Some might find Suggested Sites useful; others might find it a worrisome intrusion on their privacy. If you're among the latter, you can disable the Suggested Sites feature by clicking the Tools button and unchecking Suggested Sites.

Working with Accelerators

Also new to IE8 is the concept of *accelerators*. An accelerator is a means to send text you select on a web page to another page or application.

For example, you can select a piece of text on a web page and then use an accelerator to send that text to another user via email, or post that text to your blog. Or you could select an address on a web page and use another accelerator to map the address. Or you could select a word and use the accelerator to initiate a Google search for that word.

Using an Accelerator

To use an accelerator, follow these steps:

1. Use your mouse to select a word or block of text on a web page.

2. IE now displays an Accelerator button next to the selected text, as shown in Figure 14.23; click this button and you see a pop-up menu of available accelerators.

3. Click the accelerator you want to use, and Internet Explorer performs the appropriate action.

Selecting text on a web page…

…causes an accelerator button to appear

author Michael Miller:

FIGURE 14.23

Select a block of text to display the Accelerator button.

tip

Some accelerators display a preview of results when you hover over that accelerator option in the pop-up menu.

Managing Accelerators

IE8 comes with a short list of accelerators preinstalled. You can delete accelerators from this list, or add new ones as you like. Just follow these steps:

1. Click the Page button and select All Accelerators, Manage Accelerators.

2. When the Manage Add-Ons window appears, as shown in Figure 14.24, make sure that Accelerators is selected in the Add-On Types pane.

3. To remove an accelerator from this list, select it and click the Remove button.

4. To add a new accelerator, click the Find More Accelerators link. This launches Internet Explorer and displays the Add-Ons Gallery: Accelerators page, as shown in Figure 14.25. Find the accelerator you want; then click the Add to Internet Explorer button.

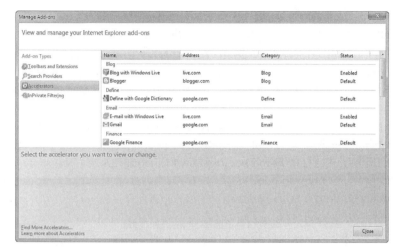

FIGURE 14.24
Managing Internet Explorer accelerators.

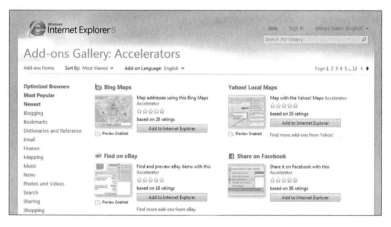

FIGURE 14.25
Browsing for new accelerators on the Web.

Working with Web Slices

Here's another new IE8 feature—the ability to easily see when content has been updated on your favorite web page, via the use of Web Slices. This is similar to subscribing to an RSS feed, but can be used with just a portion of a web page.

That's right, a Web Slice is a subscription to a part of a web page. Once you subscribe to a Web Slice, it appears as a link in the Favorites pane.

When the page for that Web Slice is updated, the link for the Slice appears in boldface. Click the link to view the updated content.

Even neater, click the link in the Favorites bar (if you have the Favorites bar displayed, that is). This displays that section of the web page to which you subscribed; the Slice folds down from the Favorites bar so you don't have to visit the web page to see the new content.

Know, however, that not all web content is available as a Web Slice. When content is available for subscribing, you'll see a green Web Slice button on IE's Command bar, as shown in Figure 14.26. (The same button appears on the web page itself when you hover your cursor over the available content.)

When content is available for subscribing,
a green icon appears on the IE Command bar.

FIGURE 14.26

This page has a Web Slice available to subscribe to.

To create a Web Slice, follow these steps:

1. Navigate to the web page you want to track.

2. Click the Web Slice button on the Command bar; then select the Slice you want to subscribe to.

3. When the confirmation dialog box appears, click Add to Favorites Bar.

For example, the MSN home page (www.msn.com) contains a slideshow of top news stories. This slideshow is a Web Slice; when you subscribe to the Slice, you can see when new content (stories) have been added to the slideshow.

I admit to not being too thrilled with the Web Slices feature, primarily because there aren't a lot of pages with Slice-compatible content—at least not yet. This may change in the future, but for now, it's a neat idea but not very useful.

Working with Compatibility View

Internet Explorer 8 is a good browser, compatible with most pages available on the Web. But what do you do if you stumble upon an older web page, designed for a previous version of Internet Explorer, that just doesn't display well in IE8? You use the new Compatibility View, that's what you do.

When you enable Compatibility View, the web page you're viewing will be displayed as if you're using an earlier version of IE. To enable Compatibility View for a given page, click the Page button and select Compatibility View. It's that easy.

Changing Web Browsers

For a number of reasons, Internet Explorer is the most popular web browser available today. It's not the only browser available, however. There are a number of worthy competitors, some of which do some things better than IE.

Evaluating the Options

Let's take a quick look at what other browsers are available. Like Internet Explorer, all of these browsers are free to download and use. Here's what's available:

- **Mozilla Firefox (www.mozilla.com/firefox/).** The number-two web browser today, behind IE. Many users praise Firefox for its advanced features and speed of operation. Like Internet Explorer, Firefox offers tabbed browsing and a host of useful security features, including private browsing and a pop-up blocker. Firefox also offers a download manager for safer and more efficient downloading of files and programs from the Internet.

- **Google Chrome (www.google.com/chrome/).** The newest competitor in the browser wars, Chrome offers tabbed browsing, private browsing, a pop-up blocker, and speedy operation; it seems particularly perky when compared to IE8. The browser's streamlined interface drops the typical title bar and search box at the top of the window, freeing up valuable space to display web pages. (You use the address box to enter both URLs and search queries.) The Chrome browser is specially designed for use with Google's many web-based applications. For example, when you use Chrome to open Google Docs or Google Calendar, the window drops all browser-specific features to appear like a standard application window. In addition, Chrome has Google Gears built in so that Google's web-based applications can be operated when you're not online.

- **Opera (www.opera.com).** Opera is an established web browser, currently at version 9.6. Like most browsers today, Opera features tabbed browsing and a pop-up blocker. Opera also offers the web-based Opera Link service, which lets you store and synchronize your bookmarks and history across multiple computers.

- **Safari (www.apple.com/safari/).** If you have an Apple Macintosh computer, Apple's Safari web browser is built into the operating system; it's also available for Windows users. Safari offers an elegant iTunes-like interface, tabbed browsing, private browsing, and a built-in pop-up blocker. Also useful is Safari's AutoFill feature, which lets you enter personal information into online forms with the click of a button.

Making the Change

How do you switch from Internet Explorer to another browser? Well, you start by downloading and installing the new browser. Then you follow these steps to make the new browser your default browser:

1. Open the Windows Start menu and select Default Programs. (Alternately, you can also open the Control Panel and select Default Programs from there.)

2. When the Default Programs window appears, click Set Program Access and Computer Defaults.

3. When the Set Program Access and Computer Defaults window opens, as shown in Figure 14.27, click the down arrow to expand the Custom section.

4. Scroll to the Choose a Default Web Browser section and check the program you want to use as your default browser.

5. Click the OK button when done.

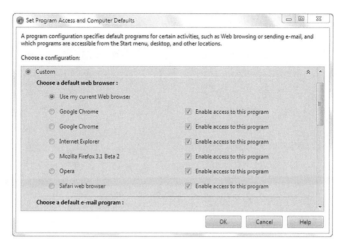

FIGURE 14.27

Changing your default browser.

The Bottom Line

I told you up front that there was a lot you could customize about Internet Explorer, and I meant it. From choosing which buttons display on the Command bar to installing new accelerators, you can really make IE work your way. (And if you don't like IE your way or any way, install another browser and make it your default!)

15

Speeding Up the Internet

Customizing Internet Explorer is one way to have the Internet your way in Windows 7, but it's just part of the picture. The other way to optimize the Internet on your system is to speed up your browsing— by whatever means possible!

Things That Slow Down Web Browsing

There are many things that can slow down your web browsing. Some of these issues have to do with your browser, others with your Internet connection itself.

Understanding Connection Speed

Let's start with your Internet connection, which is one of two types: dial-up or broadband. Dial-up is the older and much slower technology, while broadband connections are significantly faster. It goes without saying, if you're still connecting via dial-up, you will notice a significant improvement in speed by upgrading to a broadband connection of some sort.

It used to be that everyone had dial-up connections, because that was the only type of connection available. A dial-up connection works by connecting your PC to a normal phone line, using a piece of hardware called a *modem*. The modem, which physically connects between your PC and your phone line, dials into your Internet service provider (ISP) and logs in to your personal account. Your ISP plugs the signal from your computer into the Internet, so that your computer is now connected to the Internet, through your ISP. When you're done surfing the Web, you disconnect from the ISP by essentially hanging up the phone line.

---

note

Modem stands for modulate/demodulate, which describes how the device translates the digital signals from your computer to analog signals that can be sent over standard phone lines.

The problems with dial-up connections are twofold. First, you have to connect and disconnect manually; you don't have an always-on connection. Second, and most important, a dial-up connection is *sloooow*—transferring data at no more than 56.6 kilobits per second (Kbps).

In the late 1990s, slow dial-up connections began to be supplanted by faster broadband connections. Unlike an analog dial-up connection, a broadband connection is an end-to-end digital connection. When you don't have to modulate and demodulate the data from digital to analog (and back again), the all-digital data can travel much faster from your computer to other points on the Internet.

Broadband connections are typically available from either your telephone company (via what is called a digital subscriber line, or DSL, connection) or your cable company. You can also receive broadband Internet via satellite (for those locations not served by DSL or cable) or the newer FIOS (fiber optic service) technology.

Broadband speeds are considerably faster than dial-up connections, 1.5Mbps (that's 1,500Kbps) or more for DSL and 6Mbps or more for cable Internet. At the lowest speeds, we're talking 60 times dial-up speed for DSL and 120 times dial-up speed for cable broadband—more than enough of a difference to notice!

---

note

DSL Internet connections piggyback on your existing telephone line. Similarly, cable Internet piggybacks on your digital cable signal.

The speed of your actual connection, however, may differ from these general data transfer speeds. That's because different Internet service providers offer different speed plans (higher speeds for a higher price, of course)—and because your actual speed may not be the same as the promised speed. Your distance from the nearest network node affects actual speed, as do the number of other users connecting at the same time, as do numerous other factors. So just because your ISP promises blazing-fast 6Mbps rates doesn't mean that your connection will always be that fast.

That begs the obvious question, how fast is your Internet connection? There are several sites on the Web designed to test the speed of your connection; all you have to do is access the site and click the appropriate buttons. The site will download and upload some small files to and from your PC, measure how fast it all takes, and display your current upload and download speeds.

> **note**
>
> Many ISPs provide different upload and download speeds to their customers; download speeds are typically faster.

Some of my favorite speed test sites include the following:

- CNET Bandwidth Meter Speed Test (reviews.cnet.com/internet-speedtest/)
- DSL Reports Speed Test (www.dslreports.com/speedtest)
- MySpeed (myspeed.visualware.com/)

Note that your connection speed may vary from day to day, or even at different hours of the same day. Test your connection a few times on different days of the week, calculate an average, and compare that to the speeds promised by your ISP.

Understanding Browser Speed

Now let's examine your web browser, which for most of us is Microsoft's Internet Explorer. Internet Explorer 8 is the most recent version of the program, and the one included free with Windows 7.

IE is a software program, not much different from a word processor or spreadsheet application, designed specifically to display HTML pages on the Web. Like any software program, it contains numerous configuration settings—some of which affect the speed at which web pages are displayed.

As you're probably aware, a typical web page contains a mix of text, graphics, and other elements. Text is easiest to display; not a whole lot involved with that. Graphics, however, can take longer to display, primarily because image files can be quite large. These large files take longer to download and thus longer to display in your web browser.

Other page elements can include audio and video files, along with bits of JavaScript code. JavaScript is typically used to insert "applets" (small applications) into a web page; these applets often contain elements hosted on other websites. For example, a page might display a clock created with JavaScript; the code for the clock is on the web page itself, while the engine and graphics for the clock are hosted on another site. Because of this dual-hosting nature of some JavaScript code, these applets can often take longer to display than elements hosted natively.

Naturally, the more elements on a web page, the longer it will take your browser to display them. It's not just a matter of download size; all those elements must be rendered for display by the browser, and this rendering takes computing horsepower and time. It's no surprise that bigger web pages can really slow down your browser.

Here's something else that can slow down Internet Explorer: having multiple tabs open at the same time. Yes, IE8 is designed with a tabbed interface, the better to load multiple web pages simultaneously. But all those web pages have to be downloaded, rendered, and stored in memory. It's just more work for the browser—and an overworked browser can be sluggish.

Fortunately, many of these issues can be overcome by some simple configuration changes—or, in the most extreme case, a tweak to the Windows Registry. Read on to learn how to speed up your browser—and make surfing the Web go a lot smoother!

Managing Your Cache

You might not know this, but Internet Explorer stores a temporary copy of each web page you visit, called a *cache*. The intent is to speed up browsing by letting IE access the local cache when you revisit a recent page.

The cache, of course, is nothing but a file on your hard drive. As such, it takes up valuable disk space. And, although the cache is designed to speed up browsing, too big of a cache can slow Internet Explorer to a crawl.

You see, over time your browser keeps adding web pages to the cache file—and these pages aren't deleted automatically. So the more web pages you visit, the bigger the cache on your hard disk. And too large a cache file puts a drain on your web browser, because your browser has to sort through the cache every time you load a web page, looking for a cached version of that page. Simply put, a bigger cache takes longer to reference.

Clearing Your Cache

The solution to cache-based sluggishness is to clean out the cache. In essence, what you do is delete the cache file; this "empties" the cache, frees up valuable hard disk space, and makes it much easier for your browser to search for previously cached pages. Fortunately, this is easy to do—even if it must be done manually.

Here's how you clean out the cache in Internet Explorer 8:

1. Click the Safety button and select Delete Browsing History.

2. When the Delete Browsing History dialog box appears, as shown in Figure 15.1, check the Temporary Internet Files option.

3. Click the Delete button.

This deletes the temporary cache file on your computer and should speed up browser performance.

FIGURE 15.1

Deleting Internet Explorer's temporary cache file.

Clearing Your Cache Automatically

If you don't want to delete the cache on a regular basis, Internet Explorer can automate the process for you. All you have to do is enable the option that automatically clears the cache when you close the browser.

Follow these steps:

1. Click the Tools button and select Internet Options.

2. When the Internet Options dialog box appears, select the Advanced tab.

3. In the Settings list, scroll down to the Security section and check the option Empty Temporary Internet Files Folder When Browser is Closed.

4. Click OK.

Changing the Size of Your Cache

You can also change the size of the Internet Explorer cache. The smaller the cache, the speedier Internet Explorer will be.

Here's how to change the cache size in Internet Explorer 8:

1. Click the Tools button and select Internet Options.

2. When the Internet Options dialog box appears, select the General tab.

3. Click the Settings button in the Browsing History section.

4. When the Temporary Internet Files and History Settings dialog box appears, as shown in Figure 15.2, set the Disk Space setting to the desired number.

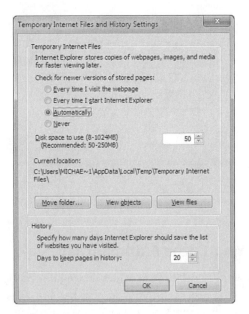

FIGURE 15.2

Configuring the size of the browser cache.

What is the best size for your cache file? While you can set a cache as small as 8MB, I recommend something in the 50MB range. Anything much smaller is less than useful, and anything much larger just takes up disk space and slows down your browser.

Dealing with Cookies

Just as your browser stores a temporary copy of each web page you visit, it also stores information about those pages, in the form of *cookies*. A cookie is a small file, created by a website but stored on your PC, which contains information about you and your activities on that website. For example, a cookie file for a particular site might contain your user name, password, and the most recent pages you visited on that site. The cookie file created by a site is accessed by that site each time you visit in the future, and the information used appropriately.

Aside from the privacy concerns of all these websites tracking your activities, cookies can also slow down your web browser. That's because, over time, you accumulate a *lot* of cookies. These files, although small, can take up significant amounts of hard disk space; in addition, your browser must sort through them all to find the cookies it needs when accessing a specific site. The more cookie files on your hard drive, the harder your browser has to work.

note

Learn more about the security aspects of cookies in Chapter 16, "Surfing Securely—And Secretly."

Deleting Cookies

As with your browser's cache file, the solution to cookie-induced sluggishness is to delete all your cookies. It's quite easy to do in Internet Explorer:

1. Click the Safety button and select Delete Browsing History.
2. When the Delete Browsing History dialog box appears, check the Cookies option.
3. Click the Delete button.

caution

Deleting all cookies may cause some websites to not remember you on your next visit.

Avoiding Cookies

You can also configure Internet Explorer not to store some or all types of cookies, by adjusting the browser's privacy level. We'll discuss this more in Chapter 16; just know that if you choose not to accept cookies, you can effect a slight improvement in browsing speed.

Reconfiguring Other Settings

As discussed previously, Internet Explorer is a web browser that has lots of built-in features, some of which can slow down the display of web pages. Given that you may or may not need all of these features, turning a few of them off can speed up your web browsing. We'll look at those features that most affect your browsing experience next.

Don't Display Graphics

Here's a big one that may or may not appeal to you. Many web pages are overloaded with photos and other images; these images are big files that can take a long time to download and display, especially if you have a slow web connection. You can speed up the loading of graphics-intensive pages by simply turning off the graphics. That leaves you with a text-only web page, of course—but that page will load a lot faster than it did with all the images intact.

To turn off the display of images in Internet Explorer, follow these steps:

1. Click the Tools button and select Internet Options.

2. When the Internet Options dialog box appears, select the Advanced tab (shown in Figure 15.3).

3. Scroll down to the Multimedia section and uncheck the Show Pictures option.

4. Click OK.

And that's not the only feature you can disable to speed up your browsing. While you're in the Internet Options dialog box, you can uncheck the Play Animations in Webpages and Play Sounds in Webpages options—which will disable animations and sounds, respectively.

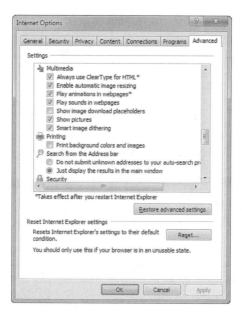

FIGURE 15.3

Speeding up IE by turning off graphics.

Disable ClearType

Internet Explorer 8 uses Windows' ClearType technology to smoothly render type at all sizes. While I haven't experienced this personally, some users have reported that ClearType has slowed down the performance of Internet Explorer on their systems. To disable ClearType, follow these steps:

1. Click the Tools button and select Internet Options.

2. When the Internet Options dialog box appears, select the Advanced tab.

3. Scroll down to the Multimedia section and uncheck the Always Use ClearType for HTML option.

4. Click OK.

Turn Off the SmartScreen Filter

Internet Explorer 8 includes a security feature called the SmartScreen Filter. This feature is designed to identify and warn you about so-called phishing websites—sites that pretend to be official sites but actually exist solely to steal your personal information. Unfortunately, the SmartScreen Filter can sometimes slow down web browsing, as it takes a bit of time to search the list of known phishing websites—which is why you can speed up your browsing by turning off the SmartScreen Filter. Here's how to do it:

note

Learn more about phishing in Chapter 16.

1. Click the Safety button and select SmartScreen Filter, Turn Off SmartScreen Filter.

2. When prompted by the next dialog box, check Turn Off SmartScreen Filter and click OK.

caution

If you turn off the SmartScreen Filter, you need to be more vigilant about clicking links in emails and on web pages to avoid becoming the victim of phishing schemes.

Disable RSS Feeds

How do you feel about a feature that few people use yet slows down everyone's browsing? Yeah, me too—get rid of it.

The feature I'm talking about is IE's RSS feeds feature, which enables you to subscribe to RSS feeds from blogs and news sites and automatically display new postings and updates in the browser. If you don't use the RSS feeds feature (and you probably don't), you can disable it and speed up your normal web browsing. Follow these steps:

1. Click the Tools button and select Internet Options.

2. When the Internet Options dialog box appears, select the Content tab.

3. Click the Settings button in the Feeds and Web Slices section.

4. When the Feed and Web Slice Settings dialog box appears, as shown in Figure 15.4, uncheck every option.

5. Click OK.

caution

Disabling RSS feeds also disables IE8's web slices feature—which uses feed technology to display updates to website content.

FIGURE 15.4

Disabling RSS feeds and web slices.

Uninstalling Unnecessary Add-Ons

Some of what slows down Internet Explorer are add-ons to the main program. These auxiliary programs require more computing power than the browser does by itself, and sometimes access third-party websites that require additional downloads. You can speed up your browsing by disabling the least essential of these add-ons.

> **note**
>
> Learn more about IE add-ons in Chapter 14, "Configuring and Customizing Internet Explorer."

Removing Third-Party Toolbars

As you learned in Chapter 14, many websites like to install their own toolbars for Internet Explorer. While these toolbars make using those sites easier, they also put an extra load on Internet Explorer, which can make your browsing seem sluggish.

To remove unwanted toolbars from Internet Explorer, follow these steps:

1. Click the Tools button and select Toolbars.
2. Uncheck those toolbars you want to disable.

> **caution**
>
> To completely remove some toolbars and their associated files from your hard drive, you may have to use Windows' Add/Remove Programs feature. (From the Control Panel, select Programs and Features.)

Removing the SSVHelper Class Add-On

Here's a somewhat esoteric plug-in that has been known to slow down IE's browsing performance. The SSVHelper Class plug-in is a nonessential part of the Java plug-in (which itself is fairly necessary). To disable this plug-in, follow these steps:

1. Click the Tools button and select Manage Add-Ons
2. When the Manage Add-Ons window appears, as shown in Figure 15.5, select Toolbars and Extensions from the Add-On Types pane.
3. Select Java(tm) Plug-In SSV Helper from the contents list.
4. Click the Disable option.

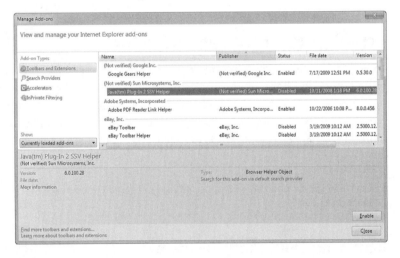

FIGURE 15.5

Managing add-ons in Internet Explorer 8.

Removing Other Add-Ons

When you open the Manage Add-Ons window and select Toolbars and Extensions, you see a full listing of all the add-ons currently running in Internet Explorer. You may need all of these add-ons; you may not. For example, you might find that a particular website has installed an add-on to view content on its site, but that add-on is not necessary when visiting other sites; that add-on is a prime candidate for removal.

Determining which add-ons to keep and which to disable is mainly a matter of trial and error; there are no universal recommendations. I might be perfectly happy disabling the Shockwave Flash add-on (I *hate* unwanted Flash animations!), but other users might balk at not having any Flash animations display in their browsers. The key is whether you frequently visit sites that use a particular add-on; if not, you might as well disable it—and help speed up your browsing!

Browsing Faster with an Alternate DNS Service

Let's move beyond the browser to consider your actual connection to the Internet—which affects every browser, not just Internet Explorer. Even the fastest broadband connection can feel slow if it takes a long time to pull up each website you want to visit. This problem is due to something called the Domain Name System (DNS) and slowness in your ISP's DNS server—and can be corrected.

What Is a DNS Server—And How Does It Affect Connection Speed?

Every website is hosted on a web server, which is a fancy type of computer connected to the Internet. To identify the millions of such servers, each server has its own unique address, called an IP address, which looks something like this: 192.111.222.333.

Of course, you don't type this address into your web browser when you want to visit a website. What you type is the URL or website address, which looks something like this: www.websiteaddress.com. The URL, then, is an alias for the site's true address.

What a DNS server does is link the site's easy-to-remember web address with its hard-to-remember IP address. For example, www.google.com is the URL for the server located at the 209.85.153.104 IP address. When you enter the URL www.google.com in your web browser, that domain request is sent to a DNS server that looks up that IP address and then routes the request to the server located at 209.85.153.104. (You can test this by entering the IP address directly into your browser; it should take you directly to the associated website.)

When you connect to the Internet via your Internet service provider (ISP), your URL requests are sent to that ISP's DNS server. That's a simple enough process—until your ISP's DNS server starts to get bogged down. When that happens, it takes longer for the DNS server to look up the IP addresses for the URLs you enter.

Unfortunately, many ISP DNS servers are notoriously slow. The result is that it takes longer to load any web page you want to visit. It's not the connection that's slow, it's the ability of your ISP to look up the web pages you want to view.

Choosing a Third-Party DNS Service

You can work around this issue by directing your URL requests to a different DNS server. To that end, several sites offer alternative DNS services, promising faster lookups and thus faster web browsing.

> **note**
>
> Some third-party DNS services offer additional features, such as parental controls, phishing protection, and more-reliable DNS lookup services.

To use a third-party DNS service, you have to configure your web browser to route your URL requests to the new server. We'll get to that in a moment. First, let's look at the two most popular DNS services today, DNS Advantage and OpenDNS. Table 15.1 provides the detail, including the information you'll need to reconfigure Windows for these services. Both of these services are free, although you may have to subscribe to gain full access.

Table 15.1   Free DNS Services

Service	URL	Preferred DNS Server	Alternate DNS Server
DNS Advantage	www.dnsadvantage.com	156.154.70.1	156.154.71.1
OpenDNS	www.opendns.com	208.67.222.222	208.67.220.220

Configuring Your System for an Alternate DNS Service

To use an alternate DNS service, you have to reconfigure Windows to send all domain requests to the new DNS server. This is a network-related procedure, and here's how it works:

1. Open the Control Panel and select Network and Sharing Center.

2. When the Network and Sharing Center opens, click Change Adapter Settings.

3. When the Network Connections window opens, right-click the icon for your connection and select Properties.

4. When the Properties dialog box appears, as shown in Figure 15.6, make sure the Networking tab is selected.

5. Select Internet Protocol Version 4 (TCP/IPv4) from the list and click the Properties button.

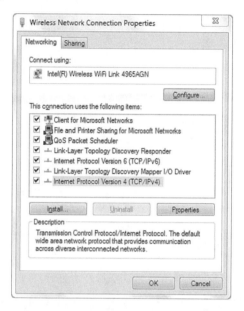

FIGURE 15.6

Editing Windows 7's Internet Protocol settings.

6. When the next Properties dialog box appears, as shown in Figure 15.7, select the Use the Following DNS Server Addresses option.

7. Enter the DNS service's preferred DNS server address into the Preferred DNS Server box.

8. Enter the DNS service's alternate DNS server address into the Alternate DNS Server box.

9. Click OK.

With Windows thus reconfigured, you'll now access the third-party DNS server whenever you're web browsing—which should be slightly faster than what you're used to with your ISP's DNS server.

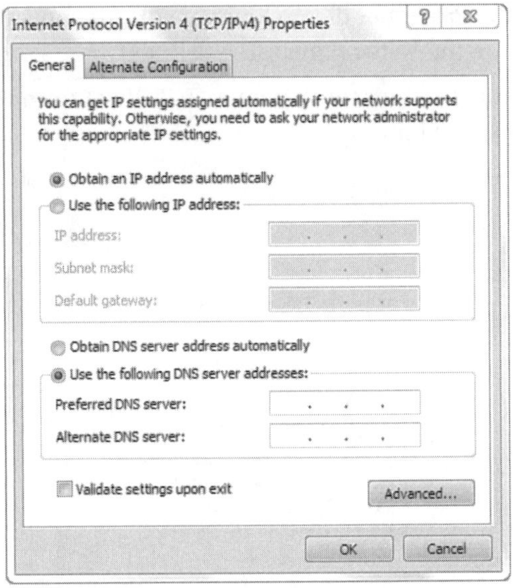

FIGURE 15.7
Entering new DNS server addresses.

Increasing the Size of Your DNS Cache

Still on the subject of DNS lookup, Windows stores your most recently visited website addresses in a special DNS cache on your hard drive. (Not to be confused with your temporary Internet cache...) Your web browser accesses this cache of known addresses before it goes out to the Internet to send a URL request to an external DNS server. If the web address you're looking for is in the cache, it gets used by your browser, saving valuable browsing time.

You can speed up your browsing by increasing the size of this DNS cache. A bigger DNS cache enables addresses for more websites to be stored locally, which means fewer external DNS lookups.

To increase the size of your computer's DNS cache, you have to edit the Windows Registry, which is the large database where all the configuration settings for your system are stored. You edit the Registry using the Registry Editor utility. Here's what you need to do:

note

Learn more about tweaking the Registry in Chapter 27, "Tweaking the Windows Registry."

1. Open the Start menu, enter **regedit** into the search box, and then press Enter.

2. When the Registry Editor, opens, as shown in Figure 15.8, navigate to the HKEY_LOCAL_MACHINE\SYSTEM\CurrentControlSet\ Services\Dnscache\Parameters key.

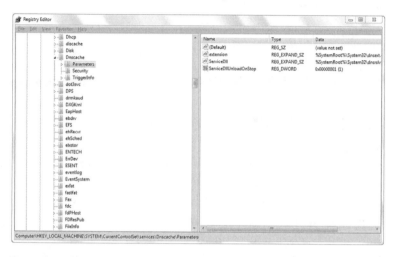

FIGURE 15.8

Managing your DNS cache via the Windows Registry.

3. Select Edit, New, DWORD (32-bit) Value.

4. Name this new item **CacheHashTableBucketSize**.

5. Right-click this new item and select Modify.

6. In the Value Data dialog box, change the value to 1.

7. Select Edit, New, DWORD (32-bit) Value.

8. Name this new item **CacheHashTableSize**.

9. Right-click this new item and select Modify.

10. In the Value Data dialog box, change the value to 180.

11. Select Edit, New, DWORD (32-bit) Value.

12. Name this new item **MaxCacheEntryTtlLimit**.

13. Right-click this new item and select Modify.

14. In the Value Data dialog box, change the value to ff00. Note, these are zeroes.

15. Select Edit, New, DWORD (32-bit) Value.

16. Name this new item **MaxSOACacheEntryTtlLimit**.

17. Right-click this new item and select Modify.

18. In the Value Data dialog box, change the value to 12d.

For these changes to take effect, you need to close the Registry Editor and restart Windows. You should notice a slight speedup when next you browse the Web.

---

caution

Take care when editing the Registry. All changes you make are immediately enabled; any mistakes you make can affect the running of your system.

Enabling More Simultaneous Connections

We'll end this chapter with another little Registry tweak that can speed up web browsing for many users. This tweak has to do with how many files you can download at the same time from a web server.

By default, Internet Explorer 8 is configured to enable six simultaneous connections to a server. The problem comes when you visit a web page that contains lots of images and JavaScript content, all of which have to download to your browser. With just a half-dozen simultaneous connections enabled, it can take awhile to download multiple images and such.

Here are the facts. Your browser has to make more than 40 requests to the server before it can assemble a typical web page. Requesting all those files a half-dozen at a time is going to take longer than requesting ten (or more) files at a time. If you can download more connections, you can significantly speed up the display of all web pages.

To enable more simultaneous connections from a single web server, you have to edit the Windows Registry, using the Registry Editor. Here's how to enable ten simultaneous connections to a server:

1. Open the Start menu, enter **regedit** into the search box, and then press Enter.

2. When the Registry Editor, opens, navigate to the HKEY_CURRENT_USER\Software\Microsoft\Windows\CurrentVersion\Internet Settings key.

3. Select Edit, New, DWORD (32-bit) Value.

4. Name this new item **MaxConnectionsPer1_0Server**.

5. Right-click this new item and select Modify.

6. In the Value Data dialog box, change the value to 10.

7. Click OK.

8. Select Edit, New, DWORD (32-bit) Value.

9. Name this new item **MaxConnectionsPerServer**.

10. Right-click this new item and select Modify.

11. In the Value Data dialog box, change the value to 10.

12. Click OK.

13. Close the Registry Editor.

When you edit the Registry Editor, close Internet Explorer. When you restart your browser, the new value will be in effect—and your web browsing should be a little speedier!

The Bottom Line

You thought web browsing was simple, didn't you? It's surprising to many users to discover all the stuff that goes on behind the scenes while you're browsing your favorite web pages. Simplify this behind-the-scenes stuff, and your browsing may get a little faster—which is yet another way to have Windows 7 and the Internet your way.

16

Surfing Securely—And Secretly

The Internet can be a worrisome place. There are all sorts of bad
things out there, just waiting for you to stumble upon them. And, if
you do, you risk not only the security of your computer system, but
also the safety of your family.

Fortunately, Windows 7 enables you to manage your online security
your way. That's right, you can configure Internet Explorer to surf
more securely—or to cover your tracks by surfing secretly.

Read on to learn more.

Protecting Against Offending Pages with the Content Advisor

Safe surfing isn't just about protecting against attacks. It's also
about safety from unwanted content—especially for your children.
The reality is, the Web today is a large, unruly, often unsavory kind
of place; far too many websites include content that most of us
would deem inappropriate, especially for younger kids.

Microsoft knows this, and includes in Internet Explorer 8 a feature
called Content Advisor. This is essentially a content filter that can
be used to block access to sites that meet specified criteria. For
example, you might configure Content Advisor to block all sites
that include nudity, or that contain bad language. Content Advisor
enables you to set your own tolerance levels for various types of
potentially offensive content, and then blocks access to sites that
don't pass muster.

Here's how to activate and configure the Content Advisor:

1. From within Internet Explorer, click the Tools button and select Internet Options. (Alternately, open the Control Panel and select Internet Options.)

2. When the Internet Options dialog box appears, select the Content tab.

3. From within the Content Advisor section, click the Enable button.

4. When the Content Advisor dialog box appears, as shown in Figure 16.1, select the Ratings tab and select a category (Language, Nudity, Sex, Violence, and so on).

FIGURE 16.1

Use the Content Advisor to filter out inappropriate language, nudity, sex, and violence.

5. Adjust the ratings slider to the right to increase the tolerance for this type of content. (Leaving the slider all the way to the left is the least tolerant level.)

6. To create a list of websites that are either always viewable or never viewable, select the Approved Sites tab. Enter the URL in the Allow This Website box, and then click the Always button (to always view the site, regardless of its rating) or the Never button (to completely block access to the site).

7. Click OK, and you'll be prompted to create a supervisor password. After you enter a password and click OK, the Content Advisor will be activated.

tip

To disable Content Advisor, return to the Content tab in the Internet Options dialog box and click the Disable button.

You should know that although Content Advisor is a great way to protect your kids, you might find it annoying when you surf the Web. That's because Content Advisor (especially when set to the least tolerant levels) is likely to block access to a lot of sites you're used to visiting on a normal basis. News sites, in particular, include stories about sex, violence, and hatred that can activate the Content Advisor filter.

If you find that Content Advisor is blocking too many sites, try turning down the tolerance level. You can also add your favorite sites to the list on the Approved Sites tab.

note

Content Advisor settings are specific to the user currently logged in. If you switch users, the Content Advisor settings change to reflect that user's preferences—which means you'll need to set separate Content Advisor settings for each of your kids, if they log on as different users.

Managing Cookies

Another worrisome aspect of web browsing is the fact that everything you do can be tracked—on your own computer. Again, however, Windows 7 offers a solution.

The primary way that your web browsing is tracked is via a small file called a *cookie*. Websites create and store cookie files on your computer's hard disk; these files contain information about you and your web activities.

For example, a cookie file for a particular site might contain your user name, the most recent pages you visited on that site, and that sort of thing. The cookie file created by a site is accessed by that site each time you visit in the future, and the information then used however the site wishes.

Understanding Cookies

A cookie is nothing more than a small text file. The file is created by the websites you visit and stored on your computer; it's a two-stage process.

First, the website's server creates the cookie file, embeds the relevant information within the file, and then stores the file on your computer, typically without your knowledge or consent. Second, when you next visit the website, the cookie file is uploaded to the site's web server, where the information is read and used accordingly.

So all that valuable information is just sitting on your computer's hard disk. Not only can it be accessed by the site that created it, anyone delving into your hard disk's contents can access the cookie file—and retrieve all the personal information stored there.

For this reason, Internet Explorer gives you the option of accepting or not accepting cookies from any given site. Obviously, not accepting cookies is the safest route—but not necessarily the one I'd recommend.

You see, as much as some users rail against the use of cookies, not accepting cookies will severely limit your use of the Web. It's kind of like the issue some people have with credit cards. Yes, obtaining a credit card creates a credit file that follows you everywhere, for the rest of your life. But trying to exist without a credit card is simply impractical. So most people trade off some degree of privacy for the convenience of using a credit card.

It's the same thing with cookies. You have to accept a compromise between complete privacy and the convenience of accessing and using a broad variety of websites. And that compromise is a personal one.

Adjusting the Privacy Level

If you value your privacy, you want to control how cookies are created and stored on your computer. To that end, Internet Explorer lets you adjust the browser's privacy level to determine which types of cookies are automatically accepted—or rejected.

You control how cookies are managed on your system by setting Internet Explorer's *privacy level*. Follow these steps:

1. From within Internet Explorer, click the Tools button and select Internet Options. (Alternately, open the Control Panel and select Internet Options.)

2. When the Internet Options dialog box appears, select the Privacy tab, shown in Figure 16.2.

3. Adjust the slider to the privacy level you want.

4. Click OK.

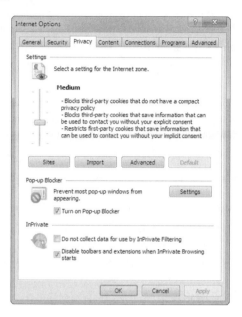

FIGURE 16.2

Managing cookies from within Internet Explorer.

Internet Explorer has six levels of cookie management, ranging from accepting all cookies to declining all cookies:

- **Accept All Cookies.** Accepts all first-party and third-party cookies.

- **Low.** Accepts all first-party cookies but blocks third-party cookies from sites that don't have privacy policies. When IE is closed, automatically deletes third-party cookies from sites that use personal information without your implicit consent.

- **Medium.** When IE is closed, automatically deletes first-party cookies from sites that use personal information without your consent. Blocks third-party cookies from sites that don't have privacy policies or from sites that use personal information without your implicit consent.

- **Medium-High.** Blocks first-party cookies from sites that use personal information without your implicit consent. Blocks third-party cookies from sites that don't have privacy policies or from sites that use personal information without your *explicit* consent.

- **High.** Blocks all cookies from sites that don't have privacy policies or from sites that use personal information without your *explicit* consent.

- **Block All Cookies.** Blocks all new cookies. Existing cookies can't be read, even by the sites that created them.

note

Internet Explorer differentiates between *first-party* and *third-party* cookies. A first-party cookie originates from the website you are currently viewing and is typically used to store your preferences regarding that site. A third-party cookie originates from a website different from the one you are currently viewing and is typically used to feed advertisements from separate ad sites to the current website. In general, third-party cookies are less desirable than first-party cookies.

The default setting is Medium, which pretty much blocks all advertising-related cookies and deletes any cookies that contain personal information when you close Internet Explorer. If you'd rather no website store any personal information you haven't explicitly approved, choose the High setting.

Deleting All Cookies

Internet Explorer also lets you automatically delete all the cookie files stored on your computer. This is useful if you want to erase all tracks of the websites you've visited; with no cookie files, your employer or spouse won't know your browsing history.

To delete all cookie files, follow these steps:

1. From within Internet Explorer, click the Safety button and select Delete Browsing History.

2. When the Delete Browsing History dialog box appears, as shown in Figure 16.3, check the Cookies option.

3. Click the Delete button.

This action deletes all the cookies from your computer—which can cause some of your favorite websites not to work properly, as all your login and browsing information will be deleted for these sites. If you prefer to keep cookies for sites on your favorites list, make sure you check the Preserve Favorites Website Data option in the Delete Browsing History dialog box.

tip

You can also use the Delete Browsing History dialog box to delete your temporary Internet files (cache), browsing history, form data, and any website passwords you've entered.

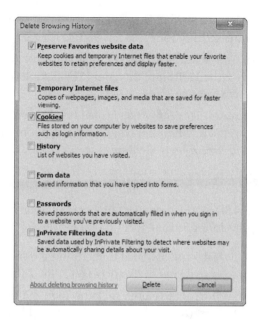

FIGURE 16.3
Deleting cookies from your computer.

Managing Security Zones

Internet Explorer incorporates a technology called ActiveX, which enables web designers to add a variety of active and multimedia content to their pages. Unfortunately, ActiveX also provides a potential "hole" into your computer system.

That's because ActiveX controls can be automatically downloaded from a web page to your PC, in the background and without your knowledge. Most of the time ActiveX controls are good things, adding functionality to web pages. On occasion, however, ActiveX controls can be configured to use your system's resources and even write to your hard disk. The result is that crafty developers can use ActiveX to breach your system, upload personal information, and download viruses and other harmful programs.

Microsoft's workaround for these ActiveX security issues is to enable you to set different *security zones* for different websites. Each security zone is assigned either a Low, Medium, or High security level.

Low security provides no warning if you're about to run potentially damaging ActiveX content. Medium security prompts you before running questionable items. High security simply won't let you run anything potentially dangerous.

These security levels are applied to different web pages by assigning each page to a specific security zone. IE8 lets you assign four different zones:

- **Internet.** This is Internet Explorer's default zone. Any website not previously visited falls into this zone. The default security level for this zone is Medium.

- **Local Intranet.** This zone is dedicated to pages on a corporate intranet. You can't manually add sites to this zone. The default security level for this zone is Medium.

- **Trusted Sites.** This zone contains sites that you know are completely safe. The default security level for this zone is Low.

- **Restricted Sites.** This zone contains sites you don't trust. The default security level for this zone is High.

By default, all websites are assigned to the Internet zone. To assign a website to either the Trusted Sites or Restricted Sites zone, follow these steps:

1. From within Internet Explorer, click the Tools button and select Internet Options. (Alternately, open the Control Panel and select Internet Options.)

2. When the Internet Options dialog box appears, select the Security tab, shown in Figure 16.4.

FIGURE 16.4

Managing security zones.

3. Select either the Trusted Sites or Restricted Sites icon.

4. Click the Sites button.

5. When the zone dialog box appears, enter the URL for the new site in the Add This Web Site To the Zone box; then click the Add button.

6. Click Close when done; then click OK again to close the Internet Options dialog box.

---

tip

The security zone for the current web page is always shown on the right side of the Internet Explorer status bar.

Protecting Against Phishing Scams with the SmartScreen Filter

One of biggest Internet-related dangers is identity theft, which is typically enabled by providing your personal information to an untrusted third party. One of the most popular scams is the *phishing scam*, and it can really trick you.

How Phishing Works

Phishing is nothing more than high-tech trickery. In a typical phishing scam, a third party with malicious intent sends you an email that looks like an official message from a trusted institution—your bank, or PayPal, or eBay, or whatever. Invariably, this email says that you need to check your account or provide more information or something similar, and provides a link for you to click to make these changes.

---

caution

If you receive an unsolicited email with a link in it do *not* click the link—even if the email looks official. Nine times out of ten, the link takes you to a phishing site.

When you click the link in the email, you're taken to a site that looks like an official site, but really isn't. This so-called phishing site is a clever forgery that exists only to extract information from unsuspecting users. You're prompted to provide your personal information, including your name, address, bank account number, and the like. When you do so, that information is fed to the identity thief, who uses it for nefarious purposes—and you're hosed.

Using the SmartScreen Filter

To protect you from phishing scams, IE8 incorporates anti-phishing technology in the form of the SmartScreen Filter. This filter automatically connects to an online service that contains a huge database of suspicious websites and alerts you if you attempt to go to one of these sites.

note

In Internet Explorer 7, the SmartScreen filter was called the Phishing Filter.

If you attempt to click a link to a known phishing site, the SmartScreen Filter blocks access to the site, changes the browser's address bar to red, navigates to a neutral page, and displays a warning message, like the one shown in Figure 16.5. In other words, if the site is fraudulent, Internet Explorer won't let you go there.

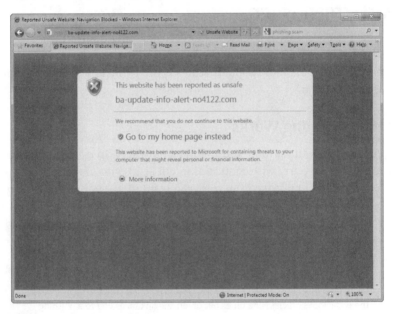

FIGURE 16.5

The SmartScreen Filter at work—this is what you see if you attempt to access a known or suspected phishing site.

In addition, the SmartScreen Filter helps protect you from sites that *might* be fake. If you attempt to click a link to a site that is not on the list of known fraudulent sites but behaves similarly to such sites, the SmartScreen Filter changes the address bar to yellow and cautions you of potentially suspicious content. Unless you're sure the site is good, don't click through.

The SmartScreen Filter is enabled by default. To disable it (not that you'd want to), click the Safety button and select SmartScreen Filter, Turn Off SmartScreen Filter.

> **tip**
>
> You can also have the filter manually check any given website. Just click the Safety button and select SmartScreen Filter, Check This Website. The filter will check the site and display its findings in a new dialog box.

Blocking Unwanted Pop-Ups

Until a few years ago, unwanted pop-up windows were legion across he Web. When you visited certain websites, all of a sudden you'd see a new, typically smaller window displayed on your desktop. This is a pop-up window, so-called because it pops up without you having to do anything; the process is automated via use of special code on the underlying web page.

Understanding the Pop-Up Blocker

Pop-up windows are extremely annoying, which is why most web browsers eventually added pop-up blocker technology. With Internet Explorer, the pop-up blocker is enabled by default so that the automatic opening of unwanted pop-up windows is blocked.

When a site tries to open a pop-up window that is blocked by Internet Explorer, a notification appears in the information bar of the browser window, just above the current web page, as shown in Figure 16.6. If you click the notification, you can choose to temporarily or permanently allow pop-ups from this site. If you ignore the notification, no further pop-ups from this site will be displayed.

FIGURE 16.6

IE8's pop-up blocker at work—note the message in the information bar.

Enabling Pop-Up Windows

In some instances, pop-up windows are necessary. For example, a website might display additional useful information in a pop-up window—but if pop-ups are blocked, you won't see this info. To enable pop-ups from a specific website, follow these steps:

1. From within Internet Explorer, click the Tools button and select Pop-up Blocker, Pop-up Blocker Settings.

2. When the Pop-up Blocker Settings dialog box appears, as shown in Figure 16.7, enter the address of the specific website.

3. Click the Add button.

This site will now be added to a list of allowed sites for pop-ups.

FIGURE 16.7

Enabling pop-up windows from a specific site.

You can also configure IE's blocking level—that is, how aggressive it is about blocking pop-ups. From within the Pop-up Blocker Settings dialog box, click the Blocking Level button and select one of these three levels:

- **High**. Blocks all pop-ups.
- **Medium**. Blocks most pop-ups.
- **Low**. Allows pop-ups from secure sites, but blocks most others.

Medium is the default level, but if you find that some pop-ups still get through, change the level to High.

Surfing Secretly with InPrivate Browsing

If you like the convenience of cookies but don't want a specific browsing session recorded, you can use Internet Explorer 8's new InPrivate Browsing feature to browse completely anonymously. With InPrivate Browsing enabled, no record of the pages you visit are kept via any means, cookies or otherwise. No one need know where you've been on the Web.

---

note

You can run normal IE and InPrivate browser windows simultaneously.

Why would you want to browse secretly? Let's be honest—InPrivate Browsing is for hiding those sites you don't want your spouse or other users to know about. While this could be the expected porn sites, it could also be an online store where you're shopping for a Christmas or anniversary gift, or just a hobby forum that you'd like to keep to yourself. InPrivate Browsing is for hiding *any* type of site; when activated, no trace of your visit is recorded anywhere on your computer.

You enable InPrivate Browsing from a normal Internet Explorer window. Just click the Safety button and select InPrivate Browsing; this opens a new browser window with the InPrivate logo displayed in the Address bar, as shown in Figure 16.8.

FIGURE 16.8

Browsing anonymously with InPrivate Browsing.

When you browse from an InPrivate window, IE stores no data about the web pages you visit. Cookies, temporary files, and history are all disabled, so after you close the InPrivate window, no trace of your visits exist.

---

note

Most other web browsers offer similar anonymous browsing features. For example, Google Chrome offers what it calls the Incognito mode; Firefox offers Private Browsing. All of these modes work similarly to IE's InPrivate Browsing.

Practicing Safe Computing

When it comes to safe surfing, the best protection is a good defense. That means using a firewall and running some sort of anti-malware program, of course, but it also means employing a good dollop of common sense. A little effort on your part will have a major impact on the security of your system.

---

note

Malware is the shorthand term for *malicious software*, typically in the form of computer viruses and spyware. Learn more in Chapter 20, "Managing System Security."

That said, because malware and other threats occur when you deal with other computers and other users, the only sure-fire way to shield your system from online threats is to completely cut off all contact with other computers. That means no Internet connection, no sharing files via CD or USB memory drive, no connecting to a home or office network. In today's connected world, however, none of these things is practical.

So know this: Because you're not going to completely quit doing any of these activities, you'll never be 100% safe from the threat of computer viruses. There are, however, some steps you can take to reduce your risk. Let's look at a few of them.

Don't Open Email Attachments

Most computer virus and spyware infections today are spread via email. The malware is typically encased in a file attached to an email message; when you click to view or open the file, you launch the malware—and your computer is automatically infected.

To that end, the best and easiest way to reduce your risk of malware infection is to never open email attachments. Never. Especially from people you don't know.

But you also shouldn't open attachments from people you *do* know, if you aren't expecting them. That's because some viruses can hijack the email address book on an infected PC, thus sending out infected email that the owner isn't even aware of.

So any email attachment is suspect, unless you were explicitly expecting it from a trusted user. Click on any other attachment, and chances are your computer will be infected.

---

caution

If you remember nothing else from this book, remember this: *Never open an unexpected file attachment.* Period!

By the way, this warning includes email sent via closed systems, such as the email components of Facebook, MySpace, and other social networks. An infected email attachment is just as infected on Facebook as it is on your private copy of Microsoft Outlook. Beware *any* attachments you receive, from any source.

Don't Open Files Sent via Instant Messaging

The previous advice goes for any files sent to you via instant messaging. IM is a growing source of virus infection, if only because users (especially younger ones) are naturally trusting of other users.

This becomes more of a problem as you grow your friends or buddies list; if you have a hundred friends, it's difficult to know whether an incoming message comes from a friend or from a stranger. And even if the IM purports to come from a friend, it could come from someone posing as your friend, or from your friend's computer that has already been hijacked by the virus.

Bottom line: Don't accept any files sent to you via instant messaging. If a trusted friend really wants to send you a file, ask him to email it to you—and then use normal caution before opening it.

Don't Click IM or Chat Links

While we're on the subject of instant messaging, here's another bit of common sense that can greatly reduce your risk of virus infection. If someone you don't know sends you a link to another site while you're instant messaging or in a chat room, don't click it! Nine times out of ten, this link either directly downloads a malware file to your PC or takes you to a website that has plenty of surreptitiously infected files to download. In any case, ignore the unsolicited links and you'll be a lot safer.

Don't Execute Files Found in Blogs, Newsgroups, or Message Boards

Email and instant messaging are not the only channels for downloading virus infected files. You can find plenty of infected files in web message boards, blogs, and USENET newsgroups. For this reason, resist downloading programs you find in these channels; although many are safe, some are not.

Don't Download Files from Suspect Websites

Many websites hold infected files. The owners of these sites are just waiting for naïve users to download the files, so that their PCs can become infected.

For this reason, you should avoid downloading files from sites with which you're not familiar. Instead, download files only from reliable file archive websites, such as Download.com (www.download.com) and Tucows (www.tucows.com), or from known sites that offer software for sale, such as Apple.com and Microsoft.com. These sites scan all their files for viruses before they're available for downloading. It's the only safe way to download files from the Internet.

Limit Your Sharing of Removable Media

Before the Internet, the most common way for your computer to get infected was through files shared through some form of removable media. Back in the day, this meant floppy disks or Zip disks; today, the preferred media are more likely to be data CDs or DVDs, or files stored on portable USB storage devices.

The logic is simple. Any file you receive has the potential to carry a computer virus. It doesn't matter what that file looks like (its filename and extension) or who gave it to you, the bottom line is that you don't know where that file came from. If you run that file on your system—either from the storage device or after you've saved it to your computer's hard disk—any malicious code contained within can infect and potentially trash your system.

To that end, the same advice applies now as it did twenty years ago: You should share disks, memory sticks, and files only with users you know and trust. (And make sure you scan the files in question with an anti-virus program before you open them on your computer.)

Or, to be completely safe, don't accept *any* files given to you on any portable storage medium.

Display and Check File Extensions

Certain types of files can carry virus and spyware infections; certain types of files can't. You need to know which files are potentially dangerous and which aren't, which you can learn by consulting the file type data in Table 16.1.

Table 16.1   Selected File Types That Can and Can't Carry Computer Viruses

Safe File Types	Unsafe File Types
AAC	ADE
AVI	ADP
BMP	BAS
DVR-MS	BAT
FLV	CHM
GIF	CMD
JPEG	COM
JPG	CPL
MOV	CRT
MPA	DOC
MP3	DOCX
MP4	DOT
MPG	EXE
MPEG	HLP
PDF	HTA
PNG	INF
QT	INS
TIF	ISP
TIFF	JS
TXT	JSE
WAV	LNK
WMA	MDB
WMV	MDE
	MSC
	MSI
	MSP

Table 16.1 Continued

Safe File Types	Unsafe File Types
	MST
	PCD
	PIF
	RAR
	REG
	SCR
	SCT
	SHB
	SHS
	SYS
	URL
	VB
	VBE
	VBS
	WSC
	WSF
	WSH
	XLS
	XLSX
	XLW
	ZIP

Of course, to guard against the riskier file types, you need to see what types of files you're dealing with. Unfortunately, since Windows 95, the Windows operating system's default configuration turns off the display of file extensions. When you look at a list of files in Windows Explorer, all you see is the main part of the filename, *not* the extension; you'll see something like **my picture file**, but not know whether it's **my picture file.jpg**, **my picture file.doc**, or **my picture file.exe**.

The solution to this dilemma is to reconfigure Windows to display file extensions—which you learned to do back in Chapter 7, "Extending File and Folder Management." I won't repeat those instructions here; re-read the pertinent section in that chapter to get the lowdown.

By the way, one of the more common ways for malware writers to trick you into opening an infected file is to disguise a bad file type as a safe file type. There are many ways to do this, but the most common is the double-dot, or double-extension, exploit. This is accomplished by adding a

.**jpg** or .**txt** to the first part of the filename, before the real extension. You
end up with a name like this:

```
thisfile.jpg.exe
```

If you're not fully alert and don't notice the trailing .**exe**, this might
appear to be a safe file. This exploit is further exacerbated by the inclu-
sion of spaces after the middle extension, like this:

```
thisfile.jpg          .exe
```

In this instance, the last part of the filename—the *real* extension—gets
pushed off the screen, so you don't see it and you think you're opening a
safe file.

Avoiding Malware-Infested Websites

Browsing the Web can be a dangerous business, as the Internet is full of
malware. If you know where you're likely to find malware programs on
the Web, however, you can avoid those sites—and thus avoid installing
malware on your system.

To that end, your worst hives of malware are the Web's illegal file-trading
networks, such as LimeWire and BitTorrent. Spyware and viruses often
hide within files that appear to be normal music and videos; try to play
the file and your computer gets infected.

In addition, the software used to access files on these networks can itself
be the source of malware infection. Sometimes the malware (typically
spyware) is installed without your knowledge, but more often than not
you actually agree to install it. That's because the installation of these
malware programs is often optional when you install the host program
with which the adware is bundled; if you look closely, you'll see that
you're given the option *not* to install these so-called "companion programs" when you install the host program. Check (or uncheck) the proper
box on the installation screen, and you avoid installing the adware.

Then there are sites that install "drive-by" malware, typically by tricking
you with a fake alert window. You know the ones; you open the site and
all of a sudden you see a new window that looks like a standard Windows
dialog box. When you click the Cancel button to close the dialog box, you
instead install a spyware program. (Better to click the "X" in the top-right
corner of the window, which should close the window without downloading any spyware.)

Also effective are sites that display what appears to be a pop-up window
advertising an anti-spyware program. The ad says something along the

lines of "your system may be infected—click here to remove all spyware from your system." Instead of removing spyware, the program you install is itself a spyware program, and your system is newly infected.

The takeaway here is to be careful what links you click and what sites you download from. The only truly safe download sites are reputable sites like Tucows.com and Download.com, as well as legitimate online media stores such as Apple's iTunes Store and Amazon.com MP3 Downloads. Most other sites offering free downloads also feature piggyback malware as part of the package. And when you do download a file, read the user agreement first—you may be able to opt out of installing piggyback adware.

In other words, look before you click.

The Bottom Line

Web browsing can be as safe or as private as you want it to be. Increase your safety by blocking sites with inappropriate content, setting high security zone levels, and choosing not to accept cookies—if you don't mind the corresponding trade-off in usability, of course. Or, if you think you have something to hide, cover all your tracks by using InPrivate Browsing. It's all about surfing the Internet your way—as safely and secretly as you like.

17

Getting the Most Out of Windows on a Notebook PC

Having Windows your way is especially important when you're
using a notebook PC. That's because there's a lot you can do to customize how your notebook works when you're on the road—from
connecting to an external projector to fine-tuning your touchpad to
installing notebook-specific gadgets. We'll look at all these issues
and more in this chapter—and then deal with battery-saving tips in
the chapter after.

Managing Notebook Settings with the Mobility Center

One of the many nice things about using Windows 7 on a notebook
PC is that the most important notebook configuration options are
consolidated into a single utility. This utility, called the Windows
Mobility Center, is the place to go when you want to configure how
your notebook PC works.

> **note**
>
> The Mobility Center is visible only if you're using a notebook PC. You
> won't find it on a desktop computer.

To launch the Mobility Center, open the Control Panel and select
Windows Mobility Center. (Alternately, you can open the Windows
Start menu and select All Programs, Accessories, Windows Mobility
Center.) As you can see in Figure 17.1, the Mobility Center includes
panels for the following settings:

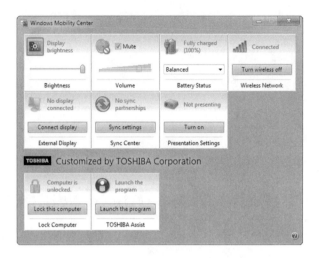

FIGURE 17.1

Manage key notebook-related settings in the Windows Mobility Center.

- **Brightness.** Adjusts the brightness of your notebook's display
- **Volume.** Adjusts the volume level of your notebook's sound
- **Battery Status.** Displays the current charge status of your notebook's battery and lets you change the selected power plan
- **Wireless Network.** Shows your current wireless status and also lets you turn on and off your notebook's wireless adapter
- **External Display.** Lets you connect your notebook to an external monitor
- **Sync Center.** Lets you connect your notebook to other devices, such as flash memory drives, and synchronize files between the two devices
- **Presentation Settings.** Lets you turn on special presentation settings for your notebook

note

Some manufacturers tack their own panels onto the generic Mobility Center. For example, Toshiba adds panels for Lock Computer and the Toshiba Assist support utility. Other manufacturers rename some of these panels; for example, Dell calls the Brightness panel Display Settings.

We'll look at each of these settings separately.

Adjusting Brightness

The first panel in the Mobility Center is labeled Brightness, and it enables quick adjustment of—you guessed it—the brightness of your notebook's display. Using this control is as easy as moving the slider; move it to the left to dim the display, or to the right to make it brighter. Simplicity itself.

Adjusting Volume

Next to the Brightness panel is the Volume panel. This control is equally self-explanatory and equally simple to use; just move the slider left to decrease your notebook's volume, or to the right to turn up the volume. There is an added wrinkle, however, in the Mute control; click this option to immediately mute your PC's sound, or unclick it to return to the previous volume level.

Managing Battery Status

Now we come to the Battery Status panel. This panel serves two functions: It displays the current charge level for your notebook's battery and lets you change Windows' power scheme. The charge level is easy enough to understand; to change power schemes, just pull down the list and select a new scheme.

note

Learn more about power schemes in Chapter 18, "Extending Battery Life."

Managing Wireless Networks

The Wireless Network panel displays the status of your current wireless connection—whether you're connected or not. If you want to quickly disable your wireless connection, just click the Turn Wireless Off button; to re-enable the wireless connection, click the resultant Turn Wireless On button.

tip

If you're not using the wireless connection, turning off your notebook's wireless feature can conserve battery power. (When the wireless feature is on, even if it's not connected to a wireless network, it's always looking for a wireless connection—which eats up valuable battery power.)

Connecting an External Display

If you want to connect an external monitor to your notebook, you can do so via the Mobility Center's External Display panel. Click the Connect Display button and select from one of the following options: Computer Only, Duplicate, Extend, or Projector Only.

note

Learn more about working with an external display in the "Using an External Monitor" section, later in this chapter.

tip

You can also display the display options by pressing Windows+P on your computer keyboard.

Managing Sync Settings

Windows 7's Sync Center enables you to synchronize data between folders in two different locations—between your home and office networks, for example, or between your notebook PC and a portable music player device. To access this feature, click the Sync Settings button to open the Sync Settings window, and then follow the instructions from there.

Activating Presentation Settings Mode

Many businesspeople use their PCs to give presentations, either on the road or down the hall in the boardroom. When you do so, however, you don't want your screen saver activating after a few minutes, or your notebook powering down if you haven't tapped a key for awhile. In other words, you want to turn your notebook computer into a somewhat dedicated presentation machine.

You do this by activating Windows' Presentation Settings mode. In this mode, your notebook always stays awake, the screen saver is disabled, and all system notifications are turned off. In other words, no unexpected distractions during your presentation.

Not surprisingly, you activate the Presentation Settings mode from the Mobility Center's Presentation Settings panel. Just click the Turn On button to enable Windows' presentation settings, or Turn Off to disable them when the presentation is over.

Using an External Monitor

Some users are just fine with the notebook's built-in display. But other users complain about the small size of some displays, preferring the larger screens available on external computer monitors.

If you want to connect an external monitor to your PC, it's easy enough to do. First, you have to physically connect the monitor; you typically do this via a VGA connection, although some notebooks and monitors have superior (and all-digital) DVI connections, which are preferred. In any case, all you have to do is run the appropriate cable between your notebook and the external monitor.

Once the monitor is connected, you have to tell Windows how you want to use the monitor. In Windows 7, you have four choices:

- **Computer Only.** Routes your computer's video to the built-in display only, leaving blank the external display.

- **Duplicate.** Sends the same video to the internal and external displays.

- **Extend.** This option lets you create a super-large desktop that stretches between the internal and external displays. You can then move your mouse from one screen to another in a single motion, as if the two displays comprised a single desktop.

- **Projector Only.** Routes your computer's video to the external display only, leaving blank the internal display.

You access these display options from the Mobility Center. Click the Connect Display button in the External Display panel and you see the four options shown in Figure 17.2. Click the option you want, and Windows does your bidding.

FIGURE 17.2

Selecting external display options.

note

Some notebook PCs let you switch between internal and external displays with the press of a function button on the keyboard or a dedicated button somewhere on the unit. Consult your computer's instructions to see what's available in this regard.

Presenting from Your Notebook

Just a few years ago, video projectors were big, bulky beasts that cost thousands of dollars—not ideal for the traveling presenter. Today, however, projectors have come down in both size and price, so that they're now small enough (some fit into the palm of your hand!) and affordable enough (as low as $500) to carry around with you in your notebook bag.

Choosing a Video Projector

Most portable video projectors today use Digital Light Processing (DLP), LCD, or liquid crystal on silicone (LCoS) technology to project images at 1024×768 or higher resolution. They're bright enough to show a clear image on a plain white wall, no special screen required (although a reflective screen will display an even better picture). You can adjust the lens and the distance from the screen or wall to display a picture sized anywhere from 30" to 300" in size.

When you're shopping for a video projector, consider the following factors:

- **Size.** Is it small enough to carry with you when you travel?
- **Weight.** Same question: Is it light enough to carry?
- **Connectors.** Does it have the right connectors to work with your notebook, or do you need to purchase an additional adapter? In addition, some projectors accept USB memory drives. This lets you load your presentation onto a keychain memory device if you want.
- **Brightness.** The brighter the picture (measured in lumens), the better the picture will be under normal lighting. Low-lumen projectors require a darkened room for the best picture.
- **Contrast ratio.** The higher the contrast ratio, the darker the blacks in the picture.
- **Resolution.** The higher the display's resolution, the more detailed the image you can display. Look for at least 1024×768 resolution; more is better.

And, of course, there's always price. Choose the best performing projector for your budget.

Making the Connection

Connecting your notebook to a projector is relatively easy, depending on the video outputs on your notebook and the video inputs on the projector.

If both your notebook and the projector have VGA connectors, just connect a simple VGA cable between the two. If the projector doesn't have a VGA input, you'll have to employ some sort of adapter or adapter cable—VGA-to-component video is the most common.

It's better if both your notebook and projector have HDMI connections. HDMI is an all-digital connection that carries both audio and video in a single cable—and delivers the best possible resolution.

tip

If your computer has a DVI output instead of HDMI, you can use a DVI-to-HDMI converter to make the connection to the projector.

Switching to External Video

Most notebooks make it easy to connect an external monitor or projector. Your notebook may automatically send a signal whenever external video is connected, or you may be able to use a keyboard shortcut to switch from internal to external video.

You can also make this switch from within Windows, using the Mobility Center. Go to the External Display panel and click the Connect Display button. From the available options, select either Duplicate (to view your presentation on both your notebook's display and the external projector) or Projector Only (to blank your internal display and view the presentation on the external projector only).

note

You should also activate Presentation Settings mode before starting a presentation. See the "Activating Presentation Settings Mode" section, earlier in this chapter.

Setting the Resolution

For the best-looking presentation, your projector's screen resolution should match the resolution of your notebook PC. If your notebook is set for a 1280×800 display and your projector is set for 1024×768, your presentation isn't going to look right when projected. You'll need to reconfigure your notebook for the projector's resolution—and make sure you create your presentation with the projected resolution in mind.

To configure the resolution for the external projector, follow these steps:

1. From the Control Panel, select Display.

2. When the Display window appears, click Adjust Resolution from the tasks pane.

3. When the Screen Resolution window appears, click the Display list and select the external projector.

4. Click the Resolution button and select the desired resolution.

5. Click OK.

---

tip

Most video projectors don't include speakers—which means you have to rely on your notebook to reproduce the sound if your presentation has an audio component. Given the puny speakers built into most notebooks, investigate whether the room or hall has a sound system you can connect to, or consider investing in a good pair of portable external speakers for your notebook.

Exploring Gadgets for Notebook Users

I assume you're already familiar with the concept of Windows gadgets—you know, those single-purpose applications that sit directly on the Windows desktop. Well, there are a number of gadgets that are targeted expressly at notebook users, and thus worth your consideration.

---

note

Learn more about gadgets in Chapter 3, "Customizing the Desktop."

You find new gadgets by opening the Control Panel and selecting Desktop Gadgets. When the Gadgets window appears, click Get More Gadgets Online; this takes you to Microsoft's Personalize Your PC website. From there you can browse through or search for specific gadgets.

Which gadgets might you be interested in? Here's a short list of my notebook-friendly favorites:

- Battery Vista, shown in Figure 17.3, displays how much charge you have left on your battery.

- Notebook Monitor, shown in Figure 17.4, displays various notebook functions—wireless connectivity, CPU status, memory use, battery status, and the like.

- Wireless Network, shown in Figure 17.5, displays the name of the wireless network to which you're connected, and the current signal strength.

FIGURE 17.3

The Battery Vista gadget.

FIGURE 17.4

The Notebook Monitor gadget.

FIGURE 17.5

The Wireless Network gadget.

Obviously, you might consider other gadgets to be even more useful. Go online and see what you can find!

Using Your Notebook to Control Your Office PC from the Road

Here's a way to have *two* computers your way. Windows 7's Remote Desktop Connection lets you connect to your office computer from your remote notebook and have access to all your programs, files, and resources as if you were actually sitting in your office.

---

note

Remote Desktop Connection is only available for host computers running Windows 7 Professional, Enterprise, and Ultimate editions—which are the editions you're likely to find in a corporate environment.

To connect to your work computer remotely, you must turn on your work computer, have a network connection, and have Remote Desktop enabled. You must also, of course, have network access to your work computer (typically via the Internet or a VPN), and you must have permission to connect.

Configuring Your Desktop PC

To set up your work computer for remote connections, you have to both activate remote access and determine who can have that access. Follow these steps:

1. Open the Control Panel and select System.

2. When the System window appears, click Advanced System Settings.

3. When the System Properties dialog box appears, select the Remote tab, shown in Figure 17.6.

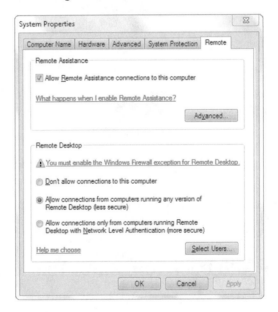

FIGURE 17.6

Setting up remote access.

4. Select either the Allow Connections from Computers Running Any Version of Remote Desktop or Allow Connections Only from Computers Running Remote Desktop with Network Level Authentication. The former option is less secure, but is easier to work with; the latter option is more secure, if you can use it.

5. Click the Select Users button.

6. When the Remote Desktop Users dialog box appears, click the Add button.

7. When the Select Users dialog box appears, enter the user name you use on your notebook PC; then click OK.

8. Back in the Remote Desktop Users dialog box, click OK.

Connecting from Your Notebook

To connect to your desktop (work) computer from your notebook, you need to follow these steps on your notebook PC:

1. Open the Control Panel and select RemoteApp and Desktop Connections.

2. When the next window appears, click Set Up a New Connection with RemoteApp and Desktop Connections in the tasks pane.

3. When the Set Up a New Connection with RemoteApp and Desktop Connections dialog box appears, as shown in Figure 17.7, enter the URL or IP address for your work computer into the Connection URL box; then click Next.

4. When the Ready to Set Up Connection screen appears, click Next.

FIGURE 17.7

Connecting to your work PC with Remote Desktop Connection.

You'll now be connected to your work PC, and the desktop from that PC will display on your current computer screen. You can use your notebook to access any program or file on your work PC, just as if you were there.

Touchpad Tricks

When it comes to making your notebook PC work your way, there's one last thing we need to discuss—the touchpad. There's a lot you can customize about it.

Most touchpads come with a configuration utility that lets you adjust sensitivity, cursor speed, and the like. Every touchpad and utility is unique, but they all operate in much the same fashion.

For our example, we'll look at the Synaptics TouchPad, which is a popular model found in many new notebook PCs. You access the touchpad utility by opening the Control Panel and selecting Mouse. This displays the Mouse Properties dialog box. The different tabs in this dialog box configure different aspects of the touchpad's operation.

Configuring Double-Click Speed

We'll start with the Buttons tab, shown in Figure 17.8. You can see that the Synaptics TouchPad is selected as the device being used for the mouse; if an external mouse was being used, something else would be selected here. Three key options appear on this tab:

- **Right-handed and Left-handed.** For most of us, we want the left mouse button to be the main mouse button; this is right-handed operation. If you're a lefty, however, you might want to reverse the button operation by selecting the left-handed option.

- **Double Click Speed.** This setting describes how fast you have to click the mouse button to achieve a double-click. Set the speed too slow and separate clicks will be counted as a single double-click; set the speed too fast and you won't be able to double-click fast enough to count.

- **ClickLock.** Normally, you drag or highlight items by holding down the mouse button and then moving the cursor. With ClickLock enabled, you don't have to hold down the mouse button; dragging/highlighting occurs simply by tapping the mouse button.

FIGURE 17.8
Configuring your touchpad's buttons in Windows 7.

Configuring Cursor Speed

How fast the cursor moves onscreen is a highly personal choice. Some people like the speed they get with a fast cursor; others like the increased precision of a slow one.

You adjust cursor speed—and a few other options—from the Pointer Options tab. As you can see in Figure 17.9, you use this tab to configure the following:

- Set pointer (cursor) speed
- Enhance pointer precision (makes the pointer more accurate when it's moving slowly)
- Automatically move the cursor to the default button in a dialog box (Snap To)
- Display visible pointer trails when the cursor is moving (helps to locate the cursor onscreen; you can make these trails shorter or longer)
- Hide the cursor when typing
- Show the position of a hidden cursor by pressing the Ctrl key

FIGURE 17.9
Configuring pointer options.

Configuring Touchpad Properties

The Device Settings tab is where you access the main configuration settings for the touchpad. Select this tab and then select the touchpad from the Devices list and click the Settings button. This displays the Properties window, shown in Figure 17.10, which is where all the fun happens.

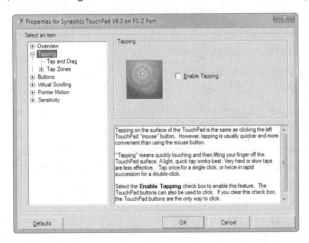

FIGURE 17.10
Configuring touchpad properties.

All the settings in the Properties window are accessed via the tree list on the left side of the window. There are more settings here than we need to discuss; let's focus on the most important ones.

Tapping via the Touchpad

By default, most touchpads come configured with "tapping" enabled. When so configured, tapping on the touchpad is the same as clicking the left mouse button. The problem with tapping is that it's all too easy to accidentally touch the touchpad with your finger or the palm of your hand, and thus click the mouse button and unwittingly select something onscreen.

This is why I disable tapping, by unchecking the Enable Tapping box. However, other users like to tap the touchpad instead of click the mouse button, so this is definitely a personal preference.

If you enable tapping, you have other options available to you. For example, you can enable tap and drag, which lets you drag the cursor by tapping first on the touchpad. You can also configure different "tap zones" on the touchpad, so that tapping in different places initiates specific actions. Again, it's a personal choice thing.

Scrolling via the Touchpad

Some touchpads let you use the touchpad for virtual scrolling. That is, instead of scrolling through a window by clicking on the window's scrollbars, you can scroll by sliding your finger up or down the side of the touchpad. I tend to like this feature, at least for normal vertical scrolling; you can also enable horizontal scrolling, for moving right and left through wide windows.

If you enable virtual scrolling, you can choose your desired scrolling speed, and whether you want the scrolling to "coast" to a stop. You can also configure what part of the touchpad is used for this scrolling.

Adjusting Pointer Motion

Many touchpads also let you fine-tune how the touchpad controls the cursor. On my particular Synaptics model, for example, I can configure EdgeMotion (the pointer continues to move when your finger hits the edge of the touchpad), constrained motion (the pointer only moves horizontally or vertically), slow motion (the pointer speed slows down for greater precision), and Sticky Borders (restricts pointer movement to within the current window borders).

Adjusting Sensitivity

Finally, most touchpads let you adjust the touchpad's sensitivity. Synaptics offers two primary adjustments: PalmCheck and Touch Sensitivity.

PalmCheck is useful for those of us who tend to rest our palms at the base of the keyboard, and thus accidentally activate the touchpad. You can adjust the PalmCheck from minimum (makes the touchpad more sensitive) to maximum (eliminates more accidental palm taps). If you find your computer mysteriously clicking and double-clicking as you type, this is probably why; adjust PalmCheck more toward the maximum setting.

A related setting is Touch Sensitivity, which determines how firm you have to touch the touchpad to make the cursor move. The slider goes from Light Touch (requires a less firm touch, sometimes resulting in unwanted taps) to Heavy Touch (requires a firmer touch, thus decreasing the number of false taps). Play around with different settings until you achieve the right touchpad feel for you.

The Bottom Line

As I said at the start of this chapter, there's a lot of personalization you can do to your notebook PC. After all, a notebook PC is a very personal kind of personal computer; it's all there under the palms of your hands. So work through all these Windows 7 notebook configuration options, and you'll soon be using your notebook PC your way.

18

Extending Battery Life

One of the key features of a notebook PC is its ability to operate on DC power, using an internal battery. Running your notebook on battery power frees you from having to connect to the nearest wall outlet; it lets you take your notebook virtually anywhere—until the battery runs out, that is.

That's why one of the key factors in using your notebook your way is figuring out how to extend the life of a battery charge. You don't want to be in the middle of an important presentation (or ten minutes from the end of a movie) and have your notebook die on you. Managing your notebook's battery life is one of the most important things you can do.

Understanding Battery Capacity

The capacity of a notebook battery—how long it will last on a charge—is determined by the number of cells in the battery. You see, a battery is composed of several individual power cells. These cells are arranged in a series, to maximize the voltage level of the battery as a whole.

The more power cells in a battery, the more voltage the battery can provide to your notebook—and the longer your notebook will run on a battery charge. An 8-cell battery will provide a longer charge than a 6-cell battery; a 12-cell battery will last longer still.

Of course, a battery with more cells weighs more than a smaller battery, is sometimes physically larger, and it costs more, too. So it's a bit of a compromise to fit the right-sized battery in a notebook PC;

the notebook manufacturer wants to minimize weight and cost while maximizing, as much as possible, the resultant battery life. Still, when you're choosing a battery for your notebook and you want the longest possible battery life for use on the road, go with the battery that offers the most cells.

---

note

Today's notebook PCs use lithium ion (Li-ion) batteries, and they're much easier to work with than older battery types. Prior to the adoption of lithium ion technology, notebooks used nickel cadmium (NiCad) batteries, which had their own unique issues, such as the dreaded "memory effect," which caused a partially discharged battery to eventually provide less charge time.

Running on Battery Power

Running your notebook on battery power is simplicity itself; there are no switches to switch or buttons to push. The battery kicks in automatically whenever you disconnect the notebook from an AC power source. Unplug the power cord, and the notebook switches to battery operation.

You'll know your notebook is operating on battery power by observing its front panel lights. There should be a separate indicator light for battery operation; this light probably changes color depending on what type of power you're using. For example, the battery indicator on my Toshiba laptop lights blue when the notebook is running on AC power (and thus charging the battery); it doesn't light at all when the notebook is running on a full battery; and it lights orange when it's running a battery that is losing its charge. Consult your notebook's documentation to see how your indicator lights work.

When your notebook is on battery operation, the power icon in the Windows notification area switches to a battery icon. The icon also begins to show a decreasing amount of fullness, reflecting the continuing discharge of the battery as it's used. Hover your cursor over the battery icon to display how much battery charge is left, as shown in Figure 18.1.

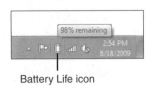

Battery Life icon

FIGURE 18.1

The battery icon in the Windows notification area.

Click the battery icon and you see even more information. As you can see in Figure 18.2, the resulting pop-up panel displays the amount of charge you have left, lets you select a new power plan, provides advice on how to get even more battery life, and provides links to adjust screen brightness and other power options.

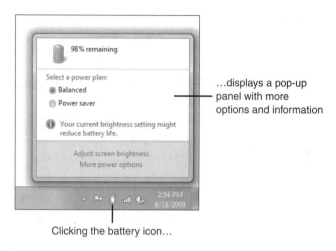

...displays a pop-up panel with more options and information

Clicking the battery icon...

FIGURE 18.2

Click the battery icon to view even more information.

> **tip**
>
> You can also view the battery level and select a power plan from the Battery Status pane in the Windows 7 Mobility Center. Learn more in Chapter 17, "Getting the Most Out of Windows on a Notebook PC."

When your battery starts running low, Windows will display an onscreen notice. When you see the low-battery notification, save your work and then either connect your notebook to AC power or turn it off. If you let your battery run down completely, Windows will automatically save your work and put itself in hibernation mode with the last amount of battery power available.

Configuring Windows 7's Power Plans

How long your battery lasts depends on a number of factors—the power drain of your PC's microprocessor, the types of programs you're running, how often your notebook accesses its hard disk or CD/DVD drive, even how bright your screen is. Many of these options are configured in what Windows calls a *power plan.* You can choose a power plan that optimizes battery life at the sacrifice of screen brightness and computing power, or one that optimizes your notebook's performance at the sacrifice of battery life.

Choosing a Power Plan

The easiest way to choose a power plan is to open the Windows Mobility Center and make a choice from the Battery Status panel, shown in Figure 18.3. From here you can choose from three different power plans: Power Saver, Balanced, and High Performance. The default settings associated with each power plan are detailed in Table 18.1.

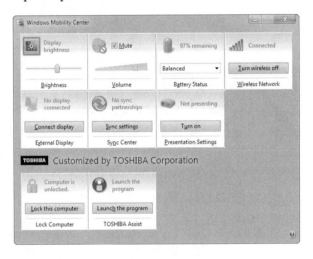

FIGURE 18.3

Choosing a power plan from the Windows Mobility Center.

Table 18.1   Windows 7 Power Plans

Settings	Power Saver Plan	Balanced Plan	High Performance Plan
Turn off display (battery mode)	3 minutes	5 minutes	20 minutes
Put computer to sleep (battery mode)	15 minutes	15 minutes	60 minutes
Screen brightness (battery mode)	40%	40%	100%
Turn off display (AC mode)	20 minutes	20 minutes	20 minutes
Put computer to sleep (AC mode)	60 minutes	60 minutes	Never

Table 18.1   **Continued**

Settings	Power Saver Plan	Balanced Plan	High Performance Plan
Screen brightness (AC mode)	100%	100%	100%
Typical uses	Best for conserving battery power	Good compromise between performance and battery life	Best for running demanding applications

Which of these power plans should you choose? For most users, the balanced plan is a good compromise between battery life and performance. However, the power saver plan will probably give you a few more minutes of battery life when operating on batteries, and the high performance plan is probably best when you're on AC power.

Customizing a Power Plan

Any of these power plans can be further customized. For example, you may want to set the high performance plan to never turn off the screen display when on AC power. To customize a power plan, follow these steps:

1. Open the Control Panel and select Power Options.

2. When the Power Options window appears, as shown in Figure 18.4, click the Change Plan Settings link under the plan you want to change.

note

By default, only the balanced and power saver plans are displayed in the Power Options window. To display the high performance plan, click the down arrow next to the Hide Additional Plans section.

3. When the Edit Plan Settings window appears, as shown in Figure 18.5, make the desired changes.

4. Click the Save Changes button when done.

What exactly can you change about a power plan? Well, it's all about conserving battery power by shutting down specific operations. Here are the options:

- **Dim the Display.** Determine how long the PC is inactive before the display is dimmed. (A dim display uses less battery power than a fully lit one.)

- **Turn Off the Display.** Determine how long the PC is inactive before the display gets turned off completely.

- **Put the Computer to Sleep.** Determine how long the PC is inactive before the computer is put into sleep mode.

- **Adjust Plan Brightness**. Determine the brightness level of the display; again, a brighter display will run down your battery faster.

All of these options can be configured separately for battery and AC power.

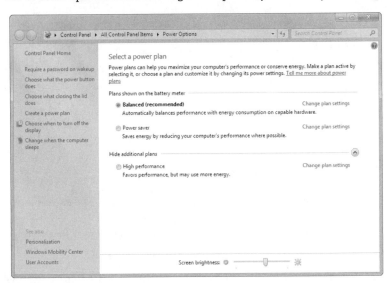

FIGURE 18.4

Managing Windows 7's power plans.

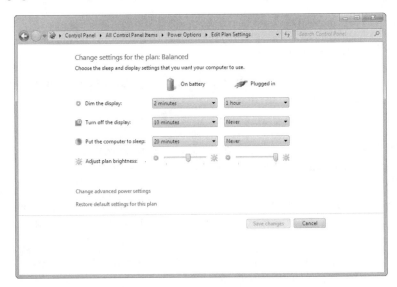

FIGURE 18.5

Editing a power plan.

Changing Advanced Plan Settings

Further plan settings can be changed by clicking the Change Advanced Power Settings link in the Edit Plan Settings window. This displays the Power Options dialog box, shown in Figure 18.6. From here you can change the following settings:

FIGURE 18.6

Changing advanced power settings.

- **Require a Password on Wakeup.** Requires that you enter a password when the computer wakes up from sleep mode.
- **Hard Disk.** Turn off hard disk after X minutes.
- **Desktop Background Settings.** Enable or disable the desktop background slideshow feature.
- **Wireless Adapter Settings.** Change the power mode for the notebook's wireless adapter (maximum performance, medium power saving, low power saving).

> **caution**
>
> Choosing anything other than maximum performance for the wireless adapter settings will reduce the range and possibly the speed of your wireless connection.

- **Sleep.** Configure sleep mode settings (sleep after X minutes, allow hybrid sleep, hibernate after X minutes).

- **USB Settings.** Enable USB selective suspend mode.

- **Power Buttons and Lid.** Change the actions for closing the lid, pressing the power button, and clicking the Start menu power button.

- **PCI Express.** Disable PCI Express link state power management.

- **Processor Power Management.** Configure your processor's minimum and maximum power states.

- **Display.** Configure several display settings: turn off display after X minutes, enable adaptive display, select screen brightness.

- **Multimedia Settings.** Configure settings for sharing media.

- **Battery.** Select what happens at critical battery levels, as well as when low-battery notification and alarm are displayed.

---

note

Not all machines show all power plan options. What settings you see sometimes varies from manufacturer to manufacturer.

Of all these settings, the most useful is probably the last. Use the Battery settings to determine when you're notified of a low-battery condition. For example, Windows is configured by default to display a low-battery-level notice when the charge drops to 10%. This may be too high for you. If so, change the Low Battery Level setting from 10% to something lower.

---

note

Depending on your notebook, the Power Options dialog box may also include some manufacturer-specific settings. For example, my Toshiba notebook includes settings for the notebook's cooling method and IEEE 1394 (FireWire) controller management.

Tips for Extending Battery Life

How long a battery charge will last depends on a number of different factors. Let's look at some of those factors now, in a series of tips that can help you extend your notebook's battery life:

- A spinning hard drive eats a lot of power. Minimize power usage by not saving your work as often to your hard drive.

- Likewise, a spinning CD/DVD drive is also tough on a battery charge. A battery that normally lasts 3 hours or more might have trouble lasting through a 2-hour DVD movie. To that end, avoid using your CD/DVD drive when on battery power—unless you're watching a movie on a plane trip, of course.

- Spreadsheet programs use virtual memory to perform complex computations, and virtual memory accesses spare storage space on your PC's hard drive. So to conserve battery power, avoid opening large Excel spreadsheets.

- Video games are processor-, graphics-, and hard disk-intensive— which means they can drain your battery fast. When playing a graphics-intensive game, plug into AC power.

- Your notebook's display is another big drain on available power. To make your battery last longer, turn down the screen brightness. (This is a big deal; tweaking the brightness down by 25% might give you an extra half-hour of battery life.)

- Audio is also a power drain. To conserve battery life, don't use your notebook to listen to music while you work.

- If you're not connecting to a Wi-Fi hotspot, turn off your notebook's built-in wireless adapter. A wireless adapter constantly sending and receiving radio signals can be a significant power drain.

- The same goes for Bluetooth wireless, if your notebook is so equipped. Turn off the Bluetooth when you're not using it to make your battery last longer.

- A cool battery lasts longer than a warm one. For that reason, avoid keeping your notebook in a hot car and try to provide adequate ventilation and cooling while working.

caution

Lithium ion batteries are particularly susceptible to heat. To that end, if you leave a notebook in a hot car all day, the computer may prevent you from powering up until it cools down enough to safely access the battery.

- Remember to use your battery from time to time. A battery that is never used has its life span reduced. Try to work on battery power at least once every 2 weeks.

- If you're not going to be using your battery for more than a month, remove it from your notebook and store it in a cool, dry place. Try to remove the battery when it has about 40% power left; some residual charge is necessary to keep the battery operational during extended storage.

- Once you have your battery broken in, avoid frequent full discharges. With lithium ion batteries, several partial discharges are better than one deep one.

- To clean dirty battery contacts, use a cotton swab and alcohol. This helps maintain a solid connection between the battery and your notebook.

- Things to avoid: Short-circuiting the battery. Dropping, hitting, or otherwise physically abusing the battery. Exposing the battery to rain or moisture. Placing the battery too close to fire or other sources of extreme heat. Storing the battery in below-freezing conditions.

- To keep working after your notebook's battery runs down, buy and carry a second battery with you. (And remember to keep that second battery fully charged!)

caution

Before you switch batteries in a notebook, you must turn off the notebook. Removing the battery while the notebook is still running on battery power may result in damaged files or applications.

Recalibrating Lithium Ion Batteries

Fortunately, today's lithium ion batteries do not suffer from the memory effect found on older NiCad batteries. You can partially discharge a lithium ion battery as often as you like with no ill effect.

Instead, notebooks that use lithium ion batteries sometimes have fuel gauge problems. In essence, short discharges with subsequent recharges mess up the calibration between the battery itself and your notebook's fuel gauge. That is, the battery and the gauge get out of sync.

To recalibrate the fuel gauge, you need to do a full discharge and subsequent recharge. In fact, to keep your notebook's fuel gauge properly calibrated, you should do a full discharge/recharge for every 30 partial discharges of your battery. If you don't do this, the fuel gauge will become increasingly less accurate.

The Bottom Line

I know, I know, that's a lot to deal with when it comes to batteries. But if you want to get every last minute's use of your PC when on battery power, you have to do some of these things. Even if it's just a matter of tweaking your power plan, you can make your battery last as long as possible for the type of computing you do. And when you're operating without a power cord, that's an important thing.

19

Backing Up and Restoring Data

Part of having Windows 7 your way is making it run faster—which is what this final section of the book is all about. Optimizing Windows 7 can take many forms, from configuring some basic settings to making hard-core registry tweaks. But before you attempt any type of optimization, you want to make sure your existing data is safe, just in case you screw something up.

Consider this chapter, then, a bit of pre-optimization advice. It's all about backing up your files and your system so that you can restore everything to its previous condition in the off chance that one of those tweaks goes bad.

Backing Up Your Files with Windows Backup

Safe optimization means protecting your system in case something you change changes more than you expected—and messes up your system. Later in this chapter I'll show you how to recover from an upgrade that actually downgrades system performance, but right now we need to discuss protecting your system against this type of screw up.

That said, the first thing on your system you want to protect is your data—all your Word documents, Excel spreadsheets, digital photos, music tracks, browser favorites, email messages, and the like. You do this by making backup copies of everything that's important to you.

Choosing a Backup Device

The easiest way to back up your data files is to use an external hard disk. These days you can get a very large drive (500GB to 1TB in size) for around a hundred dollars or so, which makes not backing up fairly inexcusable—especially if you plan on poking around under your system's hood. Make sure you get an external drive about the same size as your PC's internal hard disk, so that there's plenty of space for your backup files.

Alternately, you can back up over your network to a separate PC or server. Several companies are selling low-cost "home servers," most running Microsoft's Windows Home Server software. A home server is essentially a freestanding computer without a monitor, mouse, or keyboard; other PCs on your network can access its hard disk to store and retrieve all manner of data files—which makes it perfect as a backup device.

> **note**
>
> To learn more about Windows Home Server, see *Windows Home Server Unleashed*, by Paul McFedries (Sams Publishing).

Whether you back up to an external hard drive connected directly to your PC, or to a home server connected indirectly (over your network), you need to run a software program that automates the backup process. Most external hard drives come with their own proprietary backup programs; these are typically easy to use and get the job done. You can also use one of the many third-party backup programs sold at your local computer or electronics store, such as Acronis True Image (www.acronis.com) or CMS Bounceback (www.cmsproducts.com/product_bounceback_software.htm). You'll typically pay from $50 to $100 for one of these programs.

> **tip**
>
> Another alternative is to back up to an online backup service. This approach requires a fast Internet connection, as you copy all your files over the Internet to the backup service. The advantage to this approach is that your files are always there, even if your computer and normal backup device are both damaged, as in a flood or fire. The disadvantage is cost; you'll pay a monthly or yearly fee for this type of service. Some of the most popular online backup services include Carbonite (www.carbonite.com), IDrive (www.idrive.com), Mozy (www.mozy.com), and SOS Online Backup (www.sosonlinebackup.com).

Configuring an Automatic Backup

That said, you don't have to purchase a separate backup program. That's because Windows 7 has its own backup program built into the operating system. Like freestanding backup programs, Windows Backup lets you quickly and easily schedule automatic backups of your key data.

Follow these steps to set up an automatic backup using the Windows Backup utility:

1. Open the Control Panel and select Backup and Restore.
2. When the next window appears, click Set Up Backup.
3. This launches the Windows Backup program, shown in Figure 19.1. Select where you want to back up your data—to an external hard disk, or to a CD or DVD disc.
4. If you're running Windows 7 Professional, Enterprise, or Ultimate and want to back up to another computer on your network (including a home server), click the Save on a Network button. When the Select a Network Location window appears, as shown in Figure 19.2, click the Browse button to navigate to and select a computer and folder for the backup; then enter your network user name and password. Click OK to return to the Set Up Backup window.

---

note

The network backup option is only available on the Professional, Enterprise, and Ultimate editions of Windows 7—*not* the Home Premium edition.

---

5. Back in the Set Up Backup window, click the Next button.
6. When the next screen appears, select Let Windows Choose and click Next.
7. On the final Review Your Backup Settings screen, click Save Settings and Run Backup to perform your first backup.

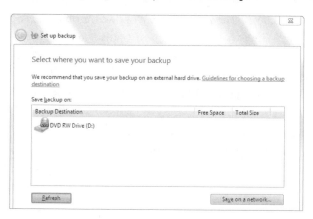

FIGURE 19.1

Use Windows Backup to back up your valuable data files.

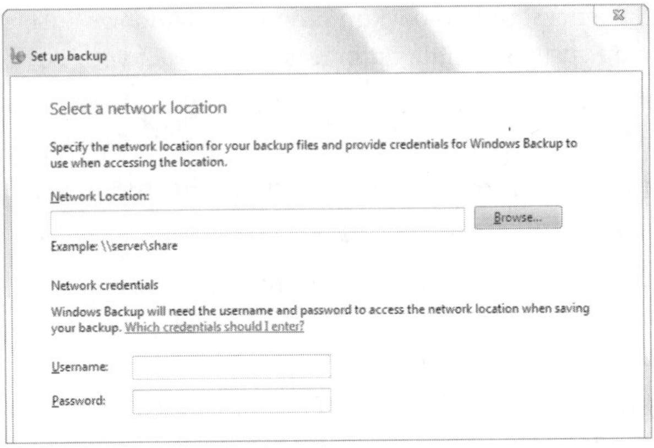

FIGURE 19.2

Backing up to a location on your network.

> **note**
>
> Windows Backup performs what is called an *incremental* backup. That is, it does-
> n't back up every file every time; it only backs up those files that are new or
> have changed since the last backup.

Choosing What to Back Up

The steps outlined in the previous section create a default backup set. This backs up all the files in your Documents folder, other key data files (including Outlook email and contact folders), and important system files. While this is sufficient for most users, you may want to back up more or fewer files than in the default set. You may also want to schedule more frequent backups, or change the time of day that backups occur. Fortunately, Windows lets you fully customize your backups.

To change *what* you backup, return to step 6 of the previous instructions—the What Do You Want to Back Up? screen. Instead of selecting the Let Windows Choose, select Let Me Choose and click Next. As you can see in Figure 19.3, you now see a tree with the following options:

- **Data Files—Back Up Data for Newly Created Users.** This backs up all the data for all users on the computer.

- **Data Files—Guest's Libraries.** This backs up any data files created by the Guest account—if the Guest account is enabled on your machine.

FIGURE 19.3

Selecting what locations to back up from.

- **Data Files—*Yourname* Libraries.** This is the one that really matters; it's all your personal files. Expand this selection to select just what files are backed up. You can opt to back up your Documents, Music, Pictures, and Videos libraries, as well as additional locations.

- **Computer.** Expand this selection to select individual drives, folders, and subfolders on your system.

Put a check mark by those items or locations you want to include in the backup; uncheck those items you don't want to back up.

Choosing *When* to Back Up

By default, Windows Backup backs up your data once a week (Sunday at 7:00 p.m.). To change the backup schedule, return to step 7 of the previous instructions and click the Change Schedule link.

You now see the window shown in Figure 19.4. Make sure the Run Backup on a Schedule option is selected; then click the How Often button and select either Daily, Weekly, or Monthly backups. If you select Weekly, click the What Day button and select which day of the week you want; if you select Monthly, click the What Day button and select which day of the month you want. Click the What Time button and select when you want the backup to start, and then click the OK button. Your backup will now be set to start on the specified schedule.

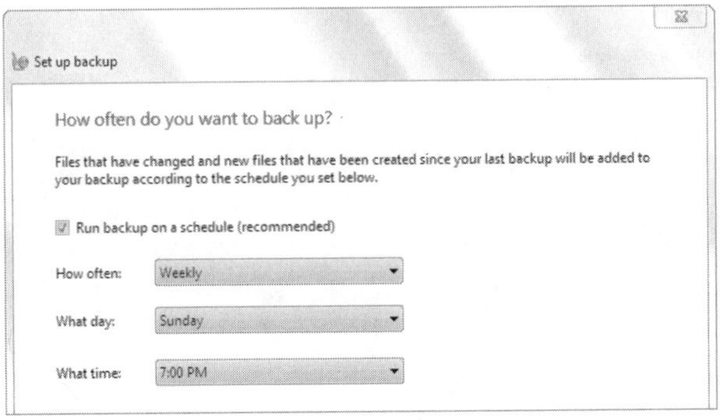

FIGURE 19.4

Setting a backup schedule.

Backing Up Your *Entire* Hard Disk

A normal back up only backs up data files—one at a time. These files can then, of course, be restored from their backup copies—again, one at a time.

Windows 7 also offers the option of making a *mirror* of your hard drive—in essence, a full system backup. This type of backup creates a carbon copy of everything loaded onto your hard drive, including documents, programs, and the Windows operating system itself. In the event of a catastrophic system failure, you can copy the mirror of your hard drive onto another hard drive, thus recreating your entire system.

You probably don't want to use this option for daily backups; it simply takes too long to do and requires too much hard disk space. That said, it's a good idea to do this type of full system backup on a periodic basis, once a month or once every few weeks, just in case the worst happens and you lose your entire hard disk.

To create a full system backup, you must have a backup device that is at least as large as the drive you're backing up. You then follow these steps:

1. Open the Control Panel and select Backup and Restore.

2. When the Backup and Restore window appears, click Create a System Image in the tasks panel.

3. When the Where Do You Want to Save the Backup? window appears, as shown in Figure 19.5, select the backup location—an external hard disk, one or more blank DVDs, or a location on your network. If necessary, select which hard drive or network computer and folder you want to use. Click Next when ready to proceed.

4. When the next window appears, confirm your backup settings and then click the Start Backup button.

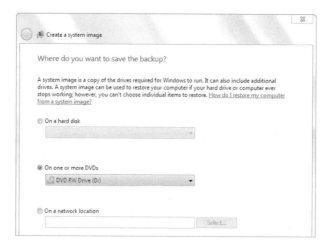

FIGURE 19.5

Configuring a full system backup.

note

A full system backup can only be done manually; you can't set up an automatic version on a schedule.

It will take some time to perform a full system backup. For that reason, it's probably good to do this overnight—and to back up to a single hard drive or network location, so that you don't have to insert new blank DVDs throughout the entire process.

Restoring Backed Up Files

Restoring files you've backed up is relatively easy, all things considered. You can restore all the files you've backed up, or restore only selected files.

To restore your data, make sure the backup disk is connected to or inserted into your computer, and then follow these steps:

1. Open the Control Panel and select Backup and Restore.

2. When the next screen appears, select Restore My Files to restore your personal files.

3. On the next screen, select Browse for Folders to select which folders to restore, or select Browse for Files to restore individual files from the backup. (You can also click the Search button to search for specific

files to restore.) When you locate a folder or file you want to restore, click the Add button.

4. When you're done adding files and folders to restore, click the Next button.

5. When the next window appears, select the In the Original Location button—unless, for some reason, you want to restore these files to a different location.

6. Click the Restore button to restore the selected files.

Restoring System Files with System Restore

While backing up document files is important—you never want to lose important data—it's more likely that any optimization gone haywire will mess with Windows' system files, not your data. In this instance, if you can restore Windows to a working condition, all your data will be where it's supposed to be, no restoring from a backup necessary.

To this end, it's important that you utilize Windows' System Restore utility. This utility can automatically restore your system to the state it was in before you messed things up. It's a great safety net for when things go wrong.

System Restore works by monitoring your system and noting any changes that are made when you install new applications. Each time it notes a change, it automatically creates what it calls a *restore point*. A restore point is basically a "snapshot" of key system files (including the Windows Registry) just before the new application is installed.

If something in your system goes bad, you can run System Restore to set things right. Pick a restore point before the problem occurred (such as right before a new installation), and System Restore will undo any changes made to monitored files since the restore point was created. This restores your system to its preinstallation—that is, *working*—condition.

To restore your system from a restore point, follow these steps:

1. Open the Start menu and select All Programs, Accessories, System Tools, System Restore.

2. When the System Restore window appears, click Next.

3. When the next window appears, as shown in Figure 19.6, select your desired restore point. (Check the Show More Restore Points option to view more restore points.) Make your choice and click Next.

4. When the confirmation screen appears, click the Finish button.

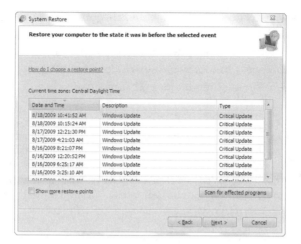

FIGURE 19.6

Use the System Restore utility to restore damaged programs or system files.

> **caution**
>
> System Restore will help you recover any damaged programs and system files, but it won't help you recover damaged documents or data files—so you'll still need to back up your data on a regular basis.

Windows now starts to restore your system. You should make sure that all open programs are closed because Windows will need to be restarted during this process.

When the process is complete, your system should be back in tip-top shape. Note, however, that it might take a half-hour or more to complete a system restore—so you'll have time to order a pizza and eat dinner before the operation is done!

Creating a System Repair Disk

There's one more safety-oriented thing you should do before attempting any major optimization of your system, and that's creating a system repair disk. You can use this disk to reinstall Windows just in case you muck things up so badly that you can't even get things started again.

First, a bit of history. Back in the old days, every PC manufacturer used to include a copy of Windows with their new PCs. Yes, Windows was installed on the PC's hard drive, but it was nice to get a physical copy of the Windows installation CD or DVD, just in case you needed to repair or reinstall Windows itself.

Well, a few years ago PC manufacturers began to discontinue this practice, probably to save a few pennies from their manufacturing costs. (They had to pay for those discs, after all.) So today, rare is the computer manufacturer who packs in a copy of the Windows installation DVD. Users are on their own if something major ever happens.

caution

Don't confuse the system restore disk provided by some manufacturers with a true Windows installation disk. The system restore disk contains a mirror of your computer's hard disk as it shipped from the factory; using this disk reverts your system to day-one condition (complete with all the preinstalled software you don't want), but doesn't let you do a clean install of Windows itself—or repair the Windows operating system.

Unless, that is, you create your own system repair disk. Now, a system repair disk is *not* a full-blown copy of Windows; for that you still have to beg and plead with your computer manufacturer's tech support, or just break down and buy a physical copy from a local retailer. A system repair disk is the next best thing, however. You can use a system repair disk to boot your system if Windows itself won't start; it also contains system recovery tools you can use to repair broken Windows, in many instances.

tip

The best combination is a system repair disk accompanied by a full system backup. Use the system repair disk to boot your computer when Windows is broken (and attempt repairs), and then restore your system from the full system backup.

So having a system repair disk is a good thing. It would be even better if Microsoft just gave you one, but no such luck. Instead, you have to create your own—which Windows makes relatively easy to do. Just follow these steps:

1. Open the Control Panel and select Backup and Restore.

2. When the Backup and Restore window opens, click Create a System Repair Disc from the tasks panel.

3. When the Create a System Repair Disc dialog box appears, as shown in Figure 19.7, pull down the Drive list and select your CD/DVD drive.

4. Insert a blank CD or DVD disc (either will do) into your PC's drive.

5. Click the Create Disc button.

FIGURE 19.7

Creating a system repair disk.

Then, in the future, if you can't get your system to start, the system backup disk is there to use.

> **note**
>
> Learn more about using the system repair disk in Chapter 28, "Troubleshooting Windows Problems."

The Bottom Line

It pays to take precautions—especially if you intend to muck about with configuration settings, the Windows Registry, and other such stuff. To that end, you should back up your data files on a daily or weekly basis; back up your entire system on a monthly basis; and learn how to use Windows' System Restore utility. You should also create a system repair disk and keep it in a safe place, just in case you run into major league problems during the optimization process.

You may never need to use any of these recovery methods, but then again you might. And if you do run into problems, you want to be able to recover from your problems as quickly and as easily as possible—without losing a single thing that's important to you.

20

Managing System Security

There's a lot of bad stuff out on the Internet. I'm talking everything from offensive content to spyware to computer viruses to computer attacks. The threats are many, but you can counter them by using the security features built into Windows 7—as well as other programs offered by Microsoft and various third parties.

Having Windows your way, then, involves not only personalization and optimization, but a large helping of security. Read on to learn more about protecting your Windows 7 computer—your way.

Understanding Computer Threats

Windows 7 has a number of security features built in, because there are a number of different threats that can potentially damage your computer or destroy your valuable data. Most of these threats are Internet-based; let's look at the major ones.

Understanding Computer Viruses

The first and probably best-known Internet-based threat is the computer virus. People fear computer viruses, justly, but don't always do all they can to protect against a virus infection.

What exactly is a computer virus? The technical definition is that it's a malicious software program designed to do damage to your computer system by deleting files or even taking over your PC to launch attacks on other systems. A virus attacks your computer when you launch an infected software program, launching a "payload" that often is catastrophic.

Many viruses are hidden in the code of legitimate software programs—programs that have been infected, that is. When the host program is launched, the code for the virus is executed and the virus loads itself into your computer's memory. From there, the virus code searches for other programs on your system that it can infect; if it finds one, it adds its code to the new program, which, now infected, can be used to infect other computers.

If all a virus did was copy itself to additional programs and computers, there would be little harm done, save for having all our programs get slightly larger (thanks to the added virus code). Unfortunately, most viruses not only replicate themselves, they also perform other operations—many of which are wholly destructive. A virus might, for example, delete certain files on your computer. It might overwrite the boot sector of your hard disk, making the disk inaccessible. It might write messages on your screen, or cause your system to emit rude noises. It might also hijack your email program and use the program to send itself to all your friends and colleagues, thus replicating itself to a large number of PCs.

Viruses that replicate themselves via email or over a computer network cause the subsidiary problem of increasing the amount of Internet and network traffic. These fast-replicating viruses—called *worms*—can completely overload a company's network, shutting down servers and forcing tens of thousands of users offline. Although no individual machines might be damaged, this type of communications disruption can be quite costly.

Other viruses open a back door to your system that can then be exploited by the virus writer. These types of backdoor viruses turn your machine into a so-called *zombie computer*, which the hacker operates via remote control to perform all manner of nefarious tasks. Hijacked computers of this sort are responsible for a large number of computer attacks and spam campaigns.

In short, viruses are nasty little bits of computer code, designed to inflict as much damage as possible, and to spread to as many computers as possible—a particularly vicious combination.

Just how can you catch a computer virus? In general, you're open for infection any time you share computer data with others. Since there are lots of ways to do this, there are also many ways a virus can be transmitted:

- Opening an infected file attached to an email message or instant message

- Launching an infected program file downloaded from the Internet
- Sharing a data CD, USB memory drive, or floppy disk that contains an infected file
- Sharing over a network a computer file that contains an infected file

Of all these methods, the most common means of virus infection is via email—with instant messaging close behind. Whenever you open a file attached to an email message or instant message, you stand a good chance of infecting your computer system with a virus—even if the file was sent by someone you know and trust. That's because many viruses "spoof" the sender's name, thus making you think the file is from a friend or colleague. The bottom line is that no email or instant message attachment is safe unless you were expressly expecting it—and even then, an expected file attachment could still be infected with a virus, without the sender knowing it.

Understanding Spyware and Adware

Spyware is similar to computer viruses. Like Trojan horse viruses, spyware typically gets installed in the background when you're installing another program, without your knowledge or consent. Unlike a virus, however, spyware doesn't replicate itself; its job is to spy on your system, not to spread itself to other computers.

That's right, spyware surreptitiously sends information about the way you use your PC to some interested third party—and that's not a good thing. Spyware can record the addresses of each web page you visit, the contents of each email and instant message you send or receive, the email addresses of people you correspond with, the user names and addresses of your IM partners, the contents of each chat room you visit, and every you keystroke you type with your computer keyboard—including user names, passwords, and other personal information.

The information recorded by the spyware is typically saved to a log file. That log file, at a predetermined time, is transmitted (via the Internet) to a central source. That source can then aggregate your information for marketing purposes, use the information to target personalized communications or advertisements, or steal any confidential data for illegal purposes.

And it's not just about the information that spyware records. Spyware can also slow down your computer; the added load of spyware programs in your system's memory inevitably leads to sluggish performance, at the very least. In addition, some spyware programs do more than just slow down your system, instead hijacking your computer and launching pop-up windows and advertisements when you visit certain web pages. If there's spyware on your computer, you definitely want to get rid of it.

Then there's a special type of spyware called *adware*, which is used by advertisers and marketers to gather information about your consumer behavior. Like other types of spyware, adware is typically placed on your PC when you install some other legitimate software, piggybacking on the main installation. After it is installed, the adware works like spyware, monitoring your various activities and reporting back to the host advertiser or marketing firm. The host firm can then use the collected data in a marketing-related fashion—totally unbeknownst to you, of course.

note

Technically, you have to agree to adware installation—although the agreement is typically buried in the boilerplate terms of a service agreement you agree to.

Unfortunately, spyware of all types is relatively easy to encounter; it can get onto your computer in many of the same ways that viruses infect your PC. Typical means of transmission include email attachments, misleading links on websites, and files downloaded from the Internet.

Some of the biggest sources of spyware are peer-to-peer music-trading networks. Not legitimate online music stores, such as Apple's iTunes Store, which are almost totally free of viruses and spyware, but instead the rogue file-trading networks, such as BitTorrent, Blubster, and LimeWire. In many instances, spyware is actually attached to the file-trading software you have to download to use the network; when you install the software, the spyware is also installed. (And you can't remove the spyware without also removing the host software—which causes some users to keep the spyware!)

Another way to have spyware installed on your system is to be tricked into doing it. You go to a website, perhaps one mentioned in a spam email message, and click on a link there. What you see next looks like a standard Windows dialog box, asking you whether you want to scan your system for spyware, or optimize your Internet browsing, or something similar. In reality, the "dialog box" is just a pop-up window designed to look like the real deal, and when you click the Yes button, you're authorizing the installation of spyware on your system. In some instances, clicking No also installs the software, so you're damned if you do and damned if you don't.

Understanding Computer Attacks

Beyond viruses and spyware (collectively dubbed malicious software, or *malware*), one of the scariest threats to your system's safety and security comes when malicious individuals stage an attack on your computer or network. Attackers access your system via some sort of back door and then steal important data, delete files and folders, or use your computer to initiate additional attacks on other computers, networks, or websites. Particularly malevolent attackers can even flood your system with data requests and emails, overloading your system until it crashes or goes offline.

This type of attack typically takes place over the Internet, with the operation executed by a remote computer or a master computer controlling a network of hijacked zombie computers. In most instances, computer attacks are directed at large computer networks or websites, typically by an individual with a grudge against the organization attacked. Malicious attacks against individual computers are more rare but not unheard of, again especially if the attacker has a grudge against the victim of the attack.

Fortunately, computer attacks can be defended against by using a *firewall* program, which blocks unauthorized users from accessing your computer or network. Most network routers come with firewalls built-in; Microsoft Windows also includes its own firewall as part of the operating system. The Windows Firewall is enabled by default, thus protecting you from most outside attacks. In addition, third-party companies sell even stronger firewall software; there's no reason not to be protected against this type of attack.

Understanding Phishing Scams and Identity Theft

The final online security threat is that of *identity theft*. This occurs when someone steals your personal identifying information—whether that be your credit card number, Social Security Number, or ATM PIN.

note

Identity theft is, more accurately, fraud rather than theft. Even though your identity is stolen, that information is used for fraudulent activities. Hence the more proper designation as *identity fraud*.

Identity theft can be the result of online negligence (responding to phishing emails or being the victim of a computer virus) or real-world theft (having your wallet stolen or credit card statements pilfered from your trash).

However it's accomplished, the identity thief obtains one or more of your valuable numbers, and then uses those numbers to access things that are yours—typically, your money.

Online, the most common cause of ID theft is *phishing*. This is a particular type of email scam that extracts valuable information from the victim, using a series of fake emails and websites.

In essence, a phishing email is one designed to look like an official email message from a trusted institution, such as your bank or eBay or PayPal. In reality, the email is a clever forgery, down to the use of the original firm's logo. The email is designed to get you to click on an enclosed link that purports to take you to an "official" website. That website, however, is also fake. Any information you provide to that website is then used for various types of fraud, from simple user name/password theft to credit card and identity theft.

note

The term *phishing* derives from the attempt to "fish" for the victim's information. The spelling is influenced by the word *phreaking*, a slang term for hacking into public telephone networks.

The key to the phishing scam is the link to the website within the original email message. At first glance, this appears to be a legitimate link. But if you hover your cursor over the link, you'll see that the actual URL is different from the one visible in the text. In other words, clicking the link doesn't take you to where you think you're going, but to a completely different web page.

note

This redirection of a link from one website to another fake one is called *pharming*.

Typically, the URL for this link in a phishing email is a very long and involved address that's actually a bit hard to read. The first part of the address might look legitimate, but the URL doesn't stop there. If you follow the complete URL, it takes you not to the expected website, but to the phisher's carefully constructed forgery.

The counterfeit website is where the final scam takes place. Like the official-looking email, the web page on which you land is designed to look as authentic as possible. But even though the site might look official, if you look closely at the address bar at the top of your web browser, you'll find that the URL listed there is not the official site's URL. This is a spoof web page; if you enter the requested information (your user name, password, account number, Social Security Number, you name it), that info is transmitted to the con artist behind the phishing scam—and used to steal your identity.

The primary defense against phishing scams is simple: Never click a link in an email message, no matter how official it may look. Even if you think it's a legitimate communication, manually enter the company's official URL into your web browser; you can then check your account for any action that might be necessary. It's clicking the link in the email that gets you into trouble.

You can also rely on technology built into Microsoft Windows and your web browser to protect against phishing scams. Windows 7 includes a SmartScreen Filter that flags suspected phishing emails and websites and warns you if you try to access known phishing sites. This works within all Microsoft email programs and the Internet Explorer browser; other web browsers have similar anti-phishing filters. Enable these filters and be aware for any warning messages they generate.

Using the Windows 7 Action Center

In Windows 7, all your security- and maintenance-related activities are monitored in a utility called the Action Center. This where you go to check to see if your system is properly protected.

You access the Action Center by opening the Control Panel and selecting Action Center. As you can see in Figure 20.1, the Action Center is divided into two main sections—Security and Maintenance. The security-related features are in the Security section; the maintenance-related features are in the Maintenance section. You expand each section by clicking the down arrow next to the section name.

The Security section of the Action Center, shown in Figure 20.2, includes information about all sorts of security-related items, from the Windows Firewall to User Account Control.

note

When you're running the Microsoft Security Essentials software, Action Center's Security section also includes a number of MSE-related items. Learn more about MSE in the "Defending Against Malware with Microsoft Security Essentials" section, later in this chapter.

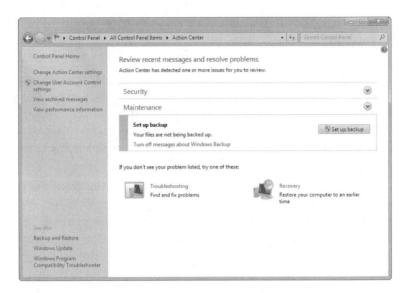

FIGURE 20.1

The Windows 7 Action Center.

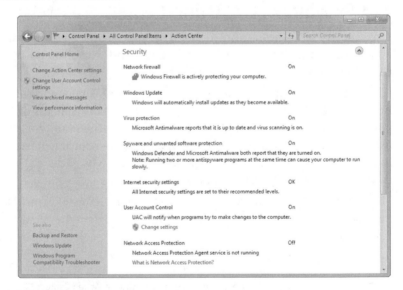

FIGURE 20.2

Security-related items in the Action Center.

If anti-virus or anti-spyware capabilities are not activated or updated on your system, an alert to that effect is displayed in the Security section of the Action Center. You can then click the button within the alert to restore these functions to normal operation.

Likewise with the Action Center's Maintenance section. If there's a maintenance-related task that needs to be performed (like backing up your data), you see an alert to that effect. Click the button within the alert to perform the requested task.

Defending Against Attacks with the Windows Firewall

While computer attacks are rare, they are also devastating. For that reason, you need to block potential attacks with a firewall program, which forms a virtual barrier between your computer and the Internet. The firewall selectively filters the data that is passed between both ends of the connection and protects your system against outside attack.

To better protect your system, Windows 7 has its own built-in firewall program. The Windows Firewall is activated by default, although you can always check to make sure that it's up and working properly. To access the Windows Firewall, open the Control Panel and select Windows Firewall. As you can see in Figure 20.3, this window displays the state of your firewall protection, as well as offering a variety of configuration options in the task panel. We'll look at each option separately.

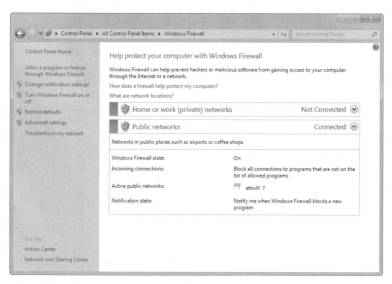

FIGURE 20.3

Monitoring the Windows Firewall.

Allow a Program or Feature Through Windows Firewall

Many programs need to get through the firewall to access the Internet and do their thing. While the Windows Firewall allows most outbound requests from programs, it blocks most inbound data—which could be responses needed for the program to work problems. With that in mind, click the Allow a Program or Feature Through Windows Firewall link to manage the list of programs that are allowed through the firewall.

When you click the link, the Allowed Programs window, shown in Figure 20.4, appears. This window lists programs that are allowed through the firewall. To edit this list, click the Change Settings button and then check those programs you want to have access.

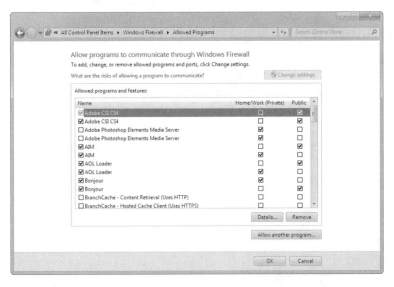

FIGURE 20.4

Managing access through the firewall.

To add more programs to this exceptions list, click the Allow Another Program button. When the Add a Program dialog box appears, as shown in Figure 20.5, select the program you want to add then click the Add button.

If you've allowed a program through the firewall by mistake and later want to revoke this access, click the Change Settings button and *uncheck* that program. You can even click the Remove button to permanently remove that item from the exceptions list, although that technically isn't necessary.

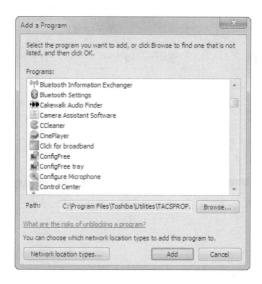

FIGURE 20.5

Enabling firewall access for a new program.

Change Notification Settings

By default, Windows Firewall notifies you whenever it blocks a new program trying to access the Internet. If you'd rather not be notified, click the Change Notification Settings link. When the Customize Settings window appears, as shown in Figure 20.6, uncheck the Notify Me When Windows Firewall Blocks a New Program, for either private or public networks. (Or both.)

> **tip**
>
> You can also use the Customize Settings window to block *all* incoming connections, which is one way to make things super safe. Know, however, that doing so will also block all incoming communications for programs you've previously approved, which can impact the way these programs run.

Turn Windows Firewall On or Off

What if you don't want to run Windows Firewall? Maybe you've installed a different firewall program and want to (need to) disable Windows Firewall. Or maybe you're having problems getting a program to run, or running into difficulties establishing a connection with another computer on your network—both issues that can be caused by an overly aggressive firewall. Bottom line, there are instances where you might want to disable the firewall.

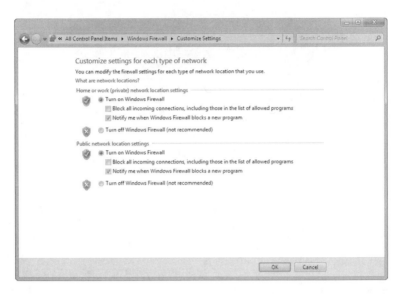

FIGURE 20.6

Changing Windows Firewall's notification settings.

To do so, click the Turn Windows Firewall On or Off link, which again opens the Customize Settings window. Check the Turn Off Windows Firewall option for whatever type of network you're on, and then click OK.

caution

Disabling the Windows Firewall leaves your system unprotected from computer attack. Do so at your own risk.

Restore Defaults

Want to restore the default settings for Windows Firewall? Then click the Restore Defaults link. That should do the job.

Advanced Settings

Finally, there are times where more technical users or IT staff might need to get their hands dirty and access the rules that Windows Firewall uses to determine what to block and what not to block. If you're so inclined, click the Advanced Settings link; this displays the Windows Firewall with Advanced Security window, shown in Figure 20.7.

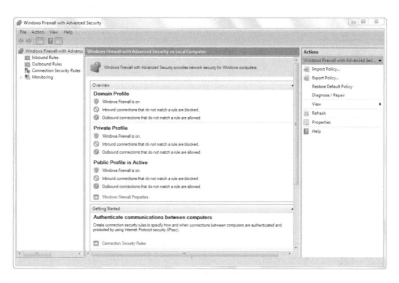

FIGURE 20.7

Configuring Windows Firewall's many advanced rules.

The actions available here are too numerous and detailed to explain in this book—although if you're an IT guy, you'll know exactly what they mean and do. Suffice to say, you can tweak these rules to block specific programs and types of programs, or let those programs through the firewall. It's a matter of editing the inbound rules, outbound rules, and connection security rules. You can also select the Monitoring option to examine what's happening with the firewall in near real-time.

Let's walk through a simple example of the kinds of things you can do. This example creates a new rule to allow inbound traffic from a specific program. Start by selecting Inbound Rules in the task pane, and then click New Rule in the Actions pane (on the right). When the New Inbound Rule Wizard window opens, select Program and click the Next button. On the next screen, click the Browse button to browse for and select the program you want to have access, and then click Next. You now see the screen shown in Figure 20.8, which prompts you for the action to take. For example, let's enable only secure inbound connections, so check the Allow the Connection If It is Secure option and click Next. On the next screen, check all the options (Domain, Private, and Public), and then click Next. Finally, you're prompted to give the rule a name and description; do so and then click the Finish button. The new inbound rule is now created and added to the inbound list you see in the Windows Firewall with Advanced Security window.

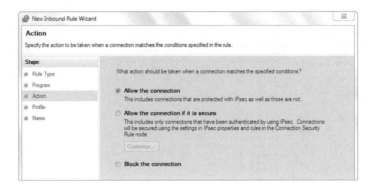

FIGURE 20.8

Creating a new inbound firewall rule.

There's a lot more here for those who need it. While casual users can pretty much ignore this stuff, IT professionals will find this a valuable tool to make the Windows Firewall work *their* way.

Defending Against Spyware with Windows Defender

Now we come to the issue of spyware. There are many anti-spyware utilities out there, but you can probably make do with the one that's included free with Windows 7.

Windows Defender is Microsoft's anti-spyware utility; it's built into Windows 7 and available as a free download for older versions of Windows. It's one of the better anti-spyware utilities out there, performing not only manual spyware scans but constantly monitoring your system for new spyware infestations.

You access Windows Defender by opening the Control Panel and selecting Windows Defender. The Defender window, shown in Figure 20.9, displays your system's current status; if no problems are present, you get a nice green message to that effect.

Scanning for Spyware

As noted, Windows Defender constantly monitors your system for spyware. You can also perform a manual scan of your system, by clicking the Scan button in the Defender toolbar. This will take a few minutes, but is a good precaution if you think you may have recently been infected.

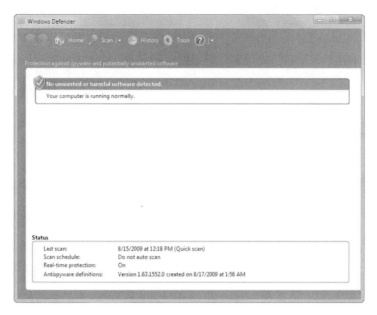

FIGURE 20.9

Defending against spyware with Windows Defender.

Configuring Windows Defender

You can also configure Windows Defender to automatically scan your system on a specified schedule. To do this, follow these steps:

1. From Windows Defender, click the Tools button.

2. When the Tools and Settings screen appears, click Options.

3. When the Options screen appears, as shown in Figure 20.10, select Automatic Scanning from the tasks panel.

4. Check the Automatically Scan My Computer option.

5. Click the Frequency button and select how often/when you want the scan performed: Daily (performed the same time every day) or on a specific day of the week (performed once a week on that day).

6. Click the Approximate Time button and select the time of day you want the scan performed.

note

Your computer must be turned on at the specific day and time for the scan to be performed.

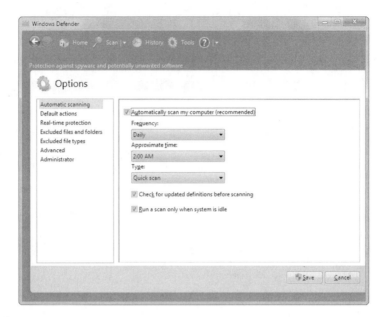

FIGURE 20.10

Configuring an automatic spyware scan.

7. Click the Type button and select either Quick Scan or Full Scan.

8. Check the Check for Updated Definitions Before Scanning option; this ensures that Defender has the latest list of spyware and adware programs before the scan commences.

9. Check the Run a Scan Only When System is Idle to keep Defender from scanning while you're using your computer—and thus slowing down system performance.

10. Click the Save button.

Defender will now perform the specified type of spyware scan on the schedule you determined.

Understanding Scan Types

When you set up automatic scanning, you had the option of doing either a Quick or Full scan. What's the difference between the two?

A Quick scan, as the name implies, is a relatively fast scan, taking no more than a few minutes. The reason this type of scan is so quick is that it doesn't scan your complete system. Instead, it scans only those locations on your hard disk that spyware is most likely to infect. It's quick, yes, but not inclusive.

For a more thorough scan, choose the Full option. This scans your entire system, leaving nothing to chance. It will take a bit longer, however—an hour or more, depending on the size of your hard disk and how fast your computer is. This type of scan is best scheduled during the overnight hours, when your computer is not otherwise in use.

Dealing with Spyware

What happens when Defender finds spyware on your system? In most instances, you'll receive an onscreen notification letting you know what was found and asking for your input. At this point you can opt to delete the offending program, quarantine it (move it to an unaccessible location on your hard drive, where it won't do any harm), or ignore it.

The first option is best when you're dealing with an obvious spyware program that's known to steal personal information or affect the running of your system. The quarantine option is best if you're not completely sure what you're dealing with; you can always restore a quarantined item or delete it completely when you receive additional information. Ignoring the file leaves it as-is on your computer, and is the best option when Defender flags what is actually a legitimate program—albeit one with spyware-like tendencies.

Additional Options

There are lots of other options available in Windows Defender, but I'm going to skip over them for the time being. That's because they essentially duplicate options found in Microsoft Security Essentials, which is Microsoft's full-fledged anti-malware program—which we discuss next.

Defending Against Malware with Microsoft Security Essentials

Defending against spyware is just part of the package. To fully protect your system, you need to protect against all types of malware—including both spyware and viruses.

To that end, I recommend using Microsoft Security Essentials (MSE for short), Microsoft's free anti-malware program. Unlike Windows Defender, which defends only against spyware and adware, MSE defends against *all* forms of malware—computer viruses, spyware, and adware.

Also unlike Windows Defender, MSE is not built into Windows 7; you have to download it separately. Since MSE is a free program, downloading it is no different than downloading any of the Windows Live applications.

note

MSE runs on Windows 7, Windows Vista, and Windows XP. Your version of Windows needs to be an official one—validated by Microsoft. In addition, you need to be using either Internet Explorer (6.0 or later) or Mozilla Firefox (2.0 or later) as your web browser.

By the way, if you've used Microsoft's previous anti-malware program, Windows Live OneCare (now discontinued), you'll find MSE somewhat but not completely familiar. That's because, while MSE is based on OneCare, it doesn't include all of OneCare's functionality. In particular, MSE drops OneCare's firewall and file backup features. (You'll have to go back to Windows' built-in firewall and backup utilities—which, in Windows 7, are quite adequate.)

Downloading and Installing MSE—For Free

Remember, MSE is a free program. Anyone can download it, and if your PC meets the requirements just stated, it will install and run on your system.

To download and install MSE, go to the Microsoft Security Essentials website, located at www.microsoft.com/security_essentials/. Click the Get It Now button and follow the onscreen instructions; when the download is finished, the installation should start automatically.

tip

The Microsoft Security Essentials website is also the place to find additional information about MSE—and about malware protection, in general.

How MSE Works

Like most anti-malware programs, MSE offers a variety of different defenses against viruses and spyware. MSE not only checks files on your hard disk, but also files you try to download or copy to your hard disk. These checks are typically done on some sort of schedule, either daily or weekly, and whenever a new file is introduced to your system.

In addition, if MSE discovers that an application running on your PC is exhibiting suspicious behavior, it enables its Dynamic Signature Service.

This feature automatically checks for updates to the definitions library, and then compares the suspect application to the definitions.

And what happens when MSE finds a virus or spyware program on your PC? First, it asks you what you want to do. You have the option of removing the suspect file from your computer, moving the file to a special quarantined section on your computer's hard disk, or just ignoring the warning and leaving the file as-is. If you don't provide input within 10 minutes, MSE performs a default action (depending on the severity of the threat) on the suspected malware file.

note

To protect your system against any possible mistakes, MSE creates a System Restore point before deleting any malware.

It's important to know that when you install MSE, it replaces and deactivates Windows Defender. That's because MSE includes Windows Defender technology as part of its own anti-malware defenses; running both MSE and Defender at the same time would be needlessly duplicative.

Using MSE

MSE launches automatically whenever you start up your computer and open Windows. It runs completely in the background; in most cases, you'll never even now it's there.

While MSE runs silently in the background, you can open the MSE window to view the program's operations and configure key settings. To open MSE, click the Microsoft Security Essentials icon in the notification area and select Open from the pop-up window. Alternately, you can open the Windows Start menu and select All Programs, Microsoft Security Essentials, Microsoft Security Essentials.

This opens the MSE window, shown in Figure 20.11. From here you can view the status of your computer's protection, deal with any imminent threat, and configure the program for your system.

To make it easy for you to understand your system's status, the MSE is color coded via a bar at the top of the window and an icon on the Home tab. Table 20.1 details the three status levels.

This bar is color-coded: Green means your computer is protected;
yellow means that there is some risk; and red means there is immediate risk.

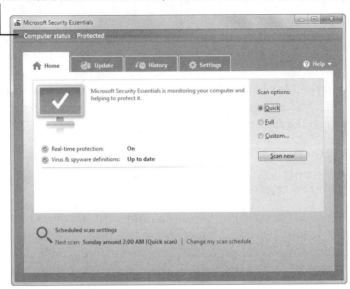

FIGURE 20.11

Microsoft Security Essentials—Microsoft's free anti-malware program.

Table 20.1 MSE Status Levels

Status Level	Description
Good (green)	MSE is running and protecting your system. No actions need to be taken.
Fair (yellow)	MSE is not fully protecting your system; some action needs to be taken. Note that this doesn't indicate a pending disaster; most often, it's for something simple such as the malware definitions being out of date or some of the program's functionality being disabled. MSE will indicate what you need to do to bring the protection back to the green level.
At risk (red)	There is an immediate threat to your system. MSE has encountered an active virus or spyware program and needs to take action.

The MSE window automatically opens when some action needs to be
taken at either the yellow or red levels. You typically don't see the window
when MSE is operating at the green level.

Setting Up Automatic Scanning

While MSE performs real-time scanning on all new files you introduce to
your system, it's still a good idea to periodically scan your entire computer
system for any malware that might already be installed. You can opt to
schedule scans once a day or once a week, at the time you specify.

To set up automatic scanning for your system, follow these steps:

1. Click the Settings tab.

2. Select Scheduled Scan from the tasks pane, as shown in Figure 20.12.

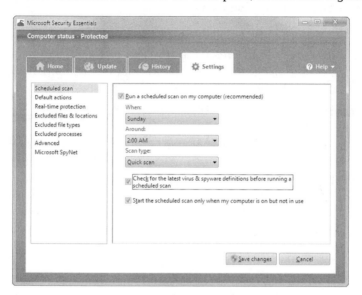

FIGURE 20.12

Configuring MSE for automatic scanning.

3. Check the Run a Scheduled Scan on My Computer option.

4. Click the When button and select how often/when you want the scan performed: Daily (performed the same time every day) or on a specific day of the week (performed once a week on that day).

5. Click the Around button and select the time of day you want the scan performed.

note

Your computer must be turned on at the specific day and time for the scan to be performed.

6. Click the Scan Type and select either Quick Scan or Full Scan.

7. If you want MSE to update its malware definitions before starting the automatic scan, check the Check for the Latest Virus & Spyware Definitions Before Running a Scheduled Scan option.

8. If you'd prefer not to initiate a scan when you're actually using your computer, check the Start the Scheduled Scan Only When My Computer Is On but Not in Use option.

9. Click the Save Changes button.

Let's examine that final option a bit. Scanning your computer requires significant use of system resources; if you try to scan and work on your computer at the same time, you'll notice your PC's performance getting quite sluggish. For that reason, you probably don't want to scan and work simultaneously, and thus select that final option to scan only when you're computer is not in use.

When should you schedule your scan? Keeping in mind that scanning affects system performance, most users schedule their scans when they know they won't be using their PCs—typically sometime in the overnight hours. That might be midnight or it might be 3:00 a.m., depending on your personal schedule. Make sure the scan starts after you stop working but ends before you start up again.

note
A scan can take anywhere from a few minutes to close to an hour, depending on the number of files on your system and the speed of your PC.

How often should you scan? I like scanning every day; this way you're protected from any malware introduced to your system within the past 24 hours. Other users consider once a week often enough, and it might be if you don't do a lot of file downloading and such. In general, though, you get more protection if you scan more frequently, and there's no harm at all in scanning daily as opposed to weekly. Just make sure that your computer is turned on when you have the scan scheduled; MSE can't scan your computer unless it's up and running!

Determining Default Actions

What does MSE do when it encounters a file it suspects as being malware? It all depends on the default actions you configure.

MSE specifies four different levels of threat: Severe, High, Medium, and Low. For each level it offers a recommended action, or you can choose from two or more optional actions (depending on the alert level). The four threat levels, as well as available actions, are detailed in Table 20.2:

note

The recommended action varies for each individual type of malware. The action is outlined in the malware definition itself; for one virus, the recommendation might be to automatically delete it, while for another it may be to quarantine it. This is also true for spyware, where some definitions dictate automatic deletion or quarantine, while other definitions (for less dangerous items) recommend leaving the file as-is.

Table 20.2   Alert Levels and Default Actions

Alert Level	Type of Threat	Available Actions
Severe	Especially malicious viruses, worms, or other malware that can damage your computer and affect your security and privacy.	Recommended action Remove Quarantine
High	Viruses or spyware that can possibly collect personal information, change system settings, and otherwise affect your privacy or impact the operation of your system.	Recommended action Remove Quarantine
Medium	Similar to a High threat, but with less serious ramifications. Typically spyware or adware that might affect your privacy or make changes to your computer settings, without your express agreement or knowledge.	Recommended action Remove Quarantine Allow
Low	Potentially unwanted software, but generally not a major threat. Typically spyware or adware that might collect information about you or your computer—but within the terms of the program's licensing agreement.	Recommended action Remove Quarantine Allow

By default, the default action for each level is Recommended Action—that is, you let MSE determine what to do. However, you may want to configure the program to be either more or less strict for specific types of threats.

For example, if you want to automatically remove any spyware or adware—even those programs that were installed with your express permission—you can set the default action for the Medium and Low levels to Remove. Likewise, if you'd rather not delete all potential malware files, you can set the Severe and High level actions to Quarantine rather than Remove; this way you can examine and, if you like, restore any suspicious files manually.

To set the default actions, follow these steps:

1. Click the Settings tab.
2. Select Default Actions from the tasks pane, as shown in Figure 20.13.

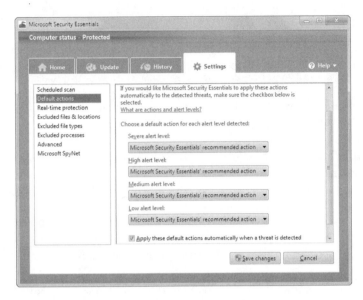

FIGURE 20.13
Configuring MSE's default actions.

3. Pull down the list for each alert level and select the desired default action.

4. Check the Apply These Default Actions Automatically When a Threat Is Detected.

5. Click the Save Changes button.

Excluding Locations, File Types, and Processes

By default, MSE scans all the files and folders on your system when doing an complete scan and when performing real-time scanning. If you have a big hard disk that's fairly well filled up, this can add a lot of time to the scan—or slow down your system during real-time scanning. You can speed things up by *excluding* certain locations, file types, and processes from the scan; the less there is to scan, the faster the scan will be.

If you have specific folders that you know don't contain malware (for example, archived photos or music tracks), you can exclude these locations from MSE's scans. To specify which locations (drives, folders, or subfolders) to exclude, follow these steps:

1. Click the Settings tab.

2. Select Excluded Files & Locations from the tasks pane.

3. Click the Add button.

4. When the next dialog box appears, navigate to and select the drive or folder you wish to exclude from the scan; then click OK.

5. Back in the MSE window, click the Save Changes button.

Some types of files are highly unlikely to contain malware, but still can add time to a typical scan. For example, JPG photo files are almost impossible to infect, and probably don't need to be scanned. To specify which types of files to exclude, follow these steps:

1. Click the Settings tab.

2. Select Excluded File Types from the tasks pane.

3. Enter the extension for the file type you wish to exclude into the first box.

4. Click the Add button.

5. Repeat steps 3 and 4 to exclude additional file types.

6. Click the Save Changes button.

Windows includes a lot of different processes as part of its system files; it takes some time to scan all of these processes, and thus you can speed up your scans by excluding them. That said, these files are the ones most likely to host malware, so excluding processes from your scans can leave your system at risk. If you want to take the risk—and speed up your scans—follow these steps:

1. Click the Settings tab.

2. Select Excluded Processes from the tasks pane.

3. Click the Add button.

4. When the next dialog box appears, navigate to and select the specific process file you want to exclude from the scan; then click OK.

5. Back in the MSE window, click the Save Changes button.

caution

Even processes you think are safe can still become infected from outside sources. For that reason, you probably should not exclude processes from your MSE scans.

Configuring Advanced Options

MSE also includes a handful of advanced options that you can configure as you like. Some of these options improve security; others make the program a little easier to use. To access these advanced options, follow these steps:

1. Click the Settings tab.

2. Select Advanced from the tasks pane, as shown in Figure 20.14.

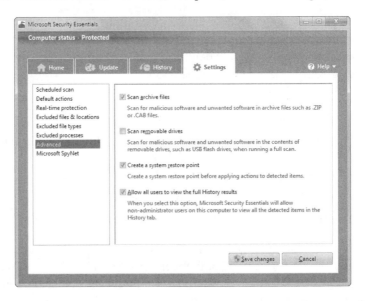

FIGURE 20.14

Configuring advanced options.

3. Check those options you want to enable, and uncheck those you don't want to run.

4. Click the Save Changes button.

What options are we talking about? Here's the list:

- **Scan Archive Files.** This scans the contents of ZIP and CAB compressed/archived files, which is a good idea; malware is often hidden in compressed files. Activated by default.

- **Scan Removable Drives**. This scans all removable drives connected to your system—external hard drives, USB drives, and the like. It's a good idea to scan these drives, even though it can slow the entire scan. Not activated by default; if you want to scan these drives, you'll have to check this option.

- **Create a System Restore Point**. This option creates a System Restore point before MSE deletes or quarantines any suspected malware files.

This is a good safety precaution; if you accidentally delete or quarantine a file necessary for Windows to run, you can use Windows' System Restore feature to restore your system to the condition it was in prior to the file action. Activated by default.

- **Allow All Users to View the Full History Results.** This enables any user of your computer to view items detected by MSE. Activated by default.

Participating in Microsoft SpyNet

There's one final option available to you, if you so desire. MSE lets you participate in Microsoft SpyNet, an online community devoted to the malware fight.

When you opt to participate in SpyNet, MSE sends information about the malware it detects to the SpyNet site. This information helps Microsoft provide better protection for its users.

One on hand, participating in SpyNet is a good thing; you're helping to provide information about malware threats. On the other hand, SpyNet itself can be viewed as a form of SpyWare; it is sending information about what's on your PC to a central database. Even though the intentions are good (and done with your approval), it's still a spyware technique.

If you decide to participate in SpyNet, you have two levels of membership to choose from:

- Basic, which sends information about any malware detected, where the item came from, actions taken, and whether those actions were successful.

- Advanced, which sends even more details, including the location of the flagged item on your hard drive, the filename, how it operates, and how it impacted your computer.

caution

Microsoft says that personal information might end up your SpyNet submissions. It also claims that this information will not be used to identify you or contact you.

SpyNet is activated by default, at the Basic level. If you want to change to the Advanced level, follow these steps:

1. Click the Settings tab.
2. Select Microsoft SpyNet from the tasks pane.

3. Select the Advanced Membership option.

4. Click the Save Changes button.

Updating MSE

As noted previously, MSE operates by comparing the files on your computer with known malware files. If it finds a match, it then takes the appropriate defensive action.

For MSE to do its thing, then, it needs to access a continually updated database of malware definitions. You can configure MSE to update its definitions library on a regular basis; you can also download the latest definitions manually, if you like.

By default, MSE downloads new malware definitions once a day. That should be often enough to catch newly created viruses and spyware. But you can also manually download the latest malware definitions. Just follow these steps:

note

Your computer must be connected to the Internet to download malware definitions.

1. Click the Update tab, shown in Figure 20.15.

2. Click the Update button.

FIGURE 20.15

Manually updating MSE's malware definitions.

That's it; MSE will now go online and retrieve the latest malware definitions.

tip

You can also use the Update tab to view when your definitions were last updated. This tab lists the date and time the current definitions file was created, as well as the version for both the virus and spyware definitions library.

Understanding Scan Types

Key to MSE's operation is the system scan—scanning the files on your computer for known or suspected malware. As discussed previously, scanning can be either automatic or manual. But you might not know that MSE offers several different types of scans, with different levels of effectiveness.

The two primary types of scans offered by MSE are Quick scans and Full scans. As you might suspect, a Quick scan takes less time than a Full scan—but doesn't scan as many files as the latter type of scan.

A Quick scan is designed to scan those areas of your hard disk that are most likely to contain malware; it skips those areas that offer little or no danger. It's likely that a Quick scan will only take a few minutes on your system.

note

What locations get scanned with a Quick scan? We're talking about any programs currently running in memory, key system files, and the Windows Registry.

Obviously, a Quick scan doesn't offer a full system check, but that's not the point. You use the Quick scan when you think you might have an immediate problem, or if your system is typically clean and you just want a quick checkup.

When you want more complete protection, do a Full scan. Unlike the Quick scan, which only scans running programs and system files, a Full scan scans all the drives and folders and files on your computer—including system files and the Windows Registry.

Obviously, a Full scan takes longer than a Quick scan—several hours on a typical system. But it will find malware buried in obscure places, if problems exist.

Because of the length of time it takes to do a Full scan, you should probably initiate it (either automatically or manually) when you expect to be away from your computer for an extended period of time. Most users schedule or start a Full scan overnight, when they're asleep.

Performing a Manual Scan

You can perform a Quick or Full scan at any time. All you have to do is follow these steps:

1. Click the Home tab.

2. Select which type of scan you want to perform—Quick, Full, or Custom.

3. Click the Scan Now button.

> **note**
>
> A Custom scan only scans those locations that you specify.

If you selected the Quick or Full options, the scan now commences. If you selected the Custom option, MSE displays a dialog box that lets you select which locations to scan. Click the + button next to a drive or folder to expand that item, and then check those locations you want to include in the scan. Click OK when all the items are selected.

MSE now begins the selected scan, displaying its progress on the Home tab. This screen displays the type of scan running, when the scan was started, how much time has elapsed, the number of items scanned, and (if you can read that fast), the current item being scanned.

> **tip**
>
> If a scan is taking longer than you'd like, you can cancel it mid-scan by clicking the Cancel Scan button.

When a scan is complete MSE displays the results on the Home tab. These results tell you how many files were scanned and whether any threats were detected.

Scanning from Windows Explorer

When you're using MSE with Windows 7, you get some nice integration with the operating system. First, MSE's status appears in the Windows 7 Action Center. Second, you can now scan individual folders and drives from within Windows 7.

That's right, you don't have to open MSE and perform a full system scan. Instead, if you suspect a problem file in a particular location (such as a file you've recently downloaded into a specific folder), you can scan just that folder.

All you have to do is open Windows Explorer and navigate to and select the drive or folder you want to scan. Right-click the folder and select Scan with Microsoft Security Essentials from the pop-up menu; MSE now scans the selected location and displays its results. If a suspicious item is found, it displays the normal alert message and asks for your action.

Alerting You to the Threat

MSE can spot a malware infection either during a system scan or while performing real-time scanning. But what happens then?

If threats are found during a scan (manual or automatic), MSE automatically acts on the flagged files as you've previously configured. Unless configured differently, MSE will automatically delete high-risk files such as viruses, and it will automatically ignore low-risk files, such as approved programs with spyware-like tendencies. For those threats in the middle, such as unauthorized spyware and adware, it will ask you what you want to do.

MSE also alerts you if it finds a threat during its real-time scanning. This typically happens if you download or copy a file to your hard drive that contains spyware or a virus.

When an issue is discovered, the Home tab in the main MSE window displays an alert, much like the one in Figure 20.16. The Home tab also displays a big Clean Computer button, which will prove useful when it comes time to address the problem.

When an alert is found during real-time scanning, MSE displays a smaller alert dialog box, like the one shown in Figure 20.17. This dialog box focuses on the specific threat at hand, and lets you directly determine the action to take.

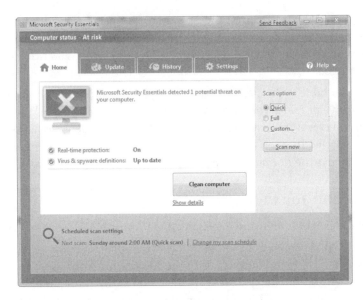

FIGURE 20.16
A malware threat detailed on MSE's Home tab.

FIGURE 20.17
Alert—MSE just discovered malware on your system!

Choosing the Right Action

When MSE prompts you to take an action about a malware threat, what should you do? Well, the action you take depends to a degree on what MSE found.

If MSE found a severe or high-level threat (typical of most viruses), your best bet is to simply delete the file. This is most easily accomplished by clicking the Clean Computer button on the Home tab.

If MSE found a medium- or low-level threat, however (typical of most spyware and adware), the course of action is less clear. Some spyware is more harmful than others; in fact, some files that exhibit spyware-like behavior are actually legitimate programs that you definitely don't want to delete.

When the course of action isn't clear, you should read more about what MSE found. You do this by clicking the Show Details link on the Home tab or in the specific alert dialog box. This opens the Potential Threat Details window, which displays more additional information about the detected item. In most instances, this will include a recommendation on how to deal with the problem.

At this point, you have either two or three options, depending on the threat level. These options are detailed in Table 20.3.

Table 20.3   Available Actions for Suspicious Files

Action	What It Does	When to Use It	When *Not* to Use It
Remove	Permanently deletes the suspicious file from your system.	The best option when you have an obvious computer virus.	Shouldn't use if you think a system file is infected; there is no way to restore a deleted file.
Quarantine	Moves the suspicious file to a quarantined area of your hard drive, where it can't affect system performance.	A good option when you think a system file might be infected, or if it's a program file that might be able to be fixed (i.e., have the virus removed).	Not the best option to use for all infections, as the quarantined area takes up valuable disk space; it's still better to permanently delete files you know you don't need to restore.
Allow	Ignores the suspicious file, enabling it to run as intended. MSE will no longer alert you to risks posed from this software.	The proper action if the suspicious file is legitimate— and you okay its behavior. You should choose this option only if you fully trust the flagged program and the company behind it.	A really bad choice if an actual spyware or virus file was flagged; it will keep doing its thing without any additional warnings being made.

If you're sure that a file is a known virus or spyware program, select Remove to permanently delete it. If you're not sure about the file, select Quarantine so that it won't harm anything, but you still keep it on your hard drive in case you change your mind in the future. And if you know a file is completely safe (and thus was wrongly flagged), select Allow to keep the file intact.

You select which action to perform from either the original alert dialog box or the Potential Threat Details window. Follow these steps:

1. Click the button in the Recommendation column. For severe and high-level threats, you'll see the Remove and Quarantine options; for medium-and low-level threats, you'll see the Remove, Quarantine, and Allow options.
2. Select the action you want to take from the list.
3. Click the Apply Actions button.

MSE will now perform the action you selected, either deleting, quarantining, or ignoring the suspicious item. When the action is completed, it displays a dialog box confirming that your actions were applied successfully.

Viewing Your Scanning History

MSE keeps a record of all items that it has found. To view this scanning history, click the History tab, shown in Figure 20.18. From here, you can view three types of items:

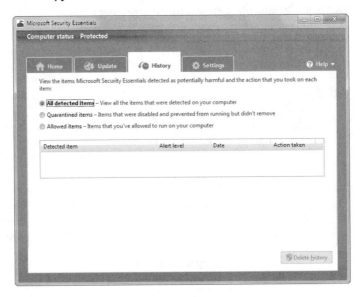

FIGURE 20.18

Viewing your complete scanning history.

- **All Detected Items.** Select this option to view every single potential threat found by MSE—including those deleted, quarantined, and ignored.

- **Quarantined Items.** Select this option to view all items that have been quarantined.

- **Allowed Items.** Select this option to view all potential threats that you have chosen to ignore.

For each item, you see the item's name, the alert level for that item (severe, high, medium, or low), the date the item was flagged, and either the recommendation for or action taken on that item. Select an item to view more details about that item from Microsoft's definitions library.

Restoring and Removing Quarantined Items

When an item has been deleted, there's not much more you can do; it's gone. But when you quarantine an item, it's still sitting on your computer, waiting for you to either remove it or restore it—both of which you do from the History tab.

Naturally, you should only take further action on a quarantined item once you determine that it's either safe to keep or safe to delete. If you're not sure which is the case, continue to keep it in quarantine.

When you think it's safe to take action against a quarantined item, follow these steps:

1. Click the History tab.
2. Select the Quarantined Items option.
3. Select the item in question.
4. To permanently delete the item, click the Remove button.
5. To restore a safe item, click the Restore button.

Removing Previously Allowed Items

What if you find an item that you previously allowed actually is causing some harm to you or your system? Well, MSE takes this contingency to mind and provides an option to remove items that you passed on removing the first time around. Again, this is done from MSE's History tab.

Follow these steps:

1. Click the History tab.
2. Select the Allowed Items option.
3. Select the item in question.
4. Click the Remove button.

> **tip**
>
> You can permanently delete all previously allowed items in a single step by clicking the Remove All button.

Protecting Your Wireless Network

If you have a wireless network installed in your home or office, you have additional potential security problems. That's because all the data on a wireless network is broadcast over the air via radio waves, for anyone within range to grab. Unless you take precautions, malicious hackers can access your PC and steal important data, delete files and folders, or use your computer (via remote control) to attack other computers.

How to Protect Your Wireless Network from Unwanted Intrusion

If the threat of unwanted intrusion scares you, that's good—you should be scared. Fortunately, you can take a number of steps to reduce your risk of attack and to minimize the impact if an intrusion does occur.

The key to protecting a network is to create as many obstacles as possible for a potential attacker. Although no network can be 100% secure, the more effort an attacker has to make, the more likely he'll give up and try a network that's easier to break into.

So how can you protect against unauthorized access to your wireless network? By using a little common sense, along with enabling basic security procedures, including the following:

- Activate the wireless security technology built into your Wi-Fi router. This wireless security, in the form of encrypted or password access, should keep all but the most dedicated hackers from accessing your wireless network.

- Change the default password for your wireless router. (You'd be surprised how many wireless networks can be accessed by entering the default "PASSWORD" password.)

- Change the default network name (also called a *service set identifier,* or *SSID*) of your wireless access router.

- Disable broadcast SSID function on your wireless router (if possible), so that the name of your network isn't publicly broadcast to the world at large.

- Physically locate your wireless router toward the center of your home or office—not near the windows, where it can extend the range of your network well outside your building.

- Install and activate a firewall program on every PC on your home network to block attacks from outside your network.

- Install and regularly update anti-virus and anti-spyware utilities on each PC on your network.

- Deactivate file sharing on your PCs, so attackers won't be able to access your personal files.

- Make regular backup copies of your important data—just in case.

Understanding Wireless Security

One of the chief defenses against unwanted intrusion is to enable wireless security on your network. This is done by assigning a fairly complex encryption code, called a *network key*, to your network. To access your network, a computer must know the code—which, unless it's officially part of your network, it won't.

There are several ways to assign a network key to your network. Most wireless routers come with configuration utilities that let you easily activate this type of wireless security, typically during the router's installation/setup process. In addition, you can use Windows' built-in wireless security function, which adds the same encryption via the operating system.

This network key may be generated automatically by your network router or adapter, or you may have to specify the key by typing it yourself. The longer the network key, the greater the encryption—and the more secure your wireless network will be.

There are four types of wireless security in use today, with the most secure listed first:

- **WPA2.** WPA stands for Wi-Fi Protected Access, and the new WPA2 standard offers the strongest level of security available today. With WPA2 (and the older WPA standard), network keys are automatically changed on a regular basis.

- **WPA.** This is the older, slightly less secure version of Wi-Fi Protected Access security, still a good choice for securing most small networks.

- **WEP 128-bit.** *WEP* stands for *Wired Equivalent Privacy*. There are two levels of WEP protection, the stronger 128-bit and the weaker 64-bit.

- **WEP 64-bit**. This is the weakest level of wireless protection available. If you have an older laptop PC or wireless adapter, you may have to use this level of protection instead of WEP 128-bit or WPA/WPA2.

You should choose the highest level of protection supported by all the equipment on your network—your wireless router, wireless adapters, and notebook PCs. If just one piece of equipment doesn't support a higher level of security, you have to switch to the next-highest level; the security level you choose has to fit the lowest common denominator, as defined by the wireless equipment in use.

So if your wireless router and all your wireless adapters and notebook PCs support WPA or WPA2 encryption, you should switch to that method because it provides the strongest protection. Otherwise, choose either WEP 128-bit (preferred) or WEP 64-bit encryption.

Enabling Wireless Security

You can assign security codes to all the PCs in your network in one of two ways. First, most wireless hubs, routers, and adapters come with configuration utilities that let you activate this type of wireless security. If your wireless equipment has this type of configuration utility, use it.

Otherwise, you can use Windows' built-in wireless security. To enable wireless security in Windows 7, follow these steps:

1. Open the Control Panel and select Network and Sharing Center.

2. From the Network and Sharing Center, click Set Up a New Connection or Network.

3. When the next window opens, select Set Up a New Network and click Next.

4. Windows should now automatically detect your network hardware and settings. Follow the onscreen instructions to enter your network's SSID name, and then either automatically assign or manually enter a network key. The type and length of the key you choose depends on the type of encryption you choose; the strongest encryption comes from a 26-character WEP key.

note

SSID stands for *Service Set Identifier*, which is a set of letters or numbers that identify a particular wireless network. You create the SSID when you initially install and configure your router.

After the network key is assigned, write it down. You'll need to run this wizard on all the other PCs on the network and manually enter this same key for each computer. (Alternatively, Windows lets you save the key to a USB drive, which you can then transfer to your other PCs.) After all the work is done, only those PCs that have been assigned this specific key can connect to your wireless network—which means no more neighbors leeching off your wireless connection.

caution

Without some form of wireless security, anyone with a wireless PC can tap into your wireless network. At the very least, they can steal bandwidth from your Internet connection. Worst case, they might be able to access the personal files stored on your PC.

Protecting Your Network's SSID

Every wireless network has a name, otherwise known as its SSID (Service Set Identifier). The SSID is assigned by your wireless router.

Many router companies use their company names as the default SSID. For example, a Linksys router might have an SSID labeled "LINKSYS." This type of common SSID could give your network the same name as other wireless networks in your neighborhood, which makes it easy for hackers to locate and gain access to your network.

note

Sometimes the router adds a unique number to this name, such as "LINKSYS123." This type of unique numbering is more secure than generic naming but still is easily found by potential hackers.

For this reason, you should override your router's default SSID and assign a more unique name to your wireless network. It's going to be tougher for a hacker to guess that your network is named "MIKE_NETWORK_1007" than if it was generically named "LINKSYS." You should be able to change the SSID from your router's configuration utility.

caution

If you change your SSID after you've set up other computers on your network, you'll need to reconfigure them to find and use the new SSID.

Along the same lines, you should also change the default password for your router. Most routers come from the factory with a simple password assigned; often, the password is "PASSWORD." As you might suspect, it's relatively easy for a hacker to access a network if the default password is still in use. So when you go to change the router's SSID, change the password, too. (And the longer and more complex the password you create, the more difficult it will be to hack.)

Disabling SSID Broadcasting

Most wireless routers, by default, constantly broadcast the network's SSID, so that all nearby computers will know that the network is there and ready to be connected to. The downside of this is that when an SSID is broadcast, anyone with a laptop PC or other wireless device receives notice of your network's name—which makes your network a more obvious target for hackers.

For this reason, you should configure your router to disable SSID broadcasting. If the SSID is not broadcast, your wireless network will be less visible to outsiders. When a hacker doesn't immediately see your network on his list of nearby wireless networks, he'll likely find another network to tap into.

As with changing the SSID, you should be able to turn off SSID broadcasting from your router's configuration utility.

> **caution**
>
> When you disable SSID broadcasting, your own wireless computers won't be able to see your network either. This means you'll have to enter the SSID manually when you go to connect.

Using Third-Party Security Tools

So far we've discussed those security tools—firewalls, anti-malware programs, and the like, either built into Windows 7 or offered free of charge by Microsoft. But there are other tools available that you may want to consider—to truly protect your computer *your way*.

Using Third-Party Firewall Software

For most users, the Windows Firewall is more than enough protection against computer attacks. That said, there are also a number of third-party firewall programs available, most of which are more robust and offer more protection than Windows' built-in firewall. The most popular of these programs include

- Comodo Firewall+AntiVirus (free, personalfirewall.comodo.com)
- Lavasoft Personal Firewall ($29.95, www.lavasoft.com)

- Outpost Firewall Pro ($39.95, www.agnitum.com/products/outpost/)
- PC Tools Firewall Plus (free, www.pctools.com/firewall/)
- Sunbelt Personal Firewall ($19.95, www.sunbelt-software.com/ Home-Home-Office/Sunbelt-Personal-Firewall/)
- ZoneAlarm Free Firewall (free, www.zonealarm.com)
- ZoneAlarm Pro ($39.95, www.zonealarm.com)

Using Anti-Virus Software

Microsoft Security Essentials is a good anti-virus program, but it's not the only one out there. Chief competitors include the following:

note

Pricing for most anti-virus software is actually for a one-year subscription. You'll end up paying this figure every year to keep the software and its virus definitions up to date.

- avast! Home Edition (free, www.avast.com)
- avast! Professional Edition ($39.95, www.avast.com)
- AVG Free (free, free.avg.com)
- AVG Anti-Virus ($34.95, www.avg.com)
- F-Secure Anti-Virus ($39.99, www.f-secure.com)
- Kaspersky Anti-Virus ($59.95, www.kaspersky.com)
- McAfee VirusScan Plus ($29.99, www.mcafee.com)
- Norton AntiVirus ($39.99, www.symantec.com)
- Panda Antivirus Pro ($39.95, www.pandasecurity.com)
- Trend Micro AntiVirus + AntiSpyware ($39.95, www.trendmicro.com)
- Webroot AntiVirus with AntiSpyware ($39.95, www.webroot.com)
- ZoneAlarm Antivirus ($29.95, www.zonealarm.com)

Some of these programs are simple anti-virus utilities; others, like MSE, are full-fledged anti-malware suites, protecting against both viruses and spyware. Still other programs include additional features, such as a firewall, content filter, and the like. In general, the more you pay the more features you get. Of course, you may not want or need all the features, so determine your needs before you buy.

caution

All of these anti-virus programs do a good job—sometimes *too* good. I have personally experienced problems with Norton and McAfee anti-virus products being too aggressive in protecting my system, resulting in system slow-downs and numerous program crashes. If you find your computer slowing down or freezing up after installing an anti-virus program, you may need to uninstall that program and try another.

caution

You might think that running multiple anti-virus programs would increase your system's security. Unfortunately, that's not the case—and, in fact, multiple anti-virus programs are likely to interfere with each other. You should only run *one* anti-virus program at a time on your system; if you want to change anti-virus programs, delete the previous program before you install the new one.

Using Anti-Spyware Software

Windows Defender is an able anti-spyware utility. But there are other equally able anti-spyware programs out there, most of them free or low-cost. The best of the bunch include the following:

- Ad-Aware Free (free, www.lavasoftusa.com)
- Ad-Aware Plus ($26.95, www.lavasoftusa.com)
- CounterSpy ($19.95, www.sunbelt-software.com)
- ParetoLogic Anti-Spyware (free, www.paretologic.com/products/paretologicas/)
- Spybot Search & Destroy (free, www.safer-networking.org)
- Spyware Doctor (free, www.pctools.com/spyware-doctor/)
- Webroot Spy Sweeper ($29.95, www.webroot.com)

tip

Some of the major Internet security suites, such as Norton Internet Security and the McAfee Internet Security Suite, include anti-spyware modules. Check the program's feature list before you buy.

Note that while any of these programs will do a good job, they won't always catch all the spyware that's out there. In fact, no single spyware program can catch everything; there's just too much spyware floating around! For that reason, I use two different anti-spyware programs—Windows Defender plus one of the other free programs. Either utility will catch spyware that the other utility misses.

The Bottom Line

Knowing everything that can happen to you and your computer system while you're on the Internet can cause some users to unplug their PCs and hide underneath the covers. While that kind of fear is understandable, it's also manageable—by utilizing all the security features available to users of Windows 7. While it's easy to be the victim of an attack, it's equally easy to protect your system—and continue using Windows your way.

21

Managing Printers, Devices, and Drivers

Having Windows your way means configuring your entire system the way you like it. This includes all the various external devices you connect to your computer—printers, scanners, iPods, digital cameras, and the like. Fortunately, it's relative easy to manage these devices—if you know what you're doing, of course.

Installing and Managing Printers

Let's start with the most popular external peripheral, the computer printer. You can connect all types of printers to your system—inkjet printers, laser printers, black and white printers, color printers, photo printers, even so-called multifunction printers that also offer scanning, copying, and faxing capabilities.

Connecting a Printer

How you connect a printer to your system depends on the printer itself. Most printers today connect via USB, which makes things relatively easy; just connect a USB cable between the printer and the PC, and your computer should recognize the new device and install the appropriate drivers.

In some instances, however, you may want or need to use the installation disc that came with your printer. This disc typically includes the printer's device drivers and some sort of printer management program—which you may not need to use, but could make managing the printer a little easier.

note

Some printers connect via the older parallel connection. Most computers still have a parallel port on the back (sometimes labeled LPT1); if you connect your printer in this fashion, you definitely will need to use the printer's installation disc to get the proper drivers installed.

Installing a New Printer from Within Windows

You can also install a new printer from within Windows itself. While this probably isn't necessary with a USB printer, it may be the only way to properly install an older parallel printer. Follow these steps:

1. Open the Start menu and select Devices and Printers.

2. When the Devices and Printers window opens, click the Add a Printer button.

3. When the What Type of Printer Do You Want to Install screen appears, click Add a Local Printer.

4. When the Choose a Printer Port screen appears, check the Use an Existing Port option; then pull down the port list and select the appropriate port. Click Next when done.

5. When the Install the Printer Driver screen appears, select the manufacturer and model number of your printer, if listed. Click Next when ready.

note

If your printer isn't listed on the Printer Driver screen, click the Have Disk button to use your printer's installation disk.

tip

To update the list of printers on the Printer Driver screen, click the Windows Update button.

6. If prompted about what version of the driver to use, choose to use the existing driver, and then click Next.

7. When prompted for a printer name, accept the recommended name or enter a new one, and then click Next.

8. When the Printer Sharing screen appears, select whether or not you want to share the printer with other computers on your network. Click Next when ready.

9. The printer driver is now installed and the printer itself added to your system. Click the Finish button to complete the installation.

Enabling Printer (and File) Sharing

One of the benefits of a home network is being able to share a single printer among multiple PCs—a definite way to save money. In this situation, a *network printer* is one that can be printed to from any properly configured computer on your network. The printer itself is connected to a single PC, and other PCs on your network access the printer through that hard-connected computer.

You install a network PC on the host computer the same way you install any printer. For most printers, that simply means connecting the USB cable and letting Windows deal with the drivers and such. However, you then have to enable printer sharing on that PC, so that the printer can be shared across the network. For machines running Windows 7, here's how to do it:

1. Open the Control Panel and select Network and Sharing Center.
2. From the Network and Sharing Center, click Change Advanced Sharing Settings.
3. On the next screen, shown in Figure 21.1, click the down arrow next to Home or Work.
4. Click Turn On File and Printer Sharing.
5. Click Save Changes.

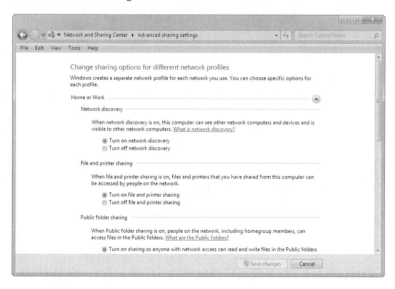

FIGURE 21.1

Enabling file and printer sharing.

> **note**
>
> You only have to enable printer sharing for the computer to which the printer is physically connected. Once printer sharing is enabled on that PC, the printer will be visible from all other computers connected to your network.

Installing a Network Printer on Other PCs

Once you have the printer physically connected and printer sharing enabled on the host PC, you then have to install the network printer on all the other computers that you want to print to this printer. From each remote PC, follow these steps:

1. Open the Start menu and select Devices and Printers.

2. When the Devices and Printers window opens, click the Add a Printer button.

3. When the What Type of Printer Do You Want to Install screen appears, click Add a Network, Wireless, or Bluetooth Printer.

4. Windows now searches for and displays all printers connected to your network. Select your printer from the list; then click Next.

5. When the next screen appears, name your printer and click Next.

6. On the next screen, print a test page if you like; then click Next.

7. If prompted to set this printer as your default printer, click Set as the Default Printer if that's what you want to do.

8. Click Finish.

After the network printer is installed, it should appear in the list of available printers whenever you choose to print a document or photo from this PC.

Managing Printers and Other Devices

Any printer you have installed on a PC—local or network—can be managed from Windows 7's Devices and Printers window. You open this window by opening the Start menu and selecting Devices and Printers. (Alternately, you can open the Control Panel and select Devices and Printers.)

Getting to Know the Devices and Printers Window

As you can see in Figure 21.2, the Devices and Printers window displays all the printers and other devices you have installed on your system. To display more information about a device, simply select it; additional information now appears in the information pane at the bottom of the window.

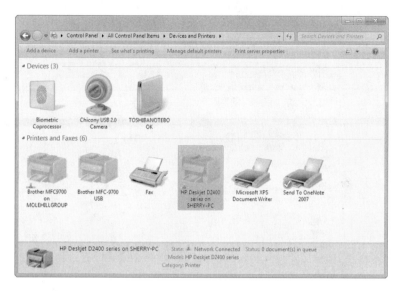

FIGURE 21.2

Use the Devices and Printers window to manage printers and other devices.

Even more information appears when you double-click the device icon. This displays a page like the one in Figure 21.3, with all sorts of useful information. In the case of a printer, you'll see whether the unit is online or offline; how many documents are currently queued up to print; and whether the printer is set for portrait or landscape printing.

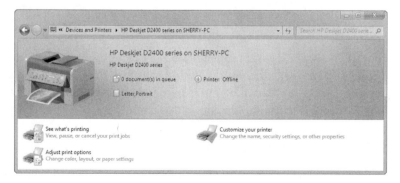

FIGURE 21.3

Viewing more information about an installed device.

Configuring Printer Settings

You can also use this screen to configure key printer settings. For example, double-click Adjust Print Options to display the Printing Preferences dialog box, shown in Figure 21.4. From here you configure the page orientation, pages per sheet, page order, paper source, and the like.

FIGURE 21.4

Configuring printing preferences for a given printer.

> **note**
>
> The options in the Printing Preferences and Properties dialog boxes differ from printer to printer.

To further customize your printer, double-click Customize Your Printer to display the Properties dialog box, shown in Figure 21.5. This dialog box lets you change a plethora of options, from the printer name to how print jobs are spooled. Have fun exploring this one!

Setting Your Default Printer

Which printer do you want to print to when you click the Print button in all your applications? That printer is called your *default* printer, and you can set your default printer from the Devices and Printers window. All you have to do is right-click the icon for the printer you want to use as your default, and then select Set as Default Printer from the pop-up menu. The default printer appears in the Devices and Printers window with a green check mark next to its icon.

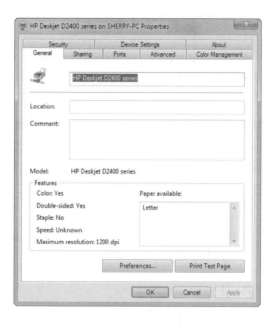

FIGURE 21.5

Configuring printer properties.

Configuring Other Devices

Of course, the Devices and Printers window isn't just about printers; you can manage all your connected devices from here. Double-click the icon for any device to open its Properties dialog box. You can then configure any and all properties for that device.

Finally, you can use the Devices and Printers window to install new devices that for some reason don't install automatically when connected. Just click the Add a Device button and Windows will look for newly connected devices; select the device from the resulting list and follow the onscreen instructions from there.

Working with Device Drivers

Throughout this chapter we've referred to something called a *device driver*. A device driver isn't a physical thing, but actually a small software program that enables your PC to communicate with and control a specific hardware device. A driver must be installed for each piece of hardware connected to your system, or Windows won't be able to work with it.

Installing Device Drivers

Fortunately, working with device drivers is relatively easy. Windows itself includes built-in device drivers for many popular peripherals. In addition, many peripherals install the proper drivers when you run their setup routine from the installation disc. More often than not, this all happens in the background.

If, for some reason, you're installing a peripheral that doesn't have an installation disc and that Windows doesn't recognize (unfortunately common with older peripherals), you can probably find and download the proper device driver from the peripheral manufacturer's website. Just go to the manufacturer's website and look for a "downloads" or "drivers" or "technical support" link. Click the link and search for your peripheral by model number. If the driver's there, you should also be able to find instructions on how to install it.

Updating Device Drivers

Once installed, you shouldn't have to worry much about a given device driver—unless, however, you begin to have trouble using the peripheral. Hardware problems like this are often caused by older device drivers that for one reason or another don't work well with recent Windows updates. That is, after a Windows update Windows itself might not be fully compatible with the version of the device driver you have installed.

In this instance, you need to update the device driver in question. Most peripheral manufacturers update their device drivers on a periodic basis; these updated drivers are available for downloading from the manufacturers' websites.

You can find and update drivers manually, from the manufacturer's website, or more easily from within Windows. Here's how to use Windows for this task:

1. Open the Control Panel and select Device Manager.

2. When the Device Manager window opens, as shown in Figure 21.6, click to expand the category for the device you want to update.

3. Double-click the device you want to update.

4. When the Properties window for that device appears, select the Driver tab, shown in Figure 21.7.

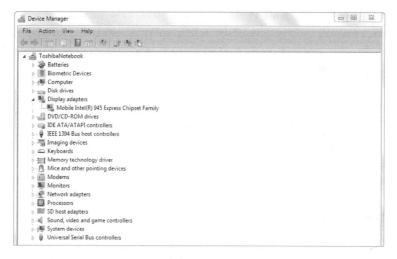

FIGURE 21.6

Managing drivers with the Device Manager.

FIGURE 21.7

Updating a driver from the Properties dialog box.

5. Click the Update Driver button.

6. When prompted, opt to Search Automatically for Updated Driver Software. This will search both your computer and the Internet for a newer version of the given driver.

If a new driver is available, follow the onscreen instructions to complete the installation. If no newer driver is available, which is often the case, you'll see a message to that effect—which means your system is as up-to-date as it can be.

caution

New problems can sometimes be introduced when you update a driver. If you experience problems after updating a driver, return to the driver Properties dialog box, select the Driver tab, and then click the Roll Back Driver button. This will uninstall the updated driver and reinstall the previous version.

The Bottom Line

While this wasn't always the case in older versions of Windows, it's relatively easy to install and manage printers and other devices on a Windows 7 PC. Just use the Devices and Printers window to configure devices your way—and, when necessary, use the Device Manager to update critical device drivers.

22

Running Problem Programs

It doesn't happen to everyone, but it could happen to you. You upgrade to Windows 7 but then find that your favorite program no longer runs. That's because not all older programs are fully compatible with Windows 7; there's no guarantee that a program written for Windows XP, let's say, will run seamlessly in the new Windows 7 environment.

Program incompatibility is particularly problematic with custom programs, such as applications written for a specific company. While it's unlikely you'll have problems running an old version of Quicken, for example, your company's six-year-old custom database program might crash and burn under Windows 7.

So if running Windows 7 your way means running whatever programs you want to run—even if they're not technically compatible with Windows 7—what do you do when you run into an incompatible program? Fortunately, there are several things to try, all of which we'll discuss in this chapter.

Running Programs as an Administrator

If you're like me, every now and then you run into a program that just won't launch. Typically it's an older program that isn't fully compatible with my current version of Windows, but other times it's a newer program that, by all accounts and purposes, should have no trouble running under Windows 7. So what gives?

Probably the most common issue behind problem newer programs is the program needs to run in *administrator mode*. That is, the program needs to do certain things that only a user with administrator access is allowed to perform. Since Windows, by default, doesn't grant administrator privileges to software programs, the application is stymied when it tries to do what it needs to do, and then shuts down.

The solution to this little conundrum is to run the program with administrator privileges. Thusly functioning as an administrator, the program can access system files, install and delete key files and registry settings, and do all that other stuff that Windows doesn't normally allow.

For example, I recently installed an update to my business's QuickBooks program. After installing the update, QuickBooks refused to run; it needed to access some protected files that it couldn't do without administrative privileges. When I reconfigured QuickBooks to run in administrative mode, it could access those previously inaccessible files and ran just fine.

Running as an Administrator—Once

Sometimes a program only needs to run as an administrator once, typically to register initial configuration settings or create some key files. Fortunately, Windows lets you launch any program as an administrator— one session at a time.

To open a program in administrator mode, follow these steps:

1. Open the Start menu and navigate to the program's shortcut.

2. Right-click the shortcut and select Run as Administrator from the pop-up menu.

At this point, User Account Control will ask you to confirm your action; you are circumventing Windows' normal security procedures, after all. Click Yes and the program launches, with full administrator privileges.

Always Running as an Administrator

What do you do if you encounter a program that always has to run with administrator privileges? Windows again supplies the answer, with the capability of configuring any program to always start in administrator mode.

Here's what to do:

1. Open the Start menu and navigate to the program's shortcut.

2. Right-click the shortcut and click Properties from the pop-up menu.

3. When the Properties dialog box appears, select the Shortcut tab.

4. Click the Advanced button.

5. When the Advanced Properties dialog box appears, as shown in Figure 22.1, check the Run as Administrator option.

6. Click OK to close this dialog box; then click OK again to close the Properties dialog box.

That's it. From now on, every time you launch the program it automatically runs with full administrator privileges.

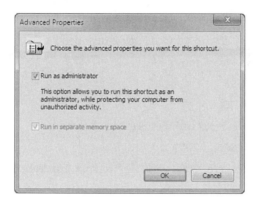

FIGURE 22.1

Configuring a program to run with administrator privileges.

Running Programs in Compatibility Mode

If it's an older program that's giving you fits, and if switching to administrative mode doesn't do the trick, chances are you have a true compatibility issue. This happens because the Windows operating system changes a lot from version to version; what's under the hood in Windows 7 is significantly different from what was under the hood in Windows XP.

The solution to an incompatible program, then, is to run that program in compatibility mode. This is a special mode that runs the program using settings from a previous version of Windows.

tip

To see if a particular program is compatible with Windows 7, visit the Windows Compatibility Center (www.microsoft.com/windows/compatibility/).

Configuring Compatibility Mode Operation

Windows 7 includes compatibility modes for several older OS versions, including the following:

- Windows Vista, no service packs installed
- Windows Vista with Service Pack 2 installed
- Windows Vista with Service Pack 1 installed
- Windows XP with Service Pack 3 installed
- Windows XP with Service Pack 2 installed
- Windows 98/Windows Me
- Windows 95
- Windows 2000
- Windows NT 4.0 with Service Pack 5 installed
- Windows Server 2003
- Windows Server 2008 with Service Pack 1 installed

caution

Running a program in compatibility mode doesn't ensure that the program will run properly in Windows 7—it only increases the chances that the program will run.

That's right, you can (at least in theory) use compatibility mode to run programs that were designed to run on Windows 95! Here's how to configure a program to run in a specific compatibility mode.

1. Open the Start menu and navigate to the program's shortcut.
2. Right-click the shortcut and click Properties from the pop-up menu.
3. When the Properties dialog box appears, select the Compatibility tab, shown in Figure 22.2.
4. In the Compatibility Mode section, check the Run This Program in Compatibility Mode For option.
5. Click the button and select the version of Windows the program is compatible with.
6. Click OK.

tip

You can also enable administrative privileges for a program from the Compatibility tab of the Properties dialog box. Just select the Run This Program as an Administrator option.

FIGURE 22.2

Configuring compatibility options for an application.

Configuring Other Program Settings

The Compatibility tab in the Properties dialog box lets you configure other settings that affect how an application runs. Sometimes changing one or more of these settings can get the program to run properly, no other adjustments necessary.

So what exactly can you configure? Here are the options:

- **Run in 256 Colors.** This option displays the program using a limited color palette. This helps run some older programs designed to run with fewer colors than is now standard.

- **Run in 640 x 480 Screen Resolution.** This opens the program in its own smaller-sized window. This helps when running programs designed for a lower screen resolution, or that you have trouble properly displaying at your system's full resolution.

- **Disable Visual Themes.** This disables Windows themes when running the program. It helps when running applications that have trouble displaying menus or buttons on the program's title bar.

- **Disable Desktop Composition.** This turns off transparency and other advanced Windows display features. This helps when running programs that have trouble displaying when the application window is moved across the screen.

- **Disable Display Scaling on High DPI Settings.** This turns off the automatic resizing of programs if large-scale fonts are in use. It helps when running an older program if that program is configured for larger print display.

---

tip

Of these settings, the ones that most often make a difference are visual themes and desktop composition.

Check the setting or settings you think will make a difference, and then click the OK button and try running the program. If this doesn't work, you can always reopen the Properties dialog box and try additional settings. (The process of trying to get an older program to run properly can be a bit of a hit or miss affair.)

Running Older Programs in XP Mode

Some organizations have their own custom-developed applications that don't translate well to the Windows 7 world. In fact, compatibility issues force many organizations from upgrading away from their older version of Windows, which is a shame; one single application is keeping users from experiencing all the good things that Windows 7 has to offer.

Compatibility becomes a big problem when shifting from Windows XP to either Windows Vista or Windows 7, which have a similar code base. It's the move away from XP that's the problem, and often no amount of compatibility mode tweaking can make the older application run.

In a move to encourage more organizations with older apps to make the upgrade (without having to rewrite the applications themselves), Microsoft introduced a new Windows XP Mode in certain editions of Windows 7. This mode, targeted expressly at business users, essentially runs a full-fledged copy of Windows XP inside a virtual machine; XP-compatible apps, then, run within Windows XP, not within Windows 7, making Win7 compatibility a moot issue.

---

note

A *virtual machine* or *virtual PC* is a software implementation of a second computer, running within the operating system already installed on that computer. In essence, it duplicates the experience of running a separate computer and enables the running of a different operating system than the one currently installed.

The way it works is that you install the Windows Virtual PC software within Windows 7. You then install Windows XP within the Virtual PC software, and then install your XP-compatible application(s) within Windows XP (running within the Virtual PC). It's a stack of things on top of or within each other, but what it boils down to is that you can now seamlessly run those old Windows XP programs without having to worry about compatibility with the newer Windows 7 operating system.

Checking Compatibility

Windows XP Mode is a good deal if you're running an app developed for Windows XP. But you can't run it on just any computer.

First of all, Windows XP Mode is only available with the Professional, Enterprise, and Ultimate editions of Windows 7. It is not available for the Home Premium or any other edition, nor is it available for Windows Vista.

Second, your computer's CPU must support hardware virtualization; not all CPUs do. To determine if your computer can work with Windows XP mode, you need to install and run a special utility provided by your CPU's manufacturer.

If your computer uses an Intel processor, install the Intel Processor Identification Utility, which you can download from www.intel.com/support/processors/tools/piu/. Once installed, run the utility and select the CPU Technologies tab. If the value in the Intel Virtualization Technology field is Yes, your CPU supports hardware virtualization and you can use the Windows XP Mode. If the value is No, then hardware virtualization is not supported and you're out of luck.

If your computer uses an AMD processor, install and run the AMD Virtualization Compatibility Check Utility, located at support.amd.com/us/Pages/dynamicDetails.aspx?ListID=c5cd2c08-1432-4756-aafa-4d9dc646342f&ItemID=172. (Sorry for the long URL; AMD doesn't make this easy.)

Enabling Hardware Virtualization

Assuming that your CPU is good to go, you need to enable hardware virtualization in your CPU's BIOS settings. This involves rebooting your PC and, before Windows loads, entering your computer's BIOS setup utility. This is typically done by pressing a designated key (F10, F12, or something similar) during the boot process. Consult your computer's manual for instructions—or just watch the screen during bootup for instructions.

Once you've entered the BIOS setup utility, you need to select the configuration or setup screen or tab. Somewhere there should be a setting for hardware virtualization or virtualization technology; enable this setting. You can then save your changes, exit the BIOS setup utility, and resume booting up your system.

Downloading and Installing Windows XP Mode

Okay, you've done a bit of work so far, and that's just the beginning. You now have to download and install two separate pieces of software—the Windows Virtual PC software and then the Windows XP Mode software.

You download both pieces of software from www.microsoft.com/windows/virtual-pc/. These are free downloads, assuming you're running a supported version of Windows 7. They also take a bit of time to download and install; remember, you're installing the complete Windows XP operating system, along with the virtual PC software. So expect to spend an hour or more downloading and installing, even on a fast Internet connection.

tip

Windows Virtual PC software isn't limited to just running Windows XP; you can install any operating system (Windows Vista, Windows 95, you name it) in its own virtual machine. All you need is a registered copy of the operating system; then select Start, All Programs, Windows Virtual PC, Windows Virtual PC to launch a new virtual machine and perform the installation.

Running Windows XP Mode

Running Windows XP Mode is a piece of cake. All you have to do is open the Start menu and select All Programs, Windows Virtual PC, Windows XP Mode. This launches the virtual PC and opens Windows XP in its own window. As you can see in Figure 22.3, this is the real deal, the Windows XP (with Service Pack 3 installed) that you know and perhaps even love.

Operating Windows XP within Windows 7 is just like operating Windows XP normally. Everything you need is there, in terms of operating system and utilities. If you prefer to run XP full-screen, click the Action button on the window menu and select View Full Screen. This displays XP full-screen but with a new toolbar at the top of the screen, as shown in Figure 22.4. To return to windowed mode, click the minimize button on this toolbar.

Windows 7 Desktop

Windows XP running in a separate window on top of Windows 7

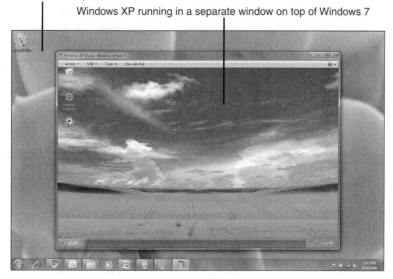

FIGURE 22.3

Windows XP running in a window within Windows 7.

Click the minimize button to return to windowed mode.

FIGURE 22.4

Windows XP running in full-screen mode in Windows 7—note the new toolbar at the top of the screen.

Note that when you're running XP Mode, even in full-screen mode, you can easily switch between XP and any open Windows 7 application. Win7 treats XP as just another application, so all the normal window-switching operations work as usual.

Installing an Application in XP Mode

To use your XP-compatible applications, you have to install them from within Windows XP—*not* from within Windows 7. To do this, follow these steps:

1. Insert the application's installation disk into the appropriate drive on your computer. Do *not* opt to install the application when the Windows 7 prompt appears.

2. From within Windows XP Mode, open the Start menu and select My Computer.

3. When My Computer opens, double-click the drive that holds the application's installation disk.

4. Navigate to and double-click the setup or installation program (typically **setup.exe**).

5. Follow the onscreen prompts to complete the installation.

Running an XP Application in Seamless Mode

Once installed, you can launch an XP application from Windows XP's Start menu—or from within Windows 7. Thanks to what Microsoft calls *seamless mode*, all applications you install in Windows XP Mode also appear on the Windows 7 Start menu under All Programs, Windows Virtual PC, Windows XP Mode Applications.

> **tip**
>
> You can also create desktop shortcuts for any XP Mode application, or pin any XP application to the Windows 7 taskbar.

Seamless mode lets you open the XP application without first launching Windows XP itself. Once launched, the program appears in its own window within Windows 7, without the whole XP desktop appearing, as shown in Figure 22.5. As you can see, the window for the XP application looks like an XP window, instead of the translucent Windows 7 window. It's an odd kind of juxtaposition, but it lets you run all your old XP applications just the way they used to run.

The Windows XP app runs inside its own Windows XP window.

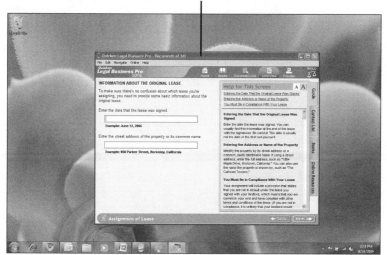

FIGURE 22.5

A Windows XP application running in seamless mode in Windows 7.

The Bottom Line

Windows 7 not only lets you run Windows 7 applications your way, but
also applications developed for older versions of Windows. And, with
Windows XP Mode, you get to run Windows 7 like Windows XP—or more
accurately, run Windows XP within Windows 7. It kind of makes the
whole operating system version thing moot, which can be a good thing if
you have a lot of critical older applications.

23

Removing Unnecessary Files and Programs

Having Windows 7 your way also means that you get to decide which files and programs you store on your computer's hard disk drive. That's important, because bad things can happen if your hard disk gets too full. Not only do you run out of space to store new stuff, but it also affects your computer's performance; a too-full hard drive slows down your PC.

So it's important that you learn how to remove the stuff you don't use or need from your hard drive. That's what this chapter is about.

Hard Disk Capacity—Enough Is Never Enough

It always seems like you have more than enough space on your hard disk—when you first get it. Back in the mid-1980s, we marveled at the huge 10MB (that's *megabytes*—not *gigabytes*) of storage available on early IBM PCs. In 1991, we wondered how we would ever fill the 100MB of capacity on that era's newest drives. By the year 2000, those older drives appeared tiny next to the first 1GB drives. In 2005, 500GB seemed like it would hold a lifetime of data. And today, in mid-2009, the latest 1TB (that's one *terabyte*—or one million megabytes) drives look to be big enough to hold entire collections of digital photos and music, with plenty of room to spare.

But here's the deal. Over time, even the largest hard drives get smaller—at least in perception. That's because when the space is available, we fill it. As the weeks and the months and the years go by after you purchase a new PC, you install lots of new programs and create tons of data files—letters, memos, email messages, digital photographs, music tracks, videos, you name it. And all this stuff fills up even the largest hard drive.

There's more to it, of course. The fuller your hard drive gets, the slower your computer runs. Oh, the sluggishness comes gradually, maybe you don't even notice it for the first year or so, but every new item that takes up space on your hard disk works to eventually slow down your system to the point that the performance change becomes noticeable. There is a direct correlation between the amount of "stuff" on your hard disk and how fast your system performs.

But why is this? Why does installing more programs and creating more files slow down your computer? And what can you do about it, after the fact?

Why a Crowded Hard Disk Slows Down Your System

Here's the rule: The more unused hard disk space your computer has, the faster it will run. There are a number of reasons for this.

First, your computer sometimes uses your hard disk as a kind of backstop when system memory fills up. In this instance, your hard disk serves as *virtual memory*, temporarily storing programs and data just as your system's random access memory (RAM) normally does. This facilitates *file swapping*, where program and data files are swapped between random access memory (for immediate access) and virtual hard disk memory (for not-quite-immediate access).

If there's a lot of free hard disk space, that means there's lots of virtual memory available for this file swapping, which lets your system run quickly. If there's not a lot of free hard disk space, that means less data can be loaded into this virtual memory—and the less stuff loaded into memory, the slower your system runs. It's a simple equation: Free up hard disk space for virtual memory and speed up your system.

But memory, virtual or otherwise, isn't the only thing that affects your system's performance. Every time you open or save a program or document, that program or document file has to be read from or written to your computer's hard disk; that's basic computer operation. If you only have a few files on your hard disk, it's relatively easy for your computer to find the right file to read or write to, which makes for speedy operation. The more files you have on your hard disk, however, the more files your computer has to sort through to find the right one to read or write to, which slows down your computer's performance. In other words, the more things stored on your hard drive, the longer it takes to access any one thing.

How Much Free Space Do You Need?

So if you want to speed up your system, you need to delete all but the most essential programs and files, and leave plenty of spare hard disk space for potential use as virtual memory and other hard disk chores. But how much free hard disk space do you need?

I recommend keeping at least 20% of your hard disk free; this should leave plenty of room for virtual memory, file swapping, temporary file storage, and the like. For example, if you have a 500GB hard drive, you want to utilize no more than 80% of the available space, leaving at least 100GB of free disk space at any given time. Do the math to figure out how much free space you need on your particular hard drive.

What's on *Your* Hard Disk—And Why?

When it comes to managing hard disk space your way, it helps to know just what kinds of files you have stored on your hard drive. Which files are essential—and which are expendable?

Understanding Computer Files

While every user's hard drive is different, you can normally organize your files into the following five major categories:

- **System files.** These are files used by the Windows operating system, and should not be deleted. (If you do delete them, Windows will probably crash.) These include executable files (typically with a .DLL or .SYS extension), device drivers (.DRV extension), configuration files (.INI extension), and the like.

- **Program files.** These are the files used by the software programs installed on your system, typically with an .EXE file extension. Obviously, files for programs you don't use can be deleted from your hard disk; programs you do use should not be deleted.

- **Data files.** These are the documents, spreadsheets, presentations, music tracks, videos, digital photographs, and the like you create and run with your software programs, or download off the Internet. You may find it better for system performance if you don't archive all your older data files on your main hard drive. Files you don't access frequently can be stored on external hard drives, CDs, or DVDs.

- **Temporary files.** These are files stored in a special "cache" on your hard drive. These may be web pages downloaded by your web browser and cached for quick viewing, or data files opened and temporarily stored by the host application. Temporary files are typically created when data used by a program is larger than the available memory space. Most temporary files are automatically deleted when the host application is closed, but sometimes, due to a program crash or ill-behaved application, they're not deleted—and continue to take up valuable hard disk space. Most temporary files have a .TMP extension and can be safely deleted.

- **Deleted files.** Here's one that might surprise you. Files that you delete from your hard drive actually aren't immediately deleted. Instead, they're moved to the Recycle Bin, a special folder that holds "deleted" files in case you want to *undelete* them in the immediate future. By default, Windows 7 allocates to the Recycle Bin 4GB plus 5% of your hard disk space—which can be a lot when you have a really big hard drive. You can, however, change the amount of space allocated, and "empty" the Recycle Bin to free up hard disk space.

To summarize, system files should not be deleted (ever), program and data files can be deleted if you don't need them, and temporary and deleted files can always be deleted.

Understanding Bundleware

There's a special category of program files that should be addressed. I'm talking about *bundleware*, those programs that come preinstalled when you purchase a new PC. More often than not, these are not programs you want on your new PC, which is why some wits (including some Microsoft managers) describe these programs as *crapware* or *craplets*.

As you can tell by the nickname, most folks hate this stuff. Users hate having their brand-new desktops cluttered with this crap, and technicians hate having to clean it off users' sluggish PCs. It's just not popular.

About the only folks who like bundleware are the hardware manufacturers. That's because they get paid by each company to install its software in this fashion. Given the slim margins inherent in computer manufacturing, the pennies that various software companies pay per machine to preload their bundleware can be the difference between profit and loss for the hardware manufacturer.

What kind of programs are we talking about? It's all the stuff you find cluttering the desktop and Start menu of a new PC. This might include sign-up utilities for one or two Internet service providers, icons for a couple of online music services, a handful of instant messaging clients, some cheapo games, a web browser toolbar or two, an anti-virus program that expires in 90 days or so, maybe even trial versions of Quicken or Adobe Photoshop Elements. Depending on the price of the PC, you might also get a functioning version of Microsoft Works or a 90-day trial version of Microsoft Office. All in all, expect at least 10% of your new PC's hard disk space to be taken up with these unwanted programs.

tip

Some retailers, such as Best Buy, offer to remove all the bundleware from a new PC you purchase—for a price. Depending on the price, this may not be a bad thing, as some retailers also install any necessary operating system updates, drivers, and the like at the same time.

And here's the really annoying thing: Much bundleware isn't even fully functioning software. More often than not what you get is a "trial" version that only works for a set period of time (30 or 90 days), or one that is somehow crippled in functionality. If you want to use the full version of the program, you have to purchase it separately. The bundleware version is just a tease or advertisement.

Even more annoying is the fact that if you don't want the bundleware taking up valuable hard disk space (or, even worse, preloading itself into system memory), you have to manually uninstall the stuff. And, not surprisingly, some bundleware makes itself quite difficult to uninstall. It's unwanted stuff that's hard to get rid of—and it slows down your PC, to boot.

tip

Because bundleware is so time-consuming and difficult to remove, the first thing many techie users do when they purchase a new PC is wipe off the hard disk (thus deleting all the bundleware) and reinstall Windows from scratch. This lets them start with a completely clean machine. (Although this doesn't work if you use the manufacturer's "restore" CD/DVD—which typically includes all the bundleware you're trying to get rid of!)

Freeing Up Hard Disk Space by Deleting Bundleware

You're probably coming to the conclusion that you have a lot of stuff on your hard disk that you just don't need and is probably slowing down your system. This is even true with a brand new PC, thanks to the problem of bundleware.

What's the best way to get rid of these unwanted trial programs? One approach is to use a utility dedicated solely to identifying and deleting this so-called crapware. One such program is PC Decrapifier, which you can download for free from www.pcdecrapifier.com.

Figure 23.1 shows PC Decrapifier at work. When you start it up, it scans your system for potential crapware and lists them for you. Check those you want to delete and click the Next button. PC Decrapifier does the dirty work of uninstalling these nuisance programs so that you don't have to deal with them.

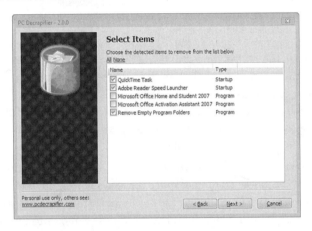

FIGURE 23.1

Removing unwanted bundleware with PC Decrapifier.

tip

If you're not sure whether you want to use a program or not, don't let PC Decrapifier delete it. Wait a few days or weeks, then if you haven't used the program, you can rerun PC Decrapifier to delete it then.

Deleting Unwanted Files with the Disk Cleanup Utility

PC Decrapifier only deletes programs it identifies as bundleware or trial versions. You may also want to delete other types of files, which you can do with the Windows Disk Cleanup utility. You use Disk Cleanup to automatically free up extra hard disk space—and speed up your PC's performance.

To use Disk Cleanup, follow these steps:

1. Click the Start button, and then select All Programs, Accessories, System Tools, Disk Cleanup.

2. If prompted, select the drive or user files you want to clean up.

3. Disk Cleanup now analyzes the contents of your hard disk drive and presents its results in the Disk Cleanup dialog box, shown in Figure 23.2.

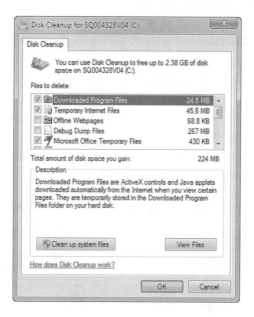

FIGURE 23.2

Use Disk Cleanup to delete unused files from your hard disk.

4. You now have the option of permanently deleting various types of files: downloaded program files, temporary Internet files, offline web pages, deleted files in the Recycle Bin, and so forth. Select which files you want to delete.

5. Click OK to begin deleting.

You can safely have Disk Cleanup delete all the listed files *except* for the setup log, content indexer, and Office setup files, which are often needed by the Windows operating system.

---

tip

Of course, you can always delete unwanted files manually. You do this by opening Windows Explorer, navigating to the files you want to delete, and then pressing the Del key on your keyboard. This moves the selected files to the Recycle Bin, so don't forget to empty the Recycle Bin to formally free up that disk space.

Emptying the Recycle Bin

As noted previously, Windows allocates 5% or so of your hard disk space to holding deleted files in the Recycle Bin. When you've deleted enough files to exceed this limit, the oldest files in the Recycle Bin are automatically and permanently deleted from your hard disk. That doesn't help you if you need an extra 10GB to 20GB of free disk space, however. In this instance, you'll want to manually empty the Recycle Bin to thus free up some of that valuable hard disk space.

To empty the Recycle Bin, all you have to do is double-click the Recycle Bin icon on your desktop. Doing so opens the Recycle Bin folder, shown in Figure 23.3. Now click the Empty the Recycle Bin button. When the Delete Multiple Items dialog box appears, click Yes to completely erase the files.

FIGURE 23.3

Emptying the contents of the Recycle Bin.

> **tip**
>
> If you accidentally move a file to the Recycle Bin, you can restore it to its original location by opening the Recycle Bin, selecting the file, and then clicking Restore This Item.

Archiving Little-Used Files

To help free up space on your main hard drive, you may want to move some of your data files to another storage device—an external hard drive, USB flash drive, CD-ROM, or data DVD. This type of *archiving* is something my wife does every year with her digital photos. Each January, she copies the previous year's photos to a series of data CDs, and then stores them in a secure location. The photos are there (on CD) if she needs to access them, but they're not taking up valuable hard disk space on her PC.

This process is as simple as inserting or attaching the backup device or medium, opening Windows Explorer, and then moving the selected files to the backup medium. This can be done using cut and paste, the Windows Move command, or by copying the files and then deleting them from their old locations. In any case, you end up with the selected files on the external device or disc, and lots of space freed up on your main hard disk.

Uninstalling Unwanted Programs

Deleting old or unwanted data files frees up a good deal of hard drive space. But if you want to make a big impact fast, you need to delete some program files, too.

If you have one or more programs that you no longer want or use, you can free up valuable hard disk space by uninstalling those programs from your system. Here's how to do it:

> **note**
>
> Some programs might require you to insert the original installation disks or CD to perform the uninstall.

1. Open the Control Panel and select Programs and Features.
2. Windows now displays a list of installed programs, as shown in Figure 23.4. Select the program you want to uninstall from this list.
3. Click the Uninstall button.

4. If prompted, confirm that you want to continue to uninstall the application. Answer any other prompts that appear onscreen; then the uninstall process will start.

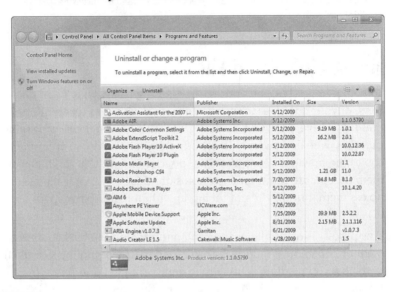

FIGURE 23.4

Deleting a program from your system.

cautioin

In some instances, the add/remove utility may not be able to completely remove all aspects of a program. If you get an error message at the end of the uninstall process, you may need to manually delete any files remaining in the program folder on your hard drive.

The Bottom Line

It pays to keep your hard disk clean. This means getting rid of files and programs that you no longer use or need. The more free hard disk space you have, the more space you have to store newer stuff—and the faster your system will run.

24

Removing Auto-Loading Programs

Memory is important, not just for you personally but also for your personal computer. The more memory your computer has, the more things it can do at once—and the faster it will run.

Unfortunately, your computer's limited memory capacity can quickly get eaten by a plethora of programs and processes. It gets even worse when these are items you really don't need or want—or even know are running. All this stuff automatically loading without your knowledge or consent is the antithesis of having Windows your way.

Too Many Running Programs Slows Things Down

Running too many software programs at the same time can slow down your system, by using up valuable and limited system memory. That's right, the more programs loaded into memory, the slower your system will run. The goal, therefore, is to remove all but the most essential programs from memory, thus speeding up your system's performance.

You see, your computer uses a form of chip-based electronic memory, called *random access memory* (RAM) to temporarily store program instructions, open files, and other data while it's being used. The more memory your computer has, the faster your applications will run—and the more applications (and larger files) you can have open at one time.

That's right, the more memory you have installed on your system, that faster it will run. (To a point, anyway; 32-bit versions of

Windows 7 support a maximum of 4GB RAM.) Most new computers today come with 4GB to 8GB of memory. Naturally, the amount of memory you need is dictated by what you do with your PC. If you're just checking email and posting on Facebook, you don't need a lot of RAM; if you're doing heavy-duty video editing, however, or playing state-of-the-art PC games, you'll want to install as much memory in your PC as it can take—and that you can afford.

---

note

RAM is measured in terms of *bytes*. One byte is equal to approximately one character in a word processing document. A unit equaling approximately one thousand bytes (1,024, to be exact) is called a *kilobyte* (KB), and a unit of approximately one thousand (1,024) kilobytes is called a *megabyte* (MB). A thousand megabytes (actually, 1,024 megabytes) is a *gigabyte* (GB).

The more programs you have running (and the more documents you have open), the slower your computer will run. That's because all these programs and documents (and other system operating instructions) are stored in your system's RAM. Too many programs in not enough memory equals tepid performance.

You can easily demonstrate this yourself. Open a Word document, an Excel spreadsheet, a PowerPoint presentation, and a web page in Internet Explorer. Now open another Word document, another Excel spreadsheet, another PowerPoint presentation, and another web page. Now do this all again—and again. At some point you'll notice your system start slowing down; it will take longer to open the next window, longer for your screen to refresh, longer for a simple mouse click to have some effect. Open enough windows and your system will go beyond sluggish to frozen. That's what happens when you have too many programs loaded into your system's limited memory.

Discovering Programs That Load Automatically—Without Your Awareness

A simple way to speed up memory-related slowness is to not run so many programs at the same time. If you're web browsing, close your Word documents. If you're editing a digital photograph, close your web browser and email program. Only open those programs and documents that you're working on at this instant.

That said, there are probably some programs running on your computer that you're not aware of, and have little control over. These programs load automatically, without your explicit approval, whenever you turn on your computer and launch Windows. Once loaded, these programs stay in system memory—taking up valuable memory space and helping to slow down your system performance.

If you want to assert your control over how Windows runs, you need to know which programs are loading when Windows launches. You can then choose to allow some or all of these programs to do their thing, or stop the auto-loading of those programs you don't want or need.

What Kinds of Programs Load Automatically?

When Windows first launches, it has to load all the system files and processes necessary for the operating system to run. These include all the bits and pieces of the operating environment, as well as device drivers, background utilities, and the like. Dozens of these processes launch on startup, all are specified in the Windows Registry, and all are absolutely necessary for Windows to do its thing.

But here's the thing: Certain software programs are also loaded when Windows starts. To determine which programs to load on startup, Windows looks both in the Windows Registry and in the Startup folder.

Most users are surprised to find out just how much stuff is running in the background. You can view all the open processes on your system from the Windows Task Manager. Just right-click the Windows taskbar and select Start Task Manager. When the Task Manager opens, click the Processes tab.

As you can see in Figure 24.1, the Task Manager lists all the open processes along with how much memory is used for each process. As one example, my system has the Google Update program (GoogleUpdate.exe) running in the background; this is a minor utility that Google uses to check for updated versions of its software applications. This utility loads automatically without asking my permission and takes up 536KB of memory space, whether I ever use the program or not. This does not thrill me.

Most of these startup programs and processes are like Google Update, programs that think they need to be running all the time, *just in case* you ever decide to use them. On any given system, you're apt to find utilities of all shapes and sizes preloaded into system memory—utilities that check for program updates, help detect and download photos from attached drives and devices, preload bits of larger programs (to help those programs launch faster if you decide to run them), run sidebars and toolbars and widgets, you name it. You'll also find instant messaging programs preloaded into memory, along with utilities that manage various system operations.

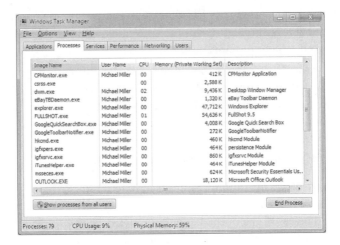

FIGURE 24.1

Viewing open processes with Windows Task Manager.

Which Startup Programs Can Be Deleted?

Do you need all of these programs and utilities running the background every time you turn on your PC? Of course not. The more of this junk that's in memory—sitting there totally unused, in most instances—the less memory is available for running the programs you do use. It's an inefficient use of system resources, and one of the most common causes for sluggish PC performance.

The challenge, of course, is identifying which programs you can safely delete and which you need to load automatically. In general, you want to keep all programs associated with Windows itself, as well as those programs that you actually use and need to be running all the time. (For example, if you use Adobe Photoshop Elements to download photos from your camera to your hard disk and do so often, it's okay to automatically load the Adobe photo downloader utility.) On the other hand, any program that you don't use or don't need to have hanging around in the background can be removed from the startup list.

But when you look at a list of auto-loading programs, what you typically see are obscure filenames. It's tough to figure out what exactly each filename means—what program it refers to, whether that program is good or bad or necessary or not, whether it's something you want to keep or not.

To help you determine what each of your startup files does, turn to one of several online databases of startup programs. These websites list tens of thousands of startup programs that you may encounter. Just enter the filename, and the site will tell you what the program does and whether it's likely to be a keeper or not.

Here are just a few of these startup program databases on the Web:

- AnswersThatWork Task List Programs (www.answersthatwork.com/ Tasklist_pages/tasklist.htm)
- Application Database (www.greatis.com/appdata/)
- Bleepingcomputer.com Startup List (www.bleepingcomputer.com/ startups/)
- Sysinfo.org Startup Applications List (www.sysinfo.org/ startuplist.php)

Deleting Auto-Loading Programs from the Startup Folder

So now you know: Many software programs have the audacity to think that you want them to run whenever you start up your PC. So they configure themselves to launch whenever Windows launches—whether or not you want them to.

To take control of your computer—to make sure that Windows launches *your* way—you need to stop those unwanted programs from launching automatically when Windows starts. To do so, of course, you have to find out from *where* it is being launched. You see, some startup programs launch from the Windows Startup folder, others from the Windows Registry—both places that Windows works through when it first starts up.

The first place to check for these auto-loading programs is the Windows Startup folder. Click the Start button, and then select All Programs, Startup. Any program or utility listed here will launch when Windows starts.

To delete a program from the Startup folder, just right-click it and select Delete from the pop-up menu.

note

Deleting a program from the Startup folder doesn't delete the program itself from your hard drive—it just removes it from the Startup folder and keeps it from loading automatically.

Deleting Auto-Loading Programs from the Windows Registry

If the offending program isn't in the Startup folder, it's probably being loaded via a setting in the Windows Registry. Several keys in the Registry can contain auto-load instructions.

> **note**
>
> Learn how to use the Registry Editor to edit settings in the Windows Registry in Chapter 27, "Tweaking the Windows Registry."

You can view and edit settings in the Registry using the Registry Editor utility. You start the Registry Editor by opening the Windows Start menu and entering **regedit** into the search box. Once the Registry Editor opens, you navigate the Registry by *key*, each of which represents a particular setting.

The Registry keys most likely to contain auto-load instructions include the following:

- HKEY_LOCAL_MACHINE\SOFTWARE\Microsoft\Windows\ CurrentVersion\RUN

- HKEY_USERS\.DEFAULT\SOFTWARE\Microsoft\Windows\ CurrentVersion\RUN

- HKEY_CURRENT_USER\SOFTWARE\Microsoft\Windows\ CurrentVersion\RUN

All programs you find listed in these keys, like those shown in Figure 24.2, are automatically loaded by Windows during the startup process. To delete a program, just highlight it and press the Del key. Once the program is deleted from the appropriate Registry key, it will no longer launch on startup.

> **caution**
>
> Make sure you really want to delete an auto-load program from the Registry before you press the Del key. Once the setting is deleted, it can't be recovered. Delete the wrong setting and you could do irreparable harm to your system!

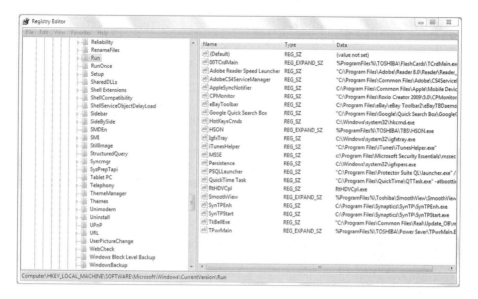

FIGURE 24.2

Viewing startup programs in the Windows Registry.

Deleting Auto-Loading Programs with the System Configuration Utility

Another way to lighten your system's load is to delete unwanted startup programs with the Windows System Configuration utility. This utility is typically used to troubleshoot your system by duplicating the procedures used by Microsoft's tech support staff when they try to diagnose system configuration problems. The System Configuration utility leads you through a series of steps that, one by one, disable various components of your system on startup, until you're able to isolate the item that's causing your specific problem. It can also be used to stop any number of programs and processes from loading at system startup.

To open the System Configuration utility, open the Start menu and enter **msconfig** into the search box. When the System Configuration utility window appears, select the Startup tab.

As you can see in Figure 24.3, the Startup tab lists all those programs and processes that load when Windows launches, along with their location (Registry key or Startup folder). To stop a program or process from loading on startup, simply uncheck that item in the list. Click OK and your changes will be applied the next time you restart Windows.

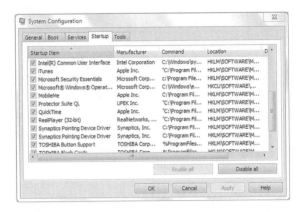

FIGURE 24.3
Managing startup programs with the System Configuration utility.

caution

Some spyware and virus programs may show up in the Startup tab with names that are very close to legitimate programs. Consult one of the startup databases mentioned previously to correctly identify all programs you want to delete.

note

When you next reboot your PC, you'll see a message warning that the System Configuration utility has been changed. Check the Do Not Show This Again option if you don't want to see this message every time you reboot.

Deleting Auto-Loading Programs with Autoruns

Microsoft recognizes the problem with auto-loading programs and has released a technical utility devoted solely to finding and managing all types of startup programs. The Autoruns utility goes beyond Windows' System Configuration Utility with its comprehensive knowledge of auto-loading programs, their locations, and in which order Windows loads them.

note

Autoruns is part of Microsoft TechNet's Sysinternals website (technet.microsoft.com/sysinternals/), which offers all manner of technical advice and utilities.

You can download Autoruns, for free, from technet.microsoft.com/sysinternals/bb963902.aspx. As you can see in Figure 24.4, Autoruns displays everything that Windows loads on launch on a series of tabs, each tab devoted to a particular type of program or process. For example, the Drivers tab lists all drivers that load on startup; the Everything tab lists everything listed on all the other tabs. Click an item to view more about it in the info pane at the bottom of the window.

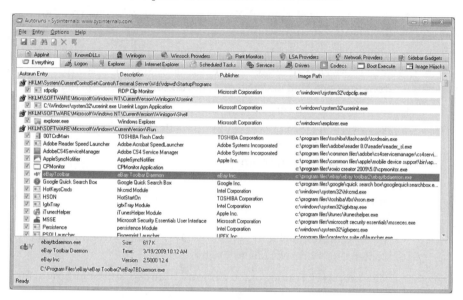

FIGURE 24.4

Advanced auto-load management with the Autoruns utility.

To stop a given item from launching when Windows starts, simply uncheck the item's check box. When next you start Windows, that item will no longer load automatically.

tip

To view the properties of a listed program or process, select the item and then click the Properties button on the Autoruns toolbar.

Turning Windows Features Off (or Back On)

Here's another way to free up some spare system memory—by turning off Windows features that you don't use. That's right, Windows loads a lot of functionality that not every user uses. If you don't need a feature, you can save some memory space by turning it off.

Features You Might Not Need

What Windows features can you disable? Here's the list:

- Games—specifically, the free games, such as Chess Titans and Solitaire, that Microsoft includes with Windows 7.

- Indexing Service, which Windows uses to index files on your hard disk for its search function.

- Internet Explorer 8. That's right, if you're using another web browser, such as Mozilla Firefox or Google Chrome, you can disconnect IE from the operating system—and free up some system memory.

- Internet Information Services—a set of Internet tools that you might not use all of. These tools include FTP Server, Web Management Tools (IIS management console, scripts, and services), and World Wide Web Services (performance and security features, application development features, and such).

- Internet Information Services Hostable Web Core, used to enable web hosting functions.

- Media Features, including Windows DVD Maker, Windows Media Center, and Windows Media Center.

- Microsoft .NET Framework, a software framework used to host a variety of third-party applications.

- Microsoft Message Queue (MSMQ) Server, which enables applications to communicate across networks.

- Print and Document Services, including the Internet Printing Client, Scan Management, and Windows Fax and Scan.

- RAS Connection Manager Application, which enables connections to remote networks and the Internet.

- Remote Differential Compression, which enables data to be synchronized to a remote source using data compression techniques.

- RIP Listener, which listens for route updates from routers using the Route Information Protocol (RIP).

- Services for NFS, which include various services used by Microsoft's Network File System (NFS).

- Simple Network Management Protocol (SNMP), a protocol used in various network management systems.

- Simple TCPIP Services, which help manage TCP/IP network and Internet connections.

- Subsystem for UNIX-based Applications, which is used to compile and run custom UNIX-based applications in the Windows environment.

- Tablet PC Components, which are used to manage the touch-screen functionality of tablet PCs.

- Telnet Client, used to manage older Telnet communications over the Internet.

- Telnet Server, also used to manage Telnet communications.

- TFTP Client, used to connect to Trivial File Transfer Protocol (TFTP) servers.

- Windows Gadget Platform—the technology that enables Windows 7's desktop gadgets.

- Windows Process Activation Service, used to manage Windows Server functions.

- Windows Search, which enables you to search for files on your hard disk.

- Windows TIFF IFilter, for advanced indexing of TIFF-format image files.

- Windows Virtual PC—if you have the Virtual PC feature installed, that is, for Windows 7's XP Mode.

- XPS Services, for managing Microsoft's new (and not widely adopted) XPS document format.

- XPS Viewer, for viewing XPS-format documents.

Of these features, which are essential and which aren't? Unfortunately there isn't a one-size-fits-all answer to this question, as what you need depends on what you do with your PC. However, you can use common sense; for example, if you don't have a tablet PC, then you can disable the Tablet PC Components feature. And if you never view XPS documents, you can disable the XPS Services and XPS Viewer features. And so on.

Disabling Features

So how do you turn off those features you don't need or use? It's easy; just follow these steps:

1. From the Control Panel, select Programs and Features.

2. When the Programs and Features window appears, select Turn Windows Features On or Off from the task pane.

3. When the Windows Features dialog box appears, as shown in Figure 24.5, uncheck those features you want to disable.

4. If you want to re-enable any features, check them in the Windows Features dialog box.

5. If prompted to confirm your choice, click Yes.

6. Click OK to close the Windows Features dialog box.

FIGURE 24.5

Disabling non-essential Windows features.

caution

Disabling some features might affect other Windows operations or installed applications. If you experience any problems after disabling a feature, return to the Windows Features dialog box and re-enable that feature.

Note that disabling a feature doesn't delete it from your system; it's still there, taking up hard disk space. This way you can easily re-enable any feature you previously disabled, without having to reinstall Windows itself.

The Bottom Line

Having Windows 7 your way means controlling all the programs and processes that Windows runs. In particular, it means having the freedom (and the means) to stop unwanted programs from automatically loading whenever Windows starts. Stopping this auto-load programs frees up valuable memory space and makes Windows run faster—which is always a good thing.

25

Managing Disks and Memory

For many users, making Windows run their way means optimizing Windows for the fastest possible performance. Two of the key factors in system performance are your computer's hard disk and memory; the more you have of each, the better your system performance will be.

But it's not just about speed. For example, a fragmented hard disk will run slower than a clean disk, as will one with bad sectors or physical errors. You need to know how to manage your computer's hard disk and system memory to get the most out of what you have—and then consider adding more, if you really need it.

Defragmenting Your Hard Disk

Your hard disk stores everything that's important to you—your documents and data, digital photographs and music, even the Windows operating system itself. So when your hard disk slows down, your entire PC slows down. That's because your computer has to access your hard drive to retrieve those programs, documents, and configuration settings; we're talking dozens of short accesses every minute. The longer it takes for each hard drive access, even if we're just talking milliseconds per access, the more your computer slows down.

What can cause a hard disk—even a relatively new one—to slow down? There are lots of possible culprits, but one of the most common problems is fragmentation—that is, having a fragmented hard disk.

Understanding Disk Fragmentation

Disk fragmentation is nothing to be afraid of. In fact, it's a common occurrence. A little bit of fragmentation happens whenever Windows writes files to your hard drive.

That's because files aren't saved as single entities on your hard drive; they're broken into smaller chunks for easier handling, and each of these chunks is stored on a separate sector of your hard disk. Because each sector holds exactly 512 bytes of data, a large file could be stored in hundreds or even thousands of separate sectors—and not all together.

When a hard disk is fresh from the factory, all the sectors for a single file can be stored contiguously—that is, all in a row. This makes it easy for the read/write head of the hard disk to access the complete file. But as more files are stored to the hard disk, and as older files are erased, contiguous hard disk space might not be available when saving a new file.

When this happens, the chunks of the file are stored in whatever sectors are available—even if those sectors are widely separated on the hard disk. When a file is fragmented in this fashion, it takes more time for the hard disk's read/write head to access each of the individual chunks and thus assemble the file for use.

It's kind of like taking the pieces of a jigsaw puzzle and storing them in different boxes along with pieces from other puzzles. The more dispersed the pieces are, the longer it takes to put the puzzle together.

So if you notice your system takes longer and longer to open and close files or run applications, it's because these file fragments are spread all over the place—in other words, your hard disk is overly fragmented. You fix this problem when you put all the pieces of the puzzle back in the right boxes, which you do by *defragmenting* your hard disk.

How Disk Defragmenting Works

To improve the performance of your hard disk—that is, to reduce how long it takes to access a file—you must defragment the disk. This is accomplished by using the Disk Defragmenter utility built in to Windows 7.

The Disk Defragmenter rearranges the chunks of data on your hard disk so that the data for a single file are stored in contiguous sectors—that is, all together in a row. To do this, the Disk Defragmenter has to temporarily store the data from noncontiguous sectors in system memory, erase those sectors to make room for new data, and then rewrite the stored data into new, contiguous sectors.

And this is how defragmenting your hard disk speeds up your PC. When necessary data is stored all together, it can be accessed much faster than if your system has to search all over your hard drive for all the assorted pieces and parts of the file. For an immediate speed boost, you can't beat a simple disk defragmentation!

note

Windows' Disk Defragmenter also rearranges where certain files are stored on the hard disk. Frequently used files are rewritten to the first sectors on the disk, where they can be accessed more quickly during normal use.

Setting a Defrag Schedule

You use Windows' Disk Defragmenter utility to defragment your PC's hard drive. In Windows 7, Disk Defragmenter runs on a once-a-week schedule, defragmenting your hard disk every Wednesday at 1:00 a.m. by default.

If you'd like to defragment your hard drive more often or at a different time, you can reconfigure Disk Defragmenter to run on a custom schedule. Follow these steps:

1. Click the Start button and select All Programs, Accessories, System Tools, Disk Defragmenter.

2. When the Disk Defragmenter window appears, as shown in Figure 25.1, click the Configure Schedule button.

3. When the Modify Schedule dialog box appears, as shown in Figure 25.2, make sure the Run on a Schedule option is selected.

4. Click the Frequency button and select how often you want to defrag: Daily, Weekly, or Monthly.

5. If you selected Weekly, click the Day button and select a day of the week. If you selected Monthly, click the Day button and select a day of the month.

6. Click the Time button and select what time of day you want the process to start.

7. If you have more than one hard disk on your system, click the Disks button and then select those disks you want to defrag.

8. Click OK.

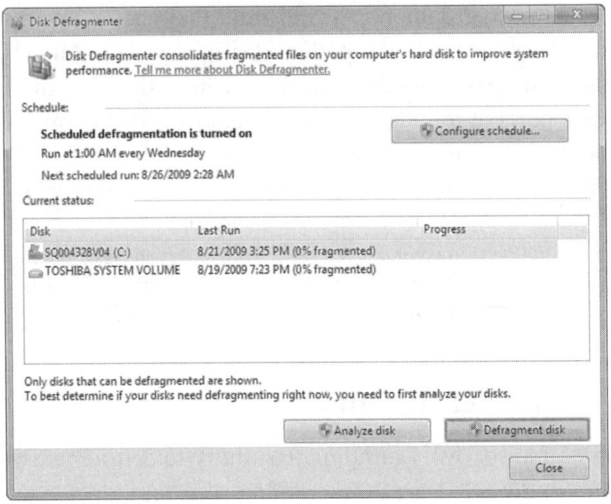

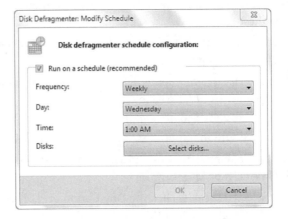

FIGURE 25.1

Running the Disk Defragmenter utility.

FIGURE 25.2

Setting a schedule for disk defragmenting.

Disk Defragmenter will now launch at the appointed day and time and do its thing.

Analyzing Your Disk

How do you know if your hard disk needs defragmenting? Disk Defragmenter can analyze your disk and let you know how fragmented it is. Here's how it works:

1. Click the Start button and select All Programs, Accessories, System Tools, Disk Defragmenter.

2. When the Disk Defragmenter window appears, click the Analyze Disk button.

Disk Defragmenter now analyzes your hard disk for fragmented files and displays the results in the Disk Defragmenter window. You'll see what percent of your disk is fragmented; the higher this number, the more urgent the need for defragmentation.

Manually Defragmenting Your Hard Disk

If your disk is overly fragmented, you may not want to wait until the scheduled time to defragment it. Fortunately, Disk Defragmenter lets you defragment your disk manually at any time. Just follow these steps:

1. Click the Start button and select All Programs, Accessories, System Tools, Disk Defragmenter.

2. When the Disk Defragmenter window appears, click the Defragment Disk button.

Disk Defragmenter now starts the defragmentation process. This can take awhile, especially if you have a large hard drive or your drive is really fragmented. So, you might want to start the utility and let it run overnight or while you're at lunch. But when it's done, you should notice that your PC feels less sluggish.

caution

You should close all applications—including your screen saver—and stop working on your system while Disk Defragmenter is running.

Scanning Your Hard Disk for Errors

Any time you run an application, move or delete a file, or accidentally turn the power off while your computer is running, you run the risk of introducing errors to your hard disk. That's because all these operations write data to your hard drive—or, in the case of an accidental shutoff, potentially interrupt the write process. And every time you write to your hard drive, errors can be introduced.

As you might suspect, it's not good to have errors on a hard drive. These errors can make it harder to open files, slow down your hard disk, or cause your system to freeze when you open or save a file or an application.

Fortunately, you can find and fix most of these errors directly from within Windows. All you have to do is run the built-in ScanDisk utility. This simple utility looks for and tries to fix errors on your hard drive—and thus speed up system performance in the process.

How ScanDisk Works

ScanDisk works like other similar "disk fix" utilities. In essence, it performs multiple tests of your hard drive's integrity, and either points out or tries to fix any problems found.

ScanDisk starts by reading the data on your hard drive, sector by sector. If there's a sector that it has trouble reading, ScanDisk attempts to move the data elsewhere, and then marks that cluster as bad. Once an area is marked bad, Windows sidesteps it in the future—thus "fixing" your hard drive by disallowing access to bad sectors.

> **note**
>
> Learn more about other hard disk utilities in Chapter 26, "Using Third-Party Utilities."

Using ScanDisk to Speed Up Your PC

To use ScanDisk, follow these steps:

1. Click the Start button and select Computer.
2. From within the Computer window, right-click the icon for the drive you want to scan, and then select the Properties option from the pop-up menu.
3. When the Properties dialog box appears, select the Tools tab.
4. Click the Check Now button in the Error-Checking section to display the Check Disk dialog box, shown in Figure 25.3.
5. Check both the options (Automatically Fix File System Errors and Scan for and Attempt Recovery of Bad Sectors).
6. Click Start.

Windows now scans your hard disk and attempts to fix any errors it encounters. If errors are found (and fixed), your PC's performance should be enhanced.

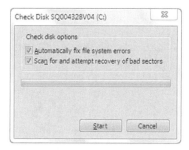

FIGURE 25.3

Running the ScanDisk utility to check your hard disk for errors.

Adding More Hard Disk Space

Even a perfectly running and defragmented hard drive can slow down over time. That's because full hard disks run slower than relatively empty ones.

Because every hard disk fills up eventually, you may want to consider adding a second hard drive to your system—or replacing the original hard drive with a bigger one. Not only will more hard disk space speed up your system, however slightly, it will also give you more valuable storage space for your programs and files. And, given the low price of hard drives today, it's not a big investment!

Viewing the Capacity of Your Hard Drive

How full is your hard disk? It's easy to find out; just follow these steps:

1. Click the Start button and select Computer.

2. When the Computer window opens, click the icon for your hard drive. This displays, at the bottom of the window, the total size of your hard drive, along with space used and space free, as shown in Figure 25.4.

3. You can view more detail by right-clicking the hard drive icon and selecting Properties from the pop-up menu. When the Properties dialog box appears, make sure the General tab is selected. As you can see in Figure 25.5, this displays a pie chart of your drive's used and free space, along with details as to capacity (in gigabytes).

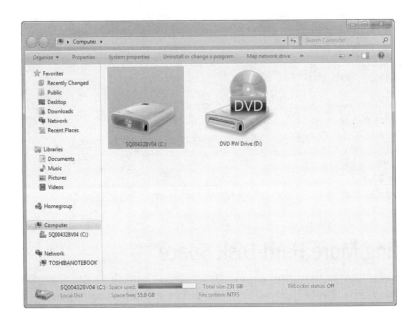

FIGURE 25.4

Viewing basic disk capacity.

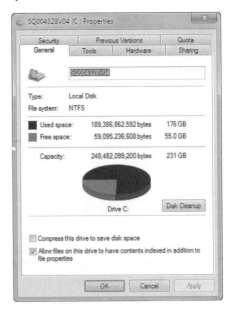

FIGURE 25.5

Viewing detailed disk capacity in the Properties dialog box.

As to the question of how much free space is enough, you should leave at least 20% of your total space free for use as virtual memory and other essential operations. So if you have a 500GB hard drive, you should always try to leave about 100GB free.

That said, the total amount of hard disk space you need depends on how much stuff you need to store on it. If all you do is browse the Web and read email, you can make do with a relatively small hard drive. On the other hand, if you store a ton of digital photos or music, or run some very large programs, you need more hard disk space. How much is something you have to determine based on your own specific needs.

Shopping for a New Hard Drive

If you don't have enough hard disk space on your computer, you can make more space by deleting programs and files you don't use—or you can just purchase a new hard drive. You can go with an external hard drive to supplement your main internal hard drive, or you can replace your existing internal drive with a larger capacity model.

note

Learn more about deleting files and programs in Chapter 23, "Removing Unnecessary Files and Programs."

Of course, it pays to do your research before you buy any type of new hard drive. You need to understand the relevant specifications to make an informed buying decision—and to get the right hard drive for your system. This information, typically available somewhere on the drive's packaging, tells you how much data the disk can hold, how fast it can access that data, and the type of interface the drive uses. (Faster is better, of course—and more expensive.)

Of the available specs, you'll want to focus your attention on form factor (internal or external), size, speed, and price.

As to form factor, you need to decide whether you want an external or internal hard drive. Naturally, if you want to replace your existing hard drive, you're talking an internal model. But if you want to *supplement* your existing drive rather than replace it, an external drive is probably the best way to go; all you have to do is connect said external drive to a free USB or FireWire port on your PC; it's that easy.

> **note**
>
> Although replacing an internal drive is a bit more work than connecting an external unit, it does result in simpler operation. That's because you only have to deal with a single drive when installing programs, opening and saving files, and the like. Get a big enough C: drive and you don't need to bother with a D: drive as well.

As to the other specs, you'll probably want to get a fairly large capacity model—something in the 500GB to 1TB range. If you're using disk-intensive applications (such as PC games or audio/video-editing programs), you'll also want to spring for the faster 7,200RPM models instead of one with a more common 5,400RPM speed. And, of course, price is always a factor; make sure you make the price/performance compromise that works best for your specific needs.

As with most electronics purchases, it pays to stick to the major manufacturers when looking for a new hard drive. These companies include the following:

- Iomega (www.iomega.com)
- LaCie (www.lacie.com)
- Maxtor (www.maxtor.com)
- Seagate (www.seagate.com)
- Western Digital (www.westerndigital.com)

When it comes to actually purchasing the drive, both external and internal hard models can be found at most computer and consumer electronics stores.

Connecting a New External Hard Drive

The easiest type of hard drive to install is the external variety. These drives typically install via either USB or FireWire, and supplement the storage space on your main internal hard drive.

Installation of an external hard drive is relatively simple. Just follow these steps:

1. If the external drive requires external power (not all do), plug it into a live electrical outlet.

2. Connect the drive to an open USB or FireWire port on your PC.

3. If your new drive came with an installation CD (and it probably did), insert the CD into your CD-ROM drive and run the installation

program. Otherwise, Windows should recognize the new drive and automatically install the proper device drivers.

> **note**
>
> Sometimes the installation program is actually on the hard drive itself and will automatically run when you connect the drive.

Your new external drive assumes the next highest available drive letter on your system. So, for example, if your current hard drive is the C: drive, the new external drive will be the D: drive. (If your CD-ROM drive was formerly the D: drive, it will now become the E: drive. When it comes to letters, your system likes to group similar types of drives together.)

Taking Full Advantage of an External Drive

Once you have the new external hard drive connected, you can install any new programs you purchase or download to that drive, as well as save new documents to that drive. But that doesn't make your existing internal disk any less congested.

What you have to do now is free up some disk space on your internal drive by moving files from there to your new external hard disk. The best candidates for relocation are data files—Word documents, Excel spreadsheets, digital photographs, music tracks, and the like. It's relatively easy to open up two Windows Explorer windows and drag and drop entire document folders from the old drive to the new one. The more files you move, the more disk space you free up and the faster your computer should run.

You can also relocate software programs from the old drive to the new one, but this is a bit more work. If you want to move a software program, you have to uninstall the program from the current hard drive and reinstall it on the external drive. This is a good idea only if you have the original software installation discs—and if you don't have to reregister a program when you reinstall it.

The one thing you definitely *can't* move to your new external drive is the Windows operating system. Windows has to be located on your computer's first (internal) hard drive, so don't even think about moving it.

Boosting System Memory with ReadyBoost

Let's now shift our attention from long-term storage to short-term memory—computer memory, that is. You see, the more memory your computer has, the faster your applications will run and the more applications (and larger files) you can have open at one time. If you don't have enough memory in your system, your computer will appear sluggish and possibly freeze up from time to time.

So here's one of the most effective ways of speeding up your PC: Add more memory!

On any Windows 7 machine, you can get an instant memory increase—without opening up the case—via ReadyBoost technology. With ReadyBoost, you can use a flash memory device to temporarily increase the amount of RAM on your personal computer. Insert one of these devices into the appropriate slot on your PC, and your system's total memory is automatically increased—and your system's performance is automatically improved.

How ReadyBoost Works

When you activate ReadyBoost, Windows duplicates the overflow data that might otherwise be sent to your computer's hard drive virtual memory. This duplicate data is then sent to the inserted flash memory device.

Windows then uses the data stored in the flash device's RAM, instead of accessing the data on the slower hard disk. Because a flash memory device is approximately 10 times faster than hard disk-based virtual memory, you'll notice an immediate speed boost.

note

Even with ReadyBoost activated, Windows continues to write the data sent to the flash memory device to your system's hard disk, as a backup.

In short, the RAM on the flash memory device is added to the available RAM on your computer's motherboard—even though the new memory runs noticeably slower than the regular memory installed on your system. This gives you that much more memory to run applications and open documents.

Speeding Up Your PC with ReadyBoost

To use ReadyBoost, you first have to insert an external memory device into one of your PC's open slots. If you have a USB memory drive, like the one in Figure 25.6, insert it into a USB slot. If you have a flash memory card, insert it into the appropriate card slot.

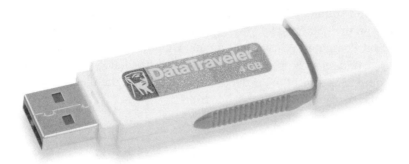

FIGURE 25.6

Use a USB memory drive, like this Kingston DataTraveler, to add instant memory to any computer running Windows 7. (Photo courtesy Kingston Technology Corporation.)

note

Windows ReadyBoost supports USB flash memory drives, as well as CompactFlash (CF) and Secure Digital (SD) memory cards.

You should now be prompted as to how you want to use that device, as shown in Figure 25.7. Select Speed Up My System Using Windows ReadyBoost, and your notebook will automatically access available memory on the device.

FIGURE 25.7

Enabling ReadyBoost to use external memory.

You can configure Windows to use all or just part of the available memory on the USB drive for your system's RAM. Just open the Start menu and select Computer. When the Computer window opens, right-click the USB drive and select Properties. From the Properties dialog box, shown in Figure 25.8, select the ReadyBoost tab and adjust the slider to select how much space to use.

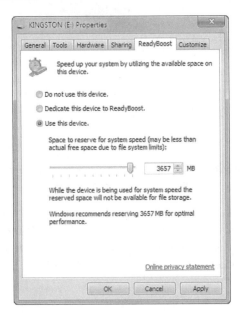

FIGURE 25.8
Configuring how much memory to use.

When you're done using the flash memory device, or if you no longer need the speed boost, simply remove the device. When the flash memory device is removed, Windows returns to using just the regular RAM installed on your system.

note

Any data still in use when the flash memory device is removed is now read from the hard disk, where it was duplicated during the ReadyBoost process. No data is lost.

Adding More System Memory

ReadyBoost aside, if you want to truly increase the amount of memory on your computer, you have to do a little physical work. That means installing new memory chips—which isn't nearly as difficult as you think.

Adding Memory to a Desktop PC

All memory today comes on modules, such as the one shown in Figure 25.9. Each module contains multiple memory chips. The capacity of each chip adds up to the total capacity of the memory module. The memory modules plug into memory sockets located on your PC's motherboard; installation is actually quite easy.

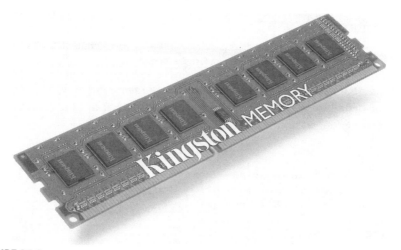

FIGURE 25.9

A typical DDR3 DIMM memory module, which plugs into the memory socket on your PC's motherboard. (Photo courtesy Kingston Technology Corporation.)

If you have a relatively new desktop PC, it's likely that it uses Dual Inline Memory Module (DIMM). This type of memory module has memory chips mounted on both sides of the module and comes in both 168-pin and 184-pin versions. DIMMs are the most popular memory modules in use today.

A DIMM can come with one of several different types of memory chips. Most DIMM chips use some form of Synchronous Dynamic RAM (SDRAM) technology. This can be basic SDRAM chips, or Double Data Rate (DDR) SDRAM chips. There are even DDR2, DDR3, and DDR4 SDRAM chips; the higher the number, the faster the memory.

Then there's the matter of how much memory to add. RAM today is typically available in 128MB, 256MB, 512MB, and 1GB increments. So, for example, if you want to add 1GB of RAM to your system, you could buy one 1GB module, two 512MB modules, four 256MB modules, or eight 128MB modules. To make the most efficient use of your system's vacant memory slots, it's always best to add the smallest number of larger-capacity modules possible.

With all these variables, you need to consult your PC's instruction manual (or look up your PC's model number in a manufacturer's website cross-listing) to determine the type of memory your machine uses. And, although it's important to get the right type of module for your specific PC, you shouldn't worry about accidentally inserting the wrong module into the wrong type of slot. It's physically impossible to insert a memory module into a slot that doesn't match it, pin-wise.

note

Some types of memory modules have to be installed in pairs. Consult your instruction manual or manufacturer's website for more details.

Then, once you've figured out what type of memory to buy, it's time for the actual upgrade. Fortunately, this is pretty much a "plug-and-go" installation, with no undo configuration necessary.

caution

It's important to protect against electrostatic discharge while you're installing memory. Use an antistatic wristband or take other precautions to make sure you don't fry your new RAM before you get to use it.

Just follow these steps:

1. Close Windows and power off your PC.
2. Disconnect your PC from its power source.
3. Open the system unit case, per the manufacturer's instructions.
4. Locate your system's memory slots on your system's motherboard—the big computer board located at the bottom or side of your system unit.
5. Insert the new memory module into an open memory slot. Release the clips at either end of the slot, line up the module, press it firmly down into the slot, and then flip the end clips back into place.
6. Reinstall the system unit's cover, reconnect your PC to an AC power supply, and power it up.

note

If you don't have an open memory slot on your PC, you'll have to remove an old lower-capacity memory module and replace it with the new higher-capacity module.

And that's all you need to do. Your PC should recognize the new memory when it reboots—and run much faster than what it did before.

Adding More Memory to a Notebook PC

Believe it or not, upgrading memory on a notebook PC is even easier than it is on a desktop machine. That's because you don't have to open up your notebook case to make the upgrade; it all happens in a little compartment on the bottom of your PC.

Most notebooks use Small Outline (SO) DIMM memory. This type of module is about half the size of a standard DIMM module, and is available in 72-pin, 144-pin, and 200-pin versions. As with desktop memory, you shop for notebook memory by plugging the manufacturer name and model number into a "configurator" program on the memory manufacturer's website.

Memory is typically added to a notebook PC through an easily accessible compartment on the bottom of the unit. A small Philips screwdriver is all you need to remove the door to this compartment; then the memory itself simply snaps into place.

Just follow these steps:

1. Close Windows and power off your notebook.

2. Remove your notebook's battery.

3. Locate and open your notebook memory compartment, typically on the bottom of your notebook case.

4. Insert the new memory module or card, per the manufacturer's instructions. Most memory modules insert into the socket at a slight angle. Apply pressure to each end of the module to fully seat it into the slot. After the module is in place, you then push the socket downward until it locks back into position.

5. Reinstall the cover to the memory compartment, reinsert the battery, and power up your notebook.

note

On some notebooks you may need to remove an old lower-capacity memory card in order to add a new higher-capacity one.

Most notebooks will automatically recognize the new additional memory when you reboot. You should notice an immediate speed improvement when you next use your notebook.

Shopping for Computer Memory

You should be able to purchase both desktop and notebook memory modules directly from your computer's manufacturer, at your local computer store, or directly from the memory manufacturers:

- Crucial Technology (www.crucial.com)
- Kingston (www.kingston.com)
- PNY (www.pny.com)

All of these manufacturers provide lots of charts and tables and "configurators" to help you find the right type of memory for your particular PC model. You'll need to know your computer's manufacturer and model number. The configurator should then direct you to the specific memory your need for your machine.

The Bottom Line

You can improve the performance of your Windows 7 computer by better managing your system's hard disk and memory. Windows 7 offers a number of utilities and technologies to manage your current hardware, or you can add new and bigger hard disks and memory to your system. When it comes to storage and memory, size does make a difference.

26

Using Third-Party Utilities

Over the past few chapters we've talked about how you can optimize your computer system to better use Windows 7 your way. While there's a lot you can do from within Windows in this regard, there are also a number of third-party software utilities that also help you optimize your Windows-based computer. So let's take a quick look at what's available—and which you might want to try on your own system.

Using PC Tune-Up Utilities

Let's start by hauling out the big guns, in the form of full-featured PC tune-up utilities. These utilities are, more often than not, suites of individual utilities, each one focusing on a specific part of your system's performance.

These tune-up suites scan your system and provide a variety of reports and recommendations on how to improve your system's performance. These utilities look for system settings that can be reconfigured to boost your PC's performance, scan your hard disk for errors that can be easily repaired, and make recommendations on other ways to speed up your PC. Some tune-up suites also include basic malware scanning, a scan for outdated device drivers, and perhaps an Internet speed test.

The most popular of these full-featured tune-up utilities include the following:

- Advanced SystemCare (www.iobit.com/ advancedwindowscareper.html), free

- Fix-It Utilities Professional (www.avanquest.com), $49.95
- Glary Utilities (www.glarysoft.com), free
- My Faster PC (www.myfasterpc.com), $29.95
- Norton SystemWorks (www.symantec.com/norton/), $69.99
- PC Booster (www.inklineglobal.com/products/pcb/), $59.95
- PC Tools Disk Suite (www.pctools.com/disk-suite/), $39.95
- System Mechanic (www.iolo.com/system-mechanic/standard/), $49.95
- TuneUp Utilities (www.tune-up.com), $49.95
- WinSettings Pro (www.filestream.com/winpro/), $69.95
- WinUtilities (www.xp-tools.com/winutilities/), $49.99

---

tip

If you want to scan your system but don't want to download and install any software, consider the PC Pitstop website (www.pcpitstop.com). This site does an online scan, no software required, and reports the results in your web browser. Plus, the basic scan is free!

Using Defragmenter Utilities

If you don't want to go to all the trouble of scanning your entire system, you can often get a good performance boost just by defragmenting your computer's hard disk—and keeping it defragmented. While Windows' Disk Defragmenter utility does a good of this, some third-party utilities are even better. These utilities keep your disk defragmented in real time and position program files on your hard disk based on prior usage patterns. (This ensures that Windows will be able to access your most-used programs without a lot of hunting.)

The most popular of these disk defragmenter utilities include

- Diskeeper (www.diskeeper.com), $29.95
- Perfect Disk (www.raxco.com), $39.99

Using File Cleanup Utilities

Need to clean up all those unused and duplicate files on your computer's hard disk? These file cleaning tools are for you—they'll find the files you don't use and get rid of them.

- CCleaner (www.ccleaner.com), free
- Duplicate File Cleaner (www.duplicatefilecleaner.com), free
- Easy Duplicate File Finder (www.easyduplicatefinder.com), free

Using Startup Optimization Utilities

As you recall, keeping unwanted or unnecessary programs from loading automatically when Windows launches can provide a huge performance benefit. To that end, these utilities manage all those auto-loading programs and utilities—and delete unwanted "bundleware" from new computers.

- Autoruns (technet.microsoft.com/en-us/sysinternals/bb963902.aspx), free
- PC Decrapifier (www.pcdecrapifier.com), free
- Security Task Manager (www.neuber.com/taskmanager/), $29
- WinPatrol (www.winpatrol.com), free

Using Browser Optimization Utilities

By now you should be aware that you can go beyond simple Windows optimization to add some speed to Internet Explorer and your web browsing. These are the tools to turn to:

- Download Accelerator Plus (www.speedbit.com), free
- Expired Cookies Cleaner (www.astatix.com/tools/expired-cookies-cleaner.php), free
- FlashGet (www.flashget.com), free
- HackCleaner (hackcleaner.en.softonic.com), free
- IE7 Pro (www.ie7pro.com), free

The Bottom Line

On your quest to optimize your PC's performance, you sometimes have to go beyond Windows. To that end, there are a number of third-party utilities that help you do everything from defragmenting your hard disk to scanning your entire system for problems. Turn to these programs when you want to wring that last ounce of performance out of your system—or just speed things up if they've slowed down.

27

Tweaking the Windows Registry

Here's something that's pretty obvious to any computer user: Windows is a complex and sophisticated piece of computer software. The operating system itself encompasses literally tens of thousands of individual system files—all of which have to be managed and monitored, as do all the devices that Windows is tasked with managing. It's a lot of information to manage.

Windows tracks all these thousands of individual configuration settings via a big database file called the Windows Registry. If you can gain control over the Registry, you take a big step in managing Windows your way—and, not coincidentally, speeding up your system's performance.

Understanding the Windows Registry

The Windows Registry is where Windows turns to when it needs to find out anything about any part of the system. The Registry houses all manner of settings for everything from window color and translucency to the brand and model number of printer you're using. This type of centralized configuration storage makes it easy for Windows to find precise settings when necessary.

The Registry also has a big impact on your PC's speed. It all comes down to what is stored in the Registry and how the Registry is configured. An overly cluttered Registry can slow down performance, while tweaking certain Registry settings can speed up performance. For that reason, learning how to clean up and tweak the Registry is an essential skill for anyone trying to speed up a Windows-based computer.

How the Registry Works

Every time you make a configuration change, that information is automatically written to the Registry. Change the system time, and the Registry is updated; change your desktop wallpaper, the Registry is updated; change the home page in Internet Explorer, the Registry is updated. The Registry is also updated whenever you install a new software program or hardware device. And it all happens automatically, in the background.

When Windows needs to do just about anything, it accesses the Registry to obtain the proper configuration information. In this sense, the Registry functions like a control center for your entire computer system; it defines how every part of your system looks and works.

Organizing the Registry

The Registry is organized into five major sections, called *hives*. Each hive is stored in its own system file on your PC's hard disk.

These hives include the following:

- **HKEY_CLASSES_ROOT.** Contains information about registered applications, including file associations and OLE object classes. (This hive displays the same settings as the HKEY_LOCAL_MACHINE\ Software\Classes key.)
- **HKEY_CURRENT_USER.** This hive is a subset of the HKEY_USERS hive, pertaining to the current user of the PC. It contains all attributes for the desktop environment and network connections.
- **HKEY_LOCAL_MACHINE.** Contains most of the settings for your PC's hardware, system software, and individual applications.
- **HKEY_USERS.** Contains subkeys corresponding to the HKEY_CURRENT_ USER hives for all users of the PC, not just the current user.
- **HKEY_CURRENT_CONFIG.** Contains information gathered when Windows first launches, such as settings pertaining to your PC's display and printers. The data stored in this hive is not permanently stored on disk, but rather is regenerated each time your PC boots.

Each hive is further organized into a variety of keys and subkeys that can be represented by a series of folders and subfolders. For example, if you want to find configuration information for which programs Windows loads at launch, you would look in the following key: HKEY_LOCAL_MACHINE\SOFTWARE\Microsoft\Windows\CurrentVersion\Run.

The settings or data for each individual key or subkey is called the *value*. Each value in the Registry is defined by a value name (often called just the value), the type of data used for that entry, and the value of that data.

Editing the Registry

Most of the time you won't need to bother with the Registry—it operates in the background, automatically updated whenever you change a Windows setting or install a new piece of software or hardware. However, if you want to speed up Windows' performance or customize some hard-to-find settings, editing the Registry may be the only way to do it.

> ### tip
>
> Most experts recommend that you make a backup of the Registry before you make any changes to it. Fortunately, backing up the Registry is as simple as setting a System Restore point before you make an edit. The System Restore point contains a backup of the Registry; if you have problems following a Registry edit, you can simply restore the Registry to its pre-edit state using the System Restore utility. (Learn how to use System Restore in Chapter 19, "Backing Up and Restoring Data."

Launching the Registry Editor

You edit the Registry with a utility imaginatively called the Registry Editor. This utility is included with all versions of Windows, including Windows 7, even though you won't find it anywhere on the Start menu or in the Control Panel. Instead, you launch Registry Editor by entering **regedit** into the Search box and pressing the Enter key.

As you can see in Figure 27.1, the Registry Editor window has two panes. The left pane displays all the Registry's hives and keys. All keys have numerous subkeys. The right pane displays the values, or configuration information, for each key or subkey. You display the different levels of subkeys by clicking on the right-arrow next to a specific item.

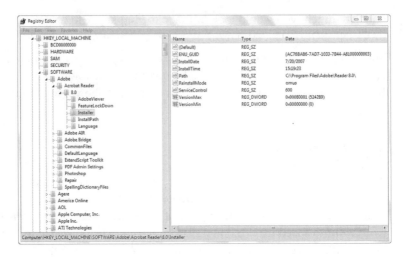

FIGURE 27.1

Editing the Windows Registry with the Registry Editor.

Editing and Adding Keys, Subkeys, and Values

You edit a particular Registry value by highlighting the subkey in the left pane and then double-clicking the value in the right pane. This displays the Edit Value or Edit String window, like the one shown in Figure 27.2. Enter a new value in the Value Data box, and then click OK.

FIGURE 27.2

Editing the value of a key.

caution

Registry settings are changed as you make the changes. There is no "save" command in the Registry Editor. There is also no "undo" command. So be very careful about the changes you make—they're final!

To add a new value to a subkey, right-click the subkey and select one of the New, Value options from the pop-up menu. Type a name for the new value, and then double-click the value to display the Edit Value (or Edit String) window. Enter the new value in the Value Data box, and then click OK.

You also can add new subkeys to the Registry. Just right-click the key where you want to add the subkey, and then select New, Key from the pop-up menu. A new subkey (with a temporary name) appears. Type a name for the new subkey, and then press Enter.

To delete a subkey or value, right-click the item and select Delete. Remember, however, that all changes are final. Once a subkey is deleted, it's gone!

Editing the Registry to Speed Up Windows

Now that you know how to edit the Windows Registry, let's examine a handful of Registry tweaks that can speed up Windows performance on your PC. They're easy to do—as long as you're comfortable using the Registry Editor.

Speeding Up Windows' Menus

Want to make Windows' menus display more quickly? You can do this by enabling this Registry tweak that removes the slight delay that is normally present between clicking a menu and Windows displaying that menu.

To perform this tweak, follow these steps:

1. Open the Registry Editor.
2. Navigate to the HKEY_CURRENT_USER\Control Panel\Desktop key.
3. Right-click the MenuShowDelay item and select Modify.
4. In the Edit String dialog box, change the current value (typically 400) to something a bit lower—something around 100 typically works well.
5. Click OK.

You can now close the Registry Editor and see how fast your menus open.

---

caution

If you set the MenuShowDelay value too low, menus will open if you merely move your mouse over them. You need a value somewhere above 0; otherwise, it will make Windows difficult to use.

Disabling Low Disk Checking

Windows constantly checks to see whether there's enough free space on your hard drive. If there isn't, it displays a low disk space warning. The problem is, all this disk space checking uses a number of system resources, and you probably know if your disk space is low, anyway.

You can speed up your PC by turning off this low disk space checking. Here's how to do it:

1. Open the Registry Editor.
2. Navigate to the HKEY_CURRENT_USER\Software\Microsoft\ Windows\CurrentVersion\Policies key.
3. If the Explorer key exists, select it. If not, right-click in the rightmost pane and select New, Key. Name this new key **Explorer**, and then select it.
4. Right-click in the rightmost pane and select New, DWORD (32-bit) Value.
5. Name the new DWORD **NoLowDiskSpaceChecks**.
6. Right-click the new NoLowDiskSpaceChecks item and select Modify.
7. In the Edit DWORD dialog box, change the value to 1.
8. Click OK.

---

note

A DWORD is a special type of data value used for some Registry entries.

Moving the Windows Kernel into Memory

Anything that runs in system memory runs faster than if it runs from your hard disk. To that end, you can speed up Windows itself by moving the Windows kernel into RAM, by executing this Registry tweak:

1. Open the Registry Editor.
2. Navigate to the HKEY_LOCAL_MACHINE\SYSTEM\ CurrentControlSet\Control\Session Manager\Memory Management key.
3. Right-click the DisablePagingExecutive item and select Modify.
4. In the Edit DWORD dialog box, change the value to 1.
5. Click OK.

You must reboot your system for this tweak to take effect.

Cleaning Up the Registry for Faster Performance

Editing Registry entries isn't the only way to use the Windows Registry to speed up Windows. That's because the Windows Registry itself can slow down your system's performance. Let me tell you how.

How the Registry Affects Your PC's Performance

Remember, the Registry holds the settings for every single program and utility stored on your system. Over time, all the different programs you install and settings you configure create lots and lots and lots of entries in the Registry—even after you uninstall the programs or no longer need the settings. That's because Registry settings often aren't deleted when you remove a program from your PC; this contributes to Registry "bloat" with lots of unnecessary or orphaned entries.

So the more programs you install over time, the larger the Registry gets. And the larger the Registry is, in terms of both file size and number of entries, the longer it takes for Windows to load it on startup—which slows down your system.

The fix for this problem is deceptively simple: Delete all the orphaned and unnecessary Registry entries. That's easier to say than to do, however. How do you know which entries are necessary and which aren't? Plus, do you really want to do all that work by hand, using the Registry Editor?

How Registry Cleaners Work

Fortunately, various third parties have recognized this issue and come up with their own solutions, in the form of Registry cleaner utilities. These programs automatically scour your Registry for redundant, invalid, or orphaned entries, and delete them. The process is easy as pie.

What kind of impact does a Registry cleaner actually have? It depends, to some degree, on how "clean" your Registry was to begin with. If a cleaner finds only a dozen or so entries to delete (out of the thousands of valid entries), the performance impact is minimal. But if you have a greater number of useless entries (or a smaller number of total entries), a Registry

cleaner will have a larger percentage impact on your system's performance. So you might notice a very small change in speed or a very large
one, depending.

caution

There is the slight chance that a poor-quality Registry cleaner program may
incorrectly identify a working entry as an unnecessary one, and thus delete a
setting that Windows needs to run. For that reason, you should set a restore
point (using System Restore) before cleaning your Registry. You can always go
back to that precleaner restore point if your system has problems after the
cleaning.

Choosing a Registry Cleaner

A large number of Registry cleaners are available today. The best of these
include the following:

tip

I recommend you choose a cleaner with backup and restore functions. This lets
you undo any changes made by the cleaner, in case the program accidentally
deletes something it shouldn't.

- Auslogics Registry Defrag (www.auslogics.com/en/software/
  registry-defrag), free
- CCleaner (www.ccleaner.com), free
- EasyCleaner (personal.inet.fi/business/toniarts/ecleane.htm), free
- Registry First Aid (www.rosecitysoftware.com/reg1aid/), $27.95
- Registry Healer (www.zoneutils.com/regheal/), $19.95
- Registry Mechanic (www.pctools.com/registry-mechanic/), $29.95
- RegSeeker (www.hoverdesk.net/freeware.htm), free
- TuneUp Utilities (www.tune-up.com/products/tuneup-utilities/),
  $49.95
- Uniblue RegistryBooster (www.liutilities.com/products/
  registrybooster/), $29.95
- WinCleaner (www.wincleaner.com), $29.95
- Wise Registry Cleaner (www.wisecleaner.com), free

All of these utilities clean up your Registry in much the same fashion, with similar results. Some utilities, however, include additional maintenance-related functionality, including file cleanup, disk defragmenting, and the like.

---

caution

Beware of so-called Trojan applications that masquerade as legitimate Registry cleaners. These malware programs typically are pushed via pop-up windows that purport to alert you of Registry problems and urge an immediate download. Once installed, they operate as spyware or adware on your system. No legitimate Registry cleaner promotes itself in this fashion.

Using a Registry Cleaner

Most Registry cleaners work in a similar fashion, scanning your Registry for entries that don't lead anywhere. This can be done automatically (the cleaner deletes every bad entry it encounters) or manually (you're asked whether you want to delete each individual entry it finds). Because most users don't know what's good and what's bad, the automatic operation is generally recommended.

Figure 27.3 shows one of the more popular cleaners, CCleaner, in action. You start the scan by clicking the Scan for Issues button. Problem entries are then listed in the rightmost pane. To delete all identified entries, leave everything checked and click the Fix Selected Issues button. Alternatively, you can manually examine all the entries and uncheck those you don't want to remove.

---

caution

In some rare instances, Registry cleaners can accidentally delete entries and DLLs that are used (if infrequently) by some programs. For this reason, make sure you create a System Restore point before running the cleaner utility; you can always restore your system to that point if any problems occur after cleaning.

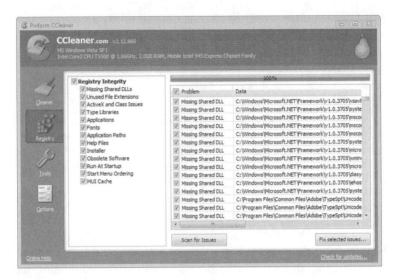

FIGURE 27.3

Cleaning the Windows Registry with CCleaner.

The Bottom Line

Configuring Windows 7 your way sometimes involves getting your hands dirty, figuratively speaking. This means tweaking and cleaning the Windows Registry, where all of the configuration settings for the Windows operating system and all the programs you install are stored. Tweak the right settings and you'll get a noticeable speed improvement.

28

Troubleshooting Windows Problems

Running Windows 7 your way also means not letting it get the best of you when things go wrong—which they sometimes will. Windows 7 is an incredibly complex operating system, and while it appears to be much better behaved than Windows Vista (especially on older PCs), it can still do lots of things you really don't want it to do, such as freezing, crashing, not starting, and the like.

So what do you do when Windows 7 starts acting like a petulant two-year-old? There's no need to panic; there are plenty of troubleshooting tools built into the operating system that you can use to your benefit.

How to Troubleshoot Computer Problems

Before we get into specific troubleshooting tips, let's examine what you need to do when you experience problems, in general terms. In my decades of experience with Windows-based computers, I've found that following six basic steps should help you track down the cause of most computer problems:

1. Check for user errors—something you've done wrong. Maybe you've clicked the wrong button or pressed the wrong key or plugged something into the wrong jack or port. Retrace your steps and try to duplicate your problem. Chances are the problem won't recur if you don't make the same mistake twice.

2. Check that everything is plugged in to the proper place, and that the PC itself is getting power. Take special care to ensure that all your cables are securely connected—loose connections can cause all sorts of strange results, especially with USB devices!

3. Be sure that you have the latest versions installed for all the software on your system. While you're at it, be sure you have the latest versions of device drivers installed for all the peripherals on your system. Incompatible software and drivers cause a lot of problems, especially when you upgrade to newer operating systems like Windows 7.

4. Run the appropriate Windows diagnostic tools, as I'll discuss later in this chapter. If you have them, use third-party tools as well.

5. Try to isolate the problem by when and how it occurs. Walk through each step of the startup process to see if you can identify which driver or service might be causing the problem.

6. When all else fails, call in professional help. That means contacting a technical support line, or taking your machine into the shop. Don't be embarrassed; if you need professional help, go and get it!

The bottom line is that whatever type of computer problem you encounter, there's no need to panic. Keep your wits about you and proceed logically, and you can probably find what's causing your problem and get it fixed. React irrationally, and you'll never figure out what's wrong—and you'll get a few gray hairs, in the bargain!

Starting Windows in Safe Mode

When Windows doesn't start normally, your first and perhaps biggest challenge is getting into Windows to fix what's wrong with Windows. How can you fix something you can't even start? The key here is to start Windows in a special mode, called *safe mode*, that lets you start Windows and do some basic troubleshooting.

Hijacking Your Computer at Startup

To launch Windows in safe mode, you first have to hijack your computer before Windows gets hold of it. You can then force Windows to load without whatever is causing the current problem.

You hijack your computer by watching the screen as your computer boots up, and pressing the F8 key just before Windows starts to load. You'll probably see some onscreen message about Windows starting, or pressing F8 for startup options, or selecting the operating system to start. When you see this message, hit the F8 key on your keyboard.

When you press F8 your computer will display the Windows startup menu. This menu lists a number of different ways that you can start Windows:

- **Normal.** This starts Windows in its normal mode as if you hadn't pressed F8 to begin with.

- **Safe Mode.** Starts Windows with a minimal number of device drivers loaded. (You use this mode for most troubleshooting procedures.)

- **Safe Mode with Networking.** A version of safe mode that also loads key network drivers; you can still connect the ailing computer to your network.

- **Safe Mode with Command Prompt.** Boots to the old DOS command prompt instead of to the Windows interface.

- **Enable Boot Logging.** This records all remaining startup operations to a special log file.

- **Enable VGA Mode.** Loads Windows as normal, but with a generic VGA video driver. (This is a good mode if you think you're having trouble with your video driver.)

- **Last Known Good Configuration.** Uses the Windows Registry information and drivers that were saved the last time you shut down your system—presumably before your system got screwed up.

note

Depending on your system configuration, you might have more, fewer, or just different options available on the Windows startup menu. The basic safe mode option is available on all systems, however.

Any time you can't load Windows normally, you should first try the Last Known Good Configuration option. If this doesn't put things right, you should reboot again and revert to safe mode. In fact, Windows will automatically start in safe mode if it encounters major problems while loading. Safe mode is a great mode for troubleshooting because Windows still works and you can make whatever changes you need to make to get it up and running again in normal mode.

Launching Safe Mode

Safe mode is a special mode of operation that loads Windows in a minimal configuration, without a bunch of pesky device drivers. This means the screen will be low-resolution VGA, and you won't be able to use a lot of your peripherals (such as your modem or your printer). But Windows will load, which it might not have, otherwise.

Once in safe mode, you can look for device conflicts, restore incorrect or corrupted device drivers, troubleshoot your startup with the System Configuration Utility (discussed later in this chapter), or restore your system to a prior working configuration with the System Restore utility. Then, once you have things working again, you can reboot your system and start Windows normally.

Starting Windows from the System Repair Disk

Sometimes you can't even get into Windows via safe mode. When you can't get your system to start by any other means, then it's time to use the system repair disk you hopefully created previously. Insert the system repair disk into your computer's CD/DVD drive and start up your machine. During the startup routine, select your Windows installation when prompted. You'll then see a list of options, as shown in Figure 28.1:

note

Learn more about creating a system repair disk in Chapter 19,"Backing Up and Restoring Data."

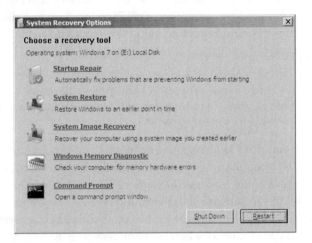

FIGURE 28.1

Using a system repair disk.

- **Startup Repair.** Select this option to troubleshoot and (hopefully) fix problems that may be preventing Windows from starting.
- **System Restore.** Select this option to run the System Restore utility and restore Windows to a previous restore point.

- **System Image Recovery.** Select this option to restore your entire system from a previously created full system backup.

- **Windows Memory Diagnostic.** Select this option to troubleshoot hardware memory problems.

- **Command Prompt.** Select this option to open a command prompt window, the better to run command-line utilities and troubleshoot from there.

The first thing to try is Startup Repair. If that doesn't work, try using System Restore to restore your system to a point before the problem occurred. If that doesn't work, select System Image Recovery to restore your system from a full system backup. (If you made such a backup, of course.) If that doesn't work, call for professional help.

Diagnosing Startup Problems with the System Configuration Utility

After you have Windows started in safe mode, you need to track down whatever is causing your startup problem. One way to do this is with the System Configuration Utility, a tool you turn to when you know you have a startup problem but you don't know what's causing it.

The System Configuration Utility troubleshoots your system by duplicating the procedures used by Microsoft's tech support staff when they try to diagnose system configuration problems. This utility leads you through a *diagnostic startup*—a series of steps that disables all the devices and programs that automatically load on Windows startup. You move through these items one-by-one until you're able to isolate the item that is causing your specific problem.

To open the System Configuration utility, open the Start menu and enter **msconfig** into the Search box. You should now select the General tab, shown in Figure 28.2, and select the Diagnostic Startup option. When you click OK, your computer restarts—but with only the most basic devices and services loaded. If you find that your problem is no longer present, you know that the problem was caused by one of the system services or programs that you *didn't* load on this diagnostic startup.

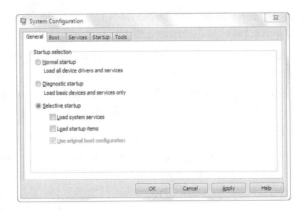

FIGURE 28.2

Use the System Configuration Utility to track down startup problems.

> **note**
>
> The System Configuration Utility is sometimes called MSCONFIG.

Now you need to determine whether it was a system service or an application that caused the problem. Return to the System Configuration utility's General tab and check the Selective Startup option. Deselect the Load Startup Items option, leaving Load System Services selected, and then click the OK button. This restarts Windows with only system services, no other applications.

If Windows started normally, you know your problem was with a program. Go to the System Configuration utility's Startup tab and work through the items, enabling one application at a time and then rebooting. This process will help you identify which application is causing the problem; you can then choose not to load that program automatically when Windows launches.

If, on the other hand, Windows did not start normally when you selected Load System Services, then your problem is with a system service, not a program. This time, go to the System Configuration utility's Services tab and work through those items, enabling one service at a time until you identify the problem.

> **note**
>
> Working through one item at a time is very time-consuming, but this is the exact same procedure that the tech professionals use. Working methodically, you can isolate the precise item that is causing your problem.

Even though this process is time-consuming, more often than not it will help you isolate your problem. Of course, after the problem is isolated, you still have to fix it—normally by reinstalling a missing or corrupted driver file.

Using the Task Manager to Deal with Program Freezes

Let's talk for a minute about frozen programs. I'm not talking about applications from the Antarctic, but rather programs that freeze while you're using them. Just what do you do when you encounter a frozen program?

Fortunately, this is a much less significant problem in Windows 7 than it used to be in Windows XP and older operating systems. Back in the bad old days, one frozen program could crash your entire system—or, at the least, force a system reboot. In Windows Vista and Windows 7, however, each running program and process is isolated from everything else running, so one bad program won't spoil the whole bunch; everything else stays running if another program freezes.

How do you unfreeze a frozen program? Well, you probably can't unfreeze it, but you can shut it down and then restart it again. To do so, you use the Windows Task Manager utility. Follow these steps:

1. Right-click the Windows taskbar and select Start Task Manager from the pop-up menu.

2. When the Task Manager appears, as shown in Figure 28.3, select the Applications tab.

3. Select the frozen program from the list.

4. Click the End Task button.

5. When prompted, confirm that you want to close that program.

This should close the frozen program; you can then close the Task Manager. You should now be able to restart the program and get back to working normally.

---

tip

If you can't open Task Manager normally (if your mouse is frozen, for instance), press Ctrl+Alt+Del to bring up the Windows menu screen; select Start Task Manager.

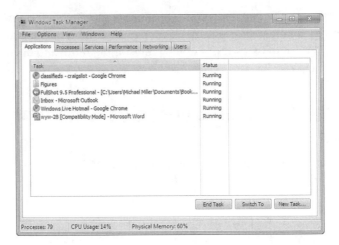

FIGURE 28.3

Closing frozen programs with the Task Manager.

Fixing Driver Problems with the Device Manager

For any piece of hardware to work with Windows, Windows has to install and configure a device driver file. If a device driver is deleted or somehow becomes corrupted, that device will no longer work.

note

Learn more about device drivers in Chapter 21,"Managing Printers, Devices, and Drivers."

You can review and hopefully fix problem device drivers by using the Device Manager, shown in Figure 28.4. You launch this utility by opening the Control Panel and selecting Device Manager.

Displaying Device Issues

When you open the Device Manager, any resource conflict on your system will be highlighted within the problematic Class group. Click the + next to the hardware device type to view all corresponding devices. If there is a problem with a specific device, it will be identified with one of the following symbols:

- A yellow triangle with a black exclamation point (!) inside indicates that the device is in what Windows calls a "problem state." Note that a device in a problem state can still be functioning, even though it has some sort of problem. The problem will be explained by the accompanying problem code.

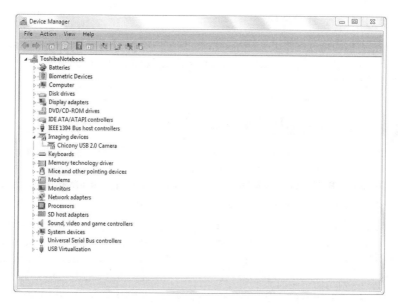

FIGURE 28.4

Managing device drivers with the Device Manager.

- A red "X" indicates that the device is currently disabled. This usually means that the device is physically present in your system, but doesn't have a driver loaded—although it could also mean that a driver is loaded but not functioning properly.

- A blue "i" on a white field indicates that the device is not using the automatic settings, but has a manual configuration instead. (This icon isn't necessarily bad, because it doesn't indicate a problem, only a different type of configuration.)

Solving Conflicts

If you have a device conflict, right-click that device and select Properties from the pop-up menu. This displays the Properties dialog box. When you select the General tab you'll see a message indicating the basic problem and the steps Windows recommends to solve the problem. The message might also display a problem code and number that can be useful when consulting with a technical support specialist—or prompt you to launch a troubleshooter for the device that is showing a problem.

Updating Drivers

Most driver-related problems can be fixed simply by updating the device driver. We learned how to do that in Chapter 21, so return there to review the specifics.

Fixing Big Problems with System Information

If none of the previous steps fixed your problem, you need to turn to a more powerful tool. That tool is called the System Information utility; you launch it by clicking the Start button and selecting All Programs, Accessories, System Tools, System Information.

As you can see in Figure 28.5, the left pane of the System Information window displays information about the three key parts of your system: Hardware Resources, Components, and Software Environment. Click the + next to one of the categories to display additional subcategories. When you highlight a specific subcategory, information about that topic appears in the right pane.

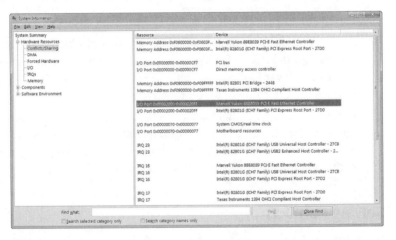

FIGURE 28.5

Use System Information to view more detailed information about your system and to access a variety of technical tools.

The Bottom Line

A lot can go wrong with Windows, but there's also a lot you can do to find and fix the causes of those problems. To me, that's the ultimate example of running Windows 7 your way: You keep control when bad things happen—and get things back to normal as quickly as possible.

Index

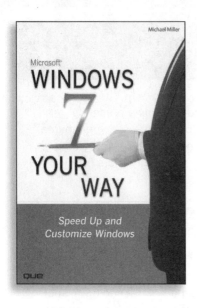

Michael Miller

Microsoft®

WINDOWS 7 YOUR WAY

Speed Up and Customize Windows

que

FREE Online Edition

Your purchase of **Microsoft Windows 7 Your Way** includes access to a free online edition for 45 days through the Safari Books Online subscription service. Nearly every Que book is available online through Safari Books Online, along with more than 5,000 other technical books and videos from publishers such as Addison-Wesley Professional, Cisco Press, Exam Cram, IBM Press, O'Reilly, Prentice Hall, and Sams.

SAFARI BOOKS ONLINE allows you to search for a specific answer, cut and paste code, download chapters, and stay current with emerging technologies.

Activate your FREE Online Edition at www.informit.com/safarifree

> **STEP 1:** Enter the coupon code: WEEPHAA.

> **STEP 2:** New Safari users, complete the brief registration form.
> Safari subscribers, just log in.

If you have difficulty registering on Safari or accessing the online edition, please e-mail customer-service@safaribooksonline.com

Safari.
Books Online